The Woman Worker, 1926-1929

The Woman Worker, 1926-1929

Margaret Hobbs and Joan Sangster, Editors

Canadian Committee on Labour History
St. John's, Newfoundland

Canadian Committee on Labour History
History Department
Memorial University of Newfoundland
St. John's, NF A1C 5S7

Manuscript was prepared for the printer by the staff of the
Canadian Committee on Labour History

Cover designed by Helen Houston

Printed and bound in Canada

The Canada Council | Le Conseil des Arts
for the Arts | du Canada

We acknowledge the support of the Canada Council for the Arts for
our publishing program.

Canadian Cataloguing in Publication Data

Main entry under title:

The Woman Worker, 1926-1929

    Includes bibliographical references.
    ISBN 1-894000-01-3

1. Women -- Employment -- Canada -- History -- 20th century.
2. Women employees -- Canada -- Social conditions. 3. Woman
worker I. Hobbs, Margaret (Margaret Helen), 1955- II. Sangster,
Joan, 1952-. III. Canadian Committee on Labour History.

HD6099.W625 1999   331.4'0971'09042   C99-950180-1

Contents

Acknowledgements

We began this project as we 'wound up' Laura Margaret in her baby swing to secure a few minutes writing peace. Thirteen years later, we went back to it in the midst of Marg's debates with Genevieve over socialist politics. We hope that our daughters and step-daughters, and a new generation of young women with a revolutionary spirit, will find something inspiring in these pages.

We want to express our thanks to the OWAHC for encouraging us to resurrect the project, and the staff at *Labour/Le Travail,* especially Michelle McBride, for their hard work on it.

Editorial Note:

The text of *The Woman Worker* was kept as much as possible in its original form. Readers may therefore notice the occasional inconsistency or error in the spelling of certain words or names in the text or in article titles. Obvious typos were normally corrected, however, and printing errors which rendered a few passages unintelligible were altered by omittting parts of the text (marked by the insertion of three dots), and/or by adding a word or two (indicated by square brackets). In addition, for the sake of stylistic consistency, minor alterations were made in the format of the reproduced text.

Margaret Hobbs and Joan Sangster

Introduction

"At last we have our magazine," wrote a triumphant Florence Custance as she launched the first issue of the *Woman Worker*, official organ of the Canadian Federation of Women's Labor Leagues, in the summer of 1926. Custance, a long time socialist and member of the Communist Party of Canada, promised her readers something very different from the usual fare in "women's" magazines: "It will not contain fashions and patterns, and we are leaving recipes for cooking to the cook book." Nor would readers find "sickly love stories." Instead, she vowed, "Everything that will be printed in our magazine will deal with life, real life, not imaginations. Its sole objective will be to champion Protection of Womanhood, and the Cause of the Workers generally."

This was no idle boast. Readers of this paper were not permitted to escape into a fantasy world where fancy souffles and romantic love obscured the difficult realities of working-class life. There were no images of carefree "flappers" or housewives in dream kitchens, no ads showing women "liberated" by the purchase of a new "Hoover" or, better still, a shiny new model Ford. During its run from July 1926 until April 1929, the *Woman Worker* gave full exposure to the ugly warts of industrial capitalism in the hope that the working-class women who constituted its primary readership would assess their female experience with a Marxist understanding of class and class conflict. Never limiting itself to simply reporting the dreary conditions of women's lives under capitalism, the paper highlighted resistance as well as victimization, encouraging women to fight the existing order by organizing against class-based economic and social injustice.

The *Woman Worker* represented the first, and for many years the last, separate English-language socialist paper for women in Canada. The best the pre-World War I socialist press had done for women was to initiate on occasion a women's column, such as the one Mary Cotton Wisdom edited for the Socialist Party of Canada's *Cotton's Weekly* from 1908-1909. Women's columns, however,

proved a controversial issue among early socialists and many papers refused to cater in any way to a specifically female audience.
For much of the interwar period the Women's Section of the United
Labour-Farmer Temple Association (ULFTA) was able to boast its
own separate publication for women, but both the *Holos Robitnytsi*
and the much longer running *Robitnytisia* ("working woman") were
edited by men. With the appearance of the Women's Labor League
paper in 1926 working-class women with English-language knowledge were offered their own monthly publication, which while not
entirely excluding the voice of male comrades, was edited and controlled by women. The *Woman Worker* documented and analyzed the
hardships of women's daily lives and presented a vision of dignity,
respect and equality which spoke to both their class and gender oppression.

   If the paper was pathbreaking for its time, the issues raised were
relevant for many years to come and some are still significant to socialist feminists. Carried through its three-year run are questions
like how can we organize women workers in ghettoized sectors like
personal service? How can the "bourgeois" ideology of the mainstream press be challenged and an alternative analysis offered?
What is the meaning of "peace" and how can we organize against imperialist war? How can women resist the state while also accepting
the modicum of "protection" it extends? How can a socialist economy be achieved? How can family life be reformulated to better meet
the needs of women? The Women's Labor Leagues' answers to these
questions were certainly partial, revealing some of the blind spots of
Marxism with its much more serious appraisal of class than gender,
and its neglect of other key axes of power such as race, sexuality,
ability, age, and region. Yet the seriousness with which the paper
took up the "woman question," as it was called, and the boundaries
that were pushed as contributors explored concerns that were not
always considered important by the Communist Party leadership,
make this paper highly significant in the history of Canadian
socialist-feminism.

* * *

Women's Labor Leagues first appeared in Canada in the pre-World
War I period. Modelled on the British WLLs, which were linked to
the British Labour Party, they were composed initially of the wives
and daughters of trade unionists and Labour Party activists. The
Canadian WLLs also closely resembled the Finnish 'sewing circles' attached to Canada's pre-war Social Democratic Party. The
Canadian WLLs, like these earlier sewing circles, combined fundraising and support work for the labour movement with political self
education. Operating as much more than mere auxiliaries to the

labour movement, the Labor Leagues developed their own priorities and initiatives as well as cooperating with labour and sometimes re-form interests.

After faltering amidst the post-war atmosphere of political repres-sion and economic depression, the WLLs were revived in the early 1920s. Not coincidentally, their revival and growth before the eco-nomic recovery was complete paralleled the emergence of the Communist Party of Canada (CPC), initially called the Workers' Party of Canada. Inspired by the 1917 Russian Revolution, by the creation in 1919 of the new Communist International (or Comin-tern), and by the major labour uprisings that followed on the heels of the armistice, the new Party was formed largely by members of the earlier socialist parties, the Socialist Party of Canada (SPC), the So-cial Democratic Party of North America (SDPC), and the small Socialist Party of North America (SPNA). Although the leadership was almost exclusively male, and not generally very interested in the particular problems of women's oppression, the new Party was di-rected by the Comintern and the Russian Party which controlled it to develop plans that would stimulate Canadian women's revolution-ary consciousness and increase their involvement in the Party. Women's militance had, after all, been crucial to the success of the Bolshevik revolution. To plan and coordinate the mobilization of women, national Communist parties were urged to establish women's departments similar to the Soviet Union's *Zhenotdel* and the Communist International's Women's Secretariat. The Canadian Party, after some stalling, set up its Women's Department in 1924. Key among its tasks was the building up of the existing Women's La-bor Leagues into a Communist-controlled WLL "movement" that would attract both wage-earning women and housewives. Under this plan and the spearheading efforts of Communist leader Flor-ence Custance, older WLLs were reinvigorated and many new ones formed, and the Leagues, which had always been socialist-leaning, became increasingly tied to the Communist Party. Not all women who joined, however, were Party members. Some were sympathizers, and others were socialists of a different stripe or social democrats who saw the Leagues as one means of moving towards socialism and women's equality. Throughout the Leagues' existence, there re-mained some tension between the firm Communist leadership provided by the Women's Department and a more politically eclectic membership.

In 1924 the ten Leagues which lay scattered across the country banded together as a Federation, with Custance elected national Secretary. Local Leagues were urged to cooperate with one another as partners in an autonomous working-class organization, but in keeping with the Communist Party's "united front" strategy they were also advised to make links with certain labour, women's and farm organizations that were "reformist" in nature. This approach reflected the Comintern's blending of Marxist theory with the practical strategies promoted by Lenin before his death in 1923, and it remained the accepted practice until late in the decade. The purpose of "boring from within" and cooperating with progressive groups was to identify potential Communist sympathizers and develop a revolutionary core that would attach itself to the Party. The work of building a WLL movement proved difficult indeed. Recalling the first years of the Federation's work, Custance complained "we received little, if any, support from 'our men' in the labour movement." Perhaps the most troubling rebuff from male unionists came when the Trades and Labour Congress of Canada—the largest federation of craft unions—refused to allow the Federation of WLLs to affiliate, almost certainly because of the Communist strength in the Leagues. Resigned to the realization that "if we were to make headway, we must do things ourselves," Custance and others in the Federation executive looked to the creation of a national paper, the *Woman Worker*, as an invaluable tool to reach out to more women and unify the Leagues. (*Woman Worker*, October 1927, p. 15) The paper's monthly publication as the mouthpiece of the Federation, together with the untiring organizing efforts of Custance herself, inspired the creation of seventeen more Leagues by October 1927, bringing the total to 37, according to the *Woman Worker*.

* * *

The appearance of the paper in the mid-1920s was timely indeed, for this decade witnessed the triumph of a mass media with the power to influence Canadian women of all classes. Mass circulation magazines and movies thrust bourgeois ideals within easy reach of working-class women, whose potential militance was endangered by the pacifying effects of "false consciousness." Although Communists worried about the effects of this "poison" on all working-class women, it was the housewife who prompted the greatest anxiety. Housewives, confined for large periods within the home, were thought to be almost completely under the influence of the capitalist class through the church, newspapers, and movies. The *Woman Worker* was seen as an important counterweight to this influence. Despite the paper's declaration that it would appeal to "all working women, whether they work in the factory, at home, or in the office," the paper was aimed most pointedly at the education and politicization of working-class women working in their homes as housewives and mothers. The Leagues themselves never brought in substantial numbers of wage-earning women. This focus revealed the Party's understanding of the pivotal role housewives played in families. As managers of domestic budgets and caretakers of family members' emotional needs, housewives could make or break the working-class unity that was needed to sustain strike action and build revolutionary resistance. Consistent with prevailing Communist fears about housewives' latent conservatism, the constitution of the Federation of WLLs proclaimed its intention to organize wives into auxiliary unions, an idea that never translated into reality.

The WLLs had always reflected the ethnic diversity of the early Canadian Left. In cities like Toronto with a heterogeneous ethnic population, Finnish, Ukrainian, Yiddish, and English-speaking groups met separately, but often joined forces to work on common causes. In the Alberta mining towns and other smaller centres, one or two ethnic locals often dominated. Despite the Comintern's push for unity of the language groups, ethnic and language barriers encouraged separation. Moreover, the exclusion of Finns, Ukrainians, and Jewish women from the seats of leadership in both the Federation and the Party produced resentment that led the non-English-speaking League members to lean inward, looking within their ethnic groups for support that was lacking outside.

* * *

Although there were many contributors to the *Woman Worker*, not all of whom were Communist, and not all of whom signed their names, without a doubt the dominant voice in the paper was that of its editor, the indomitable Florence Custance. Prominent in the Communist Party leadership, where she was one of the only women during the 1920s, Custance was a formidable force, passionately committed to socialist ideals and never one to back down from a good fight, even within her own Party where her relationships with male comrades changed with the political weather. Custance undoubtedly left her mark on the Party and was a household name in the many families receiving the *Woman Worker* every month, yet her early death in 1929 cut her political involvement short, and she is only a shadowy figure in Communist Party histories. Described in one such history as "rather prim and straight-laced" but with "revolutionary fervour," Custance had been a school teacher in England before emigrating to Canada with her husband, a carpenter. Once in Canada, she became outspoken in the labour movement, especially through the Amalgamated Carpenters of Canada Wives' Auxiliary. Just before the war she joined the SPNA, a small and short-lived organization that tried to move even farther to the Left than the Socialist Party of Canada, a party whose official refusal to cooperate with any reformist currents earned it the label "impossibilist." Custance must have outgrown the rigidity of the SPNA for after helping form what would become the new Communist Party at a secret meeting in 1919 she stood solidly behind the united front approach that dominated the 1920s. She founded the Toronto Plebs League and was active in the Ontario Labour College. During her tenure as editor of the *Woman Worker* and secretary of the Federation, Custance was also head of the Friends of Soviet Russia and secretary of the Toronto WLL.

Ever the schoolteacher, Custance was one of the strongest intellectuals in the Party and lectured frequently to Communist and non-Communist audiences. Somewhat reserved, she nonetheless whipped the paper into shape, prodding would-be contributors to send in submissions, admonishing them not to sit silent and merely read the *Woman Worker* but to make their voice heard by taking up their pens. She seemed inexhaustible. What a shock it must have been therefore when readers picked up the October 1928 issue of the *Woman Worker* and learned that Custance was seriously ill and had been ordered complete rest for three months. During her absence her comrades in the Toronto League picked up the pieces, made a special appeal to readers to contribute articles and reports, and the paper continued to publish, reporting in November that the editor was feeling much better.After an absence of three months, Custance was apparently back at her post in January 1929, but she would never fully recover. The paper contained no more references to her health, and readers must have assumed all was well, yet it is unlikely that Custance was able to be as involved with the paper as she had once been. The paper had changed appearance during her absence—the table of contents, for example, with its regular columns was replaced with a listing of "Special Contents" that allowed for more flexibility—nand after the April 1929 issue the paper fell apart.

Custance died on 12 July 1929. The *Woman Worker* had been her creation and it died with her. It is possible that changes in the Party's political tactics (already hinted at in 1928-29) and especially the more rigid left-wing rejection of the united front, may have soon led to the demise of the *Woman Worker*, or even Custance's estrangement from the Party. We will never know. What is apparent is that Custances's political determination and labour produced a paper whose appeal and message resonated with many working-class women. The result was a short-lived but significant socialist-feminist venture quite unparalleled for many years to come.

General Sources for Further Reading:

- Ian Angus, *Canadian Bolsheviks: The Early Years of the Communist Party of Canada* (Montreal: Vanguard, 1981).

- Gregory Kealey, "1919: The Canadian Labour Revolt," *Labour/Le Travail*, 13 *(Spring 1984), 11-44.*

- Linda Kealey, *Enlisting Women for the Cause: Women, Labour, and the Left in Canada, 1890-1920* (Toronto: University of Toronto Press, 1998).

- Beth Light and Ruth Roach Pierson, eds. *No Easy Road: Women in Canada 1920s to 1960s* (Toronto: New Hogtown Press, 1990).

- John Manley, "Does the International Labour Movement Need Salvaging? Communism, Labourism, and the Canadian Trade Unions, 1921-1928," *Labour/Le Travail*, 41 (Spring 1998), 147-180.

- Janice Newton, *The Feminist Challenge to the Canadian Left, 1900-1918* (Montreal: McGill-Queen's, 1995).

- Bryan Palmer, *Working Class-Experience: Rethinking the History of Canadian Labour, 1800-1991*, second edition (Toronto: McClelland and Stewart, 1992).

- William Rodney, *Soldiers of the International: A History of the Communist Party of Canada, 1919-1929* (Toronto: University of Toronto Press, 1968).

- Joan Sangster, "The Communist Party and the Woman Question, 1922-1929," *Labour/Le Travail*, 15 (Spring 1985), 25-56.

- Joan Sangster, *Dreams of Equality: Women on the Canadian Left, 1920-1950* (Toronto: McClelland and Stewart, 1989).

- Veronica Strong-Boag, *The New Day Recalled: Lives of Girls and Women in English Canada, 1919-1939* (Toronto: Copp Clark Pitman, 1988).

- Frances Swyripa, *Wedded to the Cause: Ukrainian-Canadian Women and Ethnic Identity, 1891-1991* (Toronto: University of Toronto Press, 1993).

- Catherine Vance, *Not by Gods but by People: the story of Bella Hall Gauld* (Toronto: Progress Books, 1976).

- Gerry Van Hauten, *Canada's Party of Socialism: History of the Communist Party of Canada, 1921-1976* (Toronto: Progress Books, 1982).

- Louise Watson, *She Was Never Afraid: The Biography of Annie Buller* (Toronto: Progress Books, 1976).

Left to Right: Florence Custance, Bea Colle, Becky Buhay, and Anne Buller (Thomas Fisher Rare Book Library, Kenny Collection, MS179, Box 63B).

The

Woman Worker

Published by
Canadian Federation of Women's Labor Leagues
in the Interests of Working Women

| Vol. 1 | JULY, 1926 | No. 1 |

CONTENTS THIS ISSUE

Price 10¢ per Copy   Subscription $1.00 a Year

WE HEAR FROM OUR CORRESPONDENTS

What a Woman Suffers as a Land Settler

The Woman Worker:—

Our sisters in the Old Land seem to have taken a keen interest in the new Canadian Land Settlement Scheme. The British Joint Committee of Industrial Women Workers Organizations (representing over a million working women) at a meeting held February 11th, dealt with the proposed scheme. In brief, the scheme proposes to bring some 2,000 families to Canada for the farms, and the government assistance will include a portion of the travelling expenses and a portion of the household goods. Those who come will be required to have a minimum of $125.00. The recommendation of the British Women's Committee is "That only families with $500.00 to $1,000.00 are likely to succeed without real hardship".

But what is the life of the housewife who comes to Canada to live on a farm? She is usually a mother, she has to look after her children, start her dairy, her vegetable garden and care for the poultry. Her husband must learn to make good on the land himself, and for this he must work on the other farms, and the usual rate of wage for this is from $25.00 to $30.00 per month, with food. From this they are expected to keep their families.

When her husband has received his training he may get equipment, buildings and live stock amounting to $5,000.00. This is a debt to the Canadian or British Governments. The new Canadian farmers, the man and his wife, must start to pay back this debt to the Government after the first season at the rate of about $30.00 per month.

Now, we in Canada know very well that this cannot be done. Even if provision is made by the Government to forego principal payments, the interest must be paid. The debt is never ended.

It is as well that the British women made a thorough investigation, and so were able to advise that the money spent to bring people to Canada could be used to better advantage by spending it to assist the workers on the land in Great Britain. For after all it is useless producing marketable commodities if there is not a market for the distribution of the same. Some farmers in Canada may want help, but there are farmers enough, and there are deserted farms everywhere.

Yours for the Co-operative Commonwealth,

A. CAMWELL, London, Ont.

How a Woman Worker Fared When She Stuck Out for the Rights of Women Workers

The Woman Worker:—

It may interest you to know that I have had five jobs in about just as many months. Obtaining laundry work and staying at the work is no cinch. I lasted three days in the first, being dismissed because I attacked the doctors who examined women and girls who needed relief, laundry work in this case being a form of relief. The second job lasted three weeks. The third job two days. My fourth was in an up-to-date laundry. Here I discovered that the minimum wage was not being paid and immediately registered a complaint with the Minimum Wage Board. It is true that the firm eventually came across with the money, but it was discovered that I was the one who complained and I was fired for being an agitator. I'm now in my fifth job, and I'm wondering how long I'll last.

Wishing the Woman Worker success,

Yours,
E.C. (The Peg)

The Problem of the Unmarried Woman

May 6, 1926

Dear Mrs. Custance:—

I read your letter in the paper in regard to the poor woman who had to commit suicide. Believe me, there are far too many of them. But can you blame them? I do not. I wonder if we could not do something for single women, who, like myself, have worked all their days and tried to save, yet still cannot manage to get a little home for themselves in their old age.

I think the government ought to give a pension at 45 to those who have not saved enough, through no fault of their own. I wonder if Miss McPhail would take the matter up. I am hard of hearing and this hinders me in doing much in that way.

At present I am doing the housework for a married brother and his wife and can get along, but I dread the time that will soon be here when I am past work. But, believe me, I am not thinking only of myself, but of these other poor women, some we never hear of. And so many more coming from the Old Country. I think this is a problem that will have to be met.

I think the wealthy people and all these I.O.D.E.-ers ought to help and build some cottages in the country towns for single women, rent free, and let them have a garden and a home of their own if they so wish. We hear so much of mothers and grandmothers, but never about the aunts who, in many cases have a much harder and bitter time.

I think if there was a club for single women where we could get acquainted it would help. What object has the Labor League in view? Have you a Club, and have you any reading matter?

Sincerely yours,
S.J.M., Toronto

NOTES AND HAPPENINGS

The I.O.D.E. are mentioned in our first issue on three occasions. In a letter from one of our correspondents it is intimated that the members of this organization could undertake more useful work than they are doing at the present time. In Miss McPhail's article, in which she denounces the picture patriotism of these ladies, and, lastly, in editorial comment, which deals with the discussions of these ladies in convention and which show that their patriotism ran riot. We cannot help feeling that if an anti-strike movement develops in Canada the I.O.D.E. will be the founders.

Our sister organ the Labour Woman, of Great Britain, warns the Miners' wives of the anti-strike movement. The April issue contains the following announcement:

MINERS' WIVES! BEWARE!

There is a specious organization. The Women's Guild of the Empire and Commonsense (save the mark!) going round the coalfields asking you to demonstrate against strikes and lockouts.

It offers trips to London for a demonstration.

Be cautious! Give it the cold shoulder!

Inquire where this organization gets its funds.

Keep solidly by the Trade Union of your menfolk, and Remember you are Workers, not Black-legs!

This contains the sentiment endorsed by the Women's Labor League Movement of Canada.

When Dr. Withrow lectured to the Toronto Women's Labor League on "Birth Control," many women, quite new to the League, attended the meeting, and it must be said some men were present also.

Dr. Withrow made some very frank statements about Birth Control. He said, among other things, that when he went to church to attend a wedding he did not see "two souls" being united, but instead "two bodies," and his thought always was, "Were those two bodies fit and prepared for the perpetuation of life." He contended that Birth Control knowledge was not sufficient in itself, and might even be harmful unless it were accompanied with sex knowledge. He wanted it understood that Birth Control and abortion were two entirely different things: Birth Control was the prevention of conception, while abortion was destruction of life after conception.

Dr. Withrow claimed that every woman should have the right to determine when she should have children. He scorned the quack remedies and old-fashioned ideas concerning childbearing.

The discussion which followed was interesting. Some denounced the fact that mothers and fathers were under the influence of "mock modesty," and preferred to let their children know about life and their entrance into the world from any channel and by any means other than talk properly themselves to their children. Others claimed that sex hygiene should be taught in the schools, and that this could be done by means of properly arranged courses in Nature Study. Others denounced the influence of the church in preventing a proper understanding of life. Others dealt with the need of Birth Control as a relief for working women and working class families, as in these days, it was impossible to raise a family decently if it exceeded more than three children. Evidently, the audience quite approved the Birth Control Movement, as Dr. Withrow did not meet with any objections.

It was noticeable, too, that after the meeting several women who were mothers, and young mothers at that, asked Dr. Withrow for his card.

The letter from S.J.M., Toronto, voices a great need at this time. Today there are a few millions of women who are unmarried and have no chance of marrying, they are doomed to self-maintenance for the rest of their lives. But the unmarried state of a woman is by no means a disgrace. Many lovable and good women are unmarried. Many women enter the professions because they prefer to work for themselves and prefer independence rather than be tied to the drudgery of domestic life and raising children amid all the uncertainty of life as it is today.

But there are times when loneliness and a feeling of isolation overtake some women, when, if they have only received a small wage for their labors and have not been able to save for the rainy day of failing health, that they fear the future.

It must be evident that pressure of the times should bring women together in organization for protection. Surely, the best form is that which will aid them in obtaining economic security. We claim that the Labor Movement is the best place for women who depend upon their own labors for their existence, and the Women's Labor League Movement in particular is the place for these who want help in obtaining this security.

This brings us to the point where we can discuss the great insult that has been thrown at aged workers by the House of Government Pensioners and Senile Decay, the House of Senate.

For years the labor movement of Canada has labored for "Old Age Pensions." Every local union, every part of the workers' political movement has petitioned and petitioned for Old Age Pensions. At last an Old Age Pension Bill managed to get through the House of Commons but only to be blocked by the House of Senate. Of course we know why the Senate blocked it and who were behind their action. The rich are determined they will not part with their wealth for the workers' benefit.

It is clear the workers of Canada will have to bring pressure to bear to get rid of the Senate. It would be as well, too, that they demand that the pensions paid by the government to the Senate Pensioners should be stopped and that all should go into a *common fund* and be shared by all the aged. But this is a great concession to these pensioners of the Senate. The aged workers who have been denied pensions are the ones who deserve them in recognition of their former usefulness as producers of social needs, whereas, the Senators cannot lay claim to reward by virtue of hard work and incessant toil.

But here, in Canada, like every other capitalist country, where profits are counted the first consideration, the Dollar Mind blocks the welfare of lives.

Only in one country does this appear to be different. According to the report of the British Trade Union Delegation to Land of the Soviets (Soviet Russia) things are quite different. Here, the children and the aged, those who will be the useful producers and those who have fulfilled that function and have become worn in the process, receive every possible consideration. And this consideration is not on the basis of charity, but entirely on basis of a social duty on the part of those who are able to work.

Old age and infirmity are protected in the land where the workers and peasants are the rulers. There are rest homes, permanent and otherwise, for all the aged workers. They have not to worry about payments, they can do just what they like in the way of passing their time. The workers have experienced, while they are under the rule of the rich, the bitterness of the "beggarly charity." This makes them considerate for the feelings of their fellows. This proves that a Workers' Government can bring happiness to the aged.

Peaceful Picketing has just been declared unlawful by the Supreme Court of Canada. This means that when the workers go out on strike against a reduction of wage or any form of industrial oppression inflicted by the employers, they will not be allowed to go near, or confer with, or communicate to other workers that there is a strike in a certain factory, workshop, mill, or mine.

It is clear to all who know what conditions are like to-day, that this decision was brought in in the interests of the employers. Just now the employers want to cut the wages of the workers all along the line. This will aid the masters better than anything else. But the workers will have to make a stand for their rights.

CONTRIBUTED ARTICLES

MILITARIZING THE SCHOOL CHILDREN

Agnes McPhail, M.P.

John Stuart Mill has said, "All attempts by the State to bias the conclusions of its subjects on disputed points are evil."

I believe the State, through the influence of the military authorities on the education of our several provinces, is seeking to bias the conclusions of children in regard to the best method of settling international disputes.

The walls of our schools are lined with pictures of military men in gold braid and with pictures of battles. It was bad enough years ago, but is much worse now, that the pictures donated by the I.O.D.E., and framed by the Provincial Government, at the expense of the people of Ontario, have been hung in the schools. The children naturally get the idea that only soldiers are heroes and worthy of admiration.

The School Readers emphasize war heroes and link together the soldier, war and glory.

This business of moulding the child to believe war is glorious and to be admired, begins in the Primer. We find a pictured flag— our flag— and these words:—

It is the Union Jack.
The flag is red, white and blue.
The red says "Be Brave!"
The white says "Be Pure!"
The blue says "Be True!"
Our soldiers fought for this flag
In the Great War

The child gets the idea that the flag is something to be fought for, and that bravery, purity and truth are somehow connected with the fighting, and so on, up through the Readers the work goes on:

In the Third Reader, we find—
"Come, cheer up, my lads,
　'tis to glory we steer,
To add something more to this
　wonderful year,
To honor we call you,
　not press you like slaves,
For who are so free as the sons
　of the waves?
We always are ready,
Hearts of oak are our ships,
　hearts of oak are our men,
Steady, boys, steady,
We'll fight and we'll conquer
　again and again."

Of all Burns' poems, breathing understanding of and love for the common people, not one has been given a place in the Ontario Readers, only his military poem, "Scots Wha Hae" was thought worthy of a place.

Near the end of the Fourth Reader we find England, my England:—
Mother of Ships whose might,
　England, my England,
Is the fierce old Sea's delight,
　England, my own,
Chosen daughter of the Lord,
Spouse-in-Chief of the ancient
　Sword,
There's the menace of the Word
In the Song on your Bugles blown,
　England—
Out of heaven on your bugles
　blown!

Probably this is the worst of all war poems.

In our histories, war is given the chief place. Our virtues are stressed and our shortcoming minimized, while our enemies' faults lose nothing in the telling and their virtues are quite carefully concealed.

The progress of the race toward a higher plane and the contribution of each nation, is given little space. History, to the child, means war—righteous, if we started it, and particularly if we win. The good people fought on our side, the bad ones on the other side.

Then, just in case the war psychology was not yet strong enough, the Department of National Defence invaded the schools. At twelve years of age boys can be formed into Cadet corps. The instructor, usually the principal or teacher in the school—receives $2.00 (Two dollars) per head for each Cadet up to fifty, and $1.00 (One dollar) for each one over that number.

The charm of music, color, pomp and class distinction is thrown around Cadet training to lure boys into the military machine. As Rev. M.E. Cameron, of Hamilton, has very truly said, "Military training teaches boys to be obedient to brass buttons and tin hats, but not to the great ideals of the country."

The best authorities agree that cadet training is not good physical training. But it captures the boy's mind. Our militarist knows that all our talks about settling international dispute by means other than war, will fall upon deaf ears if only he can instill war psychology into the minds of our youth.

The number of cadets in Canada has increased from 74,991, in 1920, to 115,677, in 1925, during the period of the last five years.

Where are you mothers? This is your great task. How soon can we say to the Department of National Defence, "Take your hands off the educational system," and to the compilers of Readers and Histories, "Give the child a true picture of war—its waste, cost, uselessness and true relationship to national and international life"?

How soon will you see that our school walls are decorated with pictures showing the scenic beauty of Canada and other countries; of children at play; of flowers and animals; children of other lands in national dress; of workers producing goods for our use? I hope very soon.

HOUSING CONDITIONS IN THE MINING TOWNS OF CAPE BRETON, NOVA SCOTIA
By Annie Whitfield.

The women of Canada should know just how the workers in the mining towns in Cape Breton live, and I think our magazine can help to impart this knowledge.

First of all it must be told that the houses in Cape Breton are owned by the British Empire Steel Corporation (called Besco for short), and it was these same houses that the Royal Commission advised the people to buy from Besco. But the reason they advised this was because the houses are so old and broken down that it would cost as much to repair them as it would to build new ones.

It is as well that it should be told that right in the midst of Besco's shacks, the homes of the miners, are the Public and Catholic Schools, the Globe House, doctors' houses and the homes of Besco's officials, which we all know have flush closets, bath rooms, proper drainage, and, of course, must be connected with the main sewerage pipe.

But, oh, the condition of the miners' homes is very different! The miners are only workers and they must be contented with dry toilets, open drains, and as for bath rooms, these are an unknown luxury. The water from the sinks must either stand in pools in the yard or it is drained from the yard into the street and there it stands the year round. It would do your eyesight good to walk around here now and see the drains full of a whole year's refuse, covered with a horrid green slime, which makes such a good breeding place for the germs of any and every kind of disease.

Three years ago we had an epidemic of typhoid and I did not know of one case other than those who were the tenants of Besco. Our health officer and doctors went about twenty miles into the country to find the origin of the germs, but the open drains and the toilets were never blamed.

Two years ago the town thought seriously of having a milk pasteurizing plant here and forcing everyone to buy nothing but pasteurized milk. They really thought by doing that it would save the lives of some of the children who really die of starvation and neglect through the greed of Besco.

Now a little about the inside of these shacks in which the miners live. By the way, even the Royal Commission said these homes were rightly named shacks. Just now the miners' wives are wanting to spring clean. Every woman one speaks to is bemoaning the fact that she cannot or dare not attempt this. The houses are in such a broken down condition that if an attempt is made to use either scrubbing or sweeping brush things are made worse by the falling plaster. And even if the work at the mines permitted one to buy wall paper and paint it would be like throwing money away to get them, for what damage the falling plaster did not accomplish the first rain storm would, because the roofs, doors and windows are like a sieve. Anyhow, what is the use of wasting strength trying to clean when in a few weeks' time everything in the houses will be black with flies from the open drains and toilets.

Besco has not any interest in the welfare of the people, otherwise something would be done to patch these places up and make them half decent.

Yet Besco wonders why its tenants do not take the same pride in its shacks as do people who own their own houses. It is clear, women will have to take a hand in making things better in this shack-town of Besco's.

Our children are the flowers of life. Tend them carefully. Do not let them become the victims of master class greed before it is compulsory. Keep them at school until they are 16. If you need more finance for household maintenance support your husband's stand for higher wages.

E D I T O R I A L S

Editor:
    FLORENCE CUSTANCE

Office: 211 Milverton Blvd.
Toronto 6, Canada

WORKING WOMEN AND THE ANTI-STRIKE MOVEMENT

DURING the first week of the month of May the eyes of the world were fixed on Great Britain. A great struggle was on. First came the Miners' strike, a struggle between coal owners and coal miners; the former determined to maintain their profits at all costs, and the latter just as determined that their already low standard of life should not be further lowered nor their hours of labor lengthened.

Within a few hours of the miners' strike both sections of workers laid down their tools, and a general strike had developed. This brought the government of Great Britain into action, and, as we know now, this action was in the interests of the class of owners.

One of the features of the strike was the part played by the women of the aristocracy and the owners in breaking the strike. Besides frying sausages, ham and eggs, in the canteens in Hyde Park, running motors and the like, some of them had been busy ere the strike began.

A few weeks prior to the strike these women initiated what was known as the Strike against Strikes. This took the form of a big demonstration in London, in which some thirty thousand women took part, about ninety per cent. being working women.

It is reported that Mrs. Flora Drummond is at this time the foremost active spirit in forming permanent anti-strike committees, composed of the wives of workers. It is as well to recall the fact that Mrs. Drummond was once a prominent figure in the militant wing of the Women's Suffrage Movement, vieing with Mrs. Pankhurst for leadership. Also, that this movement had adopted as its motto "Any means to our end"; and fulfilling that motto in deeds, its members did not hesitate to smash windows in the fashionable parts of Old London, obstruct the police on duty, and even molest the King. This was for "Votes for Women".

Time only will show to what extent the anti-strike movement has been successful. Only very ignorant and slavish working women will join it. Working women who know what the contents of the wage envelope mean to them will stick courageously by the side of their menfolk, those who slave in the dirt, the grime and the darkness of the mine for wages.

Strikes do not happen because the workers like periods of idleness. Strikes often bring severe hardship to the workers while they are pending. But resistance against those whose greed for profits makes them grind the workers down to depths of poverty, degradation and joyless lives, is absolutely necessary.

The anti-strike movement in Great Britain may be an example which others will copy. If the movement spreads to Canada, as other movements have, then the women in the labor movement will have to combat it. On no account must the homes of workers be divided when our men are forced into a struggle against the greed for profits.

Strikes are disagreeable—they cause suffering. But the strike evil is only a result of another and greater evil, this is, that production of the things people need is carried on for the sake of profits. The only way by which strikes will be ended will be in an alteration of the motive of producing life's necessities. Production must be for use, and all must take part in production. There must be no room for idlers who live by preying off the workers.

The task of working women is not to break strikes for the benefit of the owners and the rich. Their task is to join shoulder to shoulder with their men, to make strikes successful. This will help the process of ending the profit system, which benefits only a few. Into the Labor Movement for this end.

THE IMPERIAL ORDER OF THE DAUGHTERS OF THE EMPIRE DISCUSS WEIGHTY PROBLEMS

THE National Chapter of the Imperial Order of the Daughters of the Empire are, at the moment of writing, in session in St. Johns, N.B. Among the weighty problems under their consideration are: Immigration, Combatting Communist Propaganda, especially in the schools, the Support of Militia and Defense, and the Publication of a Text Book explaining the significance and use of the Union Jack.

A truly patriotic agenda, and no doubt one which gives joy to the heart of the militarist! But the Golden Rule, so often preached by our patriotic women, is never applied by themselves. They take it for granted they have special rights, and raise great objection when they discover that there are others who consider they have rights also.

We need only to take, as an example, the fact that in the schools there hang pictures which depict war. These show the wholesale slaughter of human beings and soldier heroes. These pictures are the gift of the I.O.D.E. to the schools. Was this gift without motive or purpose? Quite to the contrary. The motive is propaganda. These pictures are intended to instil in the minds of our children, the children of the workers, that war is glorious, to die in battle is heroic, to kill in battle is a duty, even if those who kill each other haven't the faintest idea "what 'twas all about". The propaganda of the imperialist war lovers is dominating at this time the minds of the children of the workers.

We have not been able to discover if the communists have been successful in getting their kind of pictures into the schools. But we have an idea that the kind of pictures they would place in the schools would be vastly different. One of their pictures would show how the workers toil in field, factory, mill and mine. By the side of that picture would be one showing the kind of people who fatten at the expense of those toilers, the kind of homes they live in, and the luxuries with which they are surrounded. Another would show the children of the workers playing amid the dangers of the street, while those of the leisure class play in spacious grounds with amusements of every kind. Another would show how simple, trusting people, who want but the right to live decent lives, are enticed into spending their few hard-earned savings on steamship passages in order to emigrate to a foreign country. Another would show how the militia is used to shoot down workers when they ask for a living wage. Another would depict the spirit and the bond of international brotherhood, symbolized in the Red Flag.

But are these pictures in the schools? We have yet to hear that they are. Why are the I.O.D.E. complaining? It can be said quite truly that the teachers are teaching only those things that please the I.O.D.E. The school syllabus makes no provision for communist theories.

However, it may be, that the I.O.D.E. have at last realized that the whole environment surrounding the lives of the workers is a living picture, and they are fearing they cannot cope with the workers' interpretation of that living picture. But this thought can be left with our patriotic women: That if big differences did not exist between people, that if there were not poor and rich, if poverty and luxury did not exist side by side, then there would not exist a force which seeks to bring about happiness for human beings, which is possible, but which does not at this time prevail.

LABOR LEAGUE ACTIVITIES

HAMILTON

The Hamilton League reports that they are collecting for the British Miners. The League is a unit of the Hamilton Central Council of the C.L.P. and takes part in the political activity of Hamilton.

REGINA

The Regina League has waged a fight against "Intimidation tactics of employers" and "Conditions under which girls have to work." At a public meeting called by the Saskatchewan Minimum Wage Board to fix wages for women and girls operating in Beauty Parlors, the League, through Mrs. Hanway, told the Board it was difficult to get girls and women working in the Regina stores and shops to organize because they were afraid of losing their jobs.

Dealing with store and shops generally, Mrs. Hanway charged that in Regina sanitary conditions were not what they ought to be. In at least one place men and women were obliged to use the same toilet accommodation. When Mrs. Hanway wanted the Board to recommend the girls to organize themselves, the chairman said, "It was up to the girls themselves." Mrs. Hanway further stated that one of the girls at the meeting had said to her, "We dare not take a stand for organization, we would lose our jobs." Another had said, "If my boss knew that I was here tonight I would get the door tomorrow."

The Regina League, with the Regina Trades and Labor Council, presented and requested the Board to consider the following:—

a. Return to the 48 hour week.

b. Return to the former minimum wage scale. This has been reduced from $15.00 to $14.00 for experienced workers.

c. Pay for overtime when the maximum hours had been exceeded.

d. That a maximum number of hours in any one day be set. Eleven hours was suggested.

e. That female employees in beauty parlors, professional offices and stenographers should be brought under the provisions of the Minimum Wage Act.

TORONTO

Among the activities reported by the Toronto League was the attempt to organize the domestic workers. At a social gathering a number of these working women came and talked with members of the League. They claimed they were willing to organize, but what was the good when the greater number of domestic workers did not bother, when so many were continually moving about, and when so many married women came to the Bureau and offered to work for next to nothing. For the moment the League will have to content itself with holding more conferences with these women workers and learn how to get them together.

The League also issued a public protest against the treatment of Ellen Kenealey, the woman who took her life because she could not find work.

At the recent convention of the Ontario Section of the C.L.P. (Canadian Labor Party) four resolutions submitted by the League were adopted. These dealt with, (a) Combatting the School Cadet System, (b) Urging the Quebec Minimum Wage Board to get to work to fix the minimum wage rates for the women workers in Quebec,

(c) Extention of the Mothers' Allowance to the mother with one child, (d) Support the Birth Control Movement.

It also organized a meeting at which Birth Control was discussed by Dr. Withrow, the President of the Ontario Birth Control League. This is reported elsewhere.

The League has decided to hold a bazaar in the early Fall in aid of the Woman Worker and general organizational work.

TORONTO (Jewish Women's League)

The Jewish Women's Labor League is conducting a summer camp for their children. The camp will be open for two months. Because their first attempt last year met with great success their plans for the camp this year are much more extensive.

___

NEW ABERDEEN, N.S.

The New Aberdeen League reports that for the moment they are engaged in work for the defense of the seven Nova Scotia miners who were sent to Dorchester Penitentiary for two and three years, imprisoned for taking part in the "food raids".

___

THE FEDERATION HAS ADDED ANOTHER UNIT. THE MONTREAL WOMEN'S LABOR LEAGUE HAS JOINED. WHO WILL BE THE NEXT?

___

TRADE UNION NOTES

___

Girls Benefit by Belonging to the Boot and Shoe Workers' Union

Girls working in the Boot and Shoe industry in Toronto are beginning to realize the benefits of organization. During the recent organizational campaign the membership increased 100 per cent. This increase brought increase of wages with it. Formerly, the minimum wage rate for skilled stitchers was $16.00-$18.00 per week; now it is $20.00.

A new worker starts right away at a minimum of $12.00.

The girls who are organized in the Fur Workers' Union are just as favorably situated. The average wage for an organized skilled fur worker is $22.00-$24.00 per week.

Compare these rates with those of the unorganized, who have to depend upon the rates fixed by the Minimum Wage Board. Compare, too, the advantages that a girl has when she can leave wage fixing to a Union and can also get her work through a Union, with that of the unorganized worker who has to bargain alone with an employer, or if she is afraid to ask what an employer pays, only gets what the employer feels like paying, and to say nothing of the weary tramping and searching for work.

The Minimum Wage Acts of Canada have been likened to the Magna Charta, that is, a great charter of liberty for working women. No one disputes that some good has been obtained for working women, especially those working in what are usually called the unskilled industries. But the loopholes in the orders of the Minimum Wage Boards provide a way of escape for some employers, especially when they have introduced piece work systems into their factories.

The task that awaits the trade union movement in Ontario and Quebec, where most of the industrial women workers are, is to organize these women into unions. There are 130,000 women workers in industry alone in Ontario. There are more than that number in Quebec.

We urge every working woman and girl to get into a union. The union is the means through which they can obtain *protection for their labor*.

THE STORY OF ELLEN KENEALEY
(A True Story from Life)
THE HUMAN SIDE.

Day after day she visited the Employment Bureau. For hours she would sit patiently waiting a call for house-help, and hoping that this would be a job she could do.

She was only a little woman, and forty years old, but she did not look her years. She had tried to preserve her youthful appearance, not only to please herself, but what was more important, for the sake of getting work. She knew increasing years brought increasing hardship for the woman wage-earner.

To make up for her small stature, she always put every ounce of energy into her work to give people value for their money. And now, after many years of toil, she was beginning to realize she was not quite as strong as she used to be, sometimes her strength gave out completely.

And this little woman was alone, not a single relative belonging to her was living. Her companions were only her chance work companions, and although many of these were sympathetic and sometimes jolly girls, yet often she felt their sympathies forced. She understood why. These were harassing and worrying times and everyone had her own troubles. So she kept most of her worries to herself and those who knew her thought all was well with Ellen Kenealey.

Each day she saw her hard-earned savings getting less. Who was there to give her shelter or assistance when her last cent was gone? No one. What would she be in the eyes of the law? A vagrant. She shuddered at the thought. But she could not help pondering over this, the thought would not leave her. It stayed with her as she sat waiting for work. It persisted in disturbing her sleep at night. Oh, the horror of unemployment! Oh, the terribleness of the uncertainty of life! What was life to her anyway? She asked herself this question hundreds of times. Why, it was just a dreary miserable existence! When she did manage to get a job cleaning up other people's dirt it was sheer slavery. Women who employed her expected her to get through a week's work in a single day. She hated them for their heartlessness. But, then, again, when there was no work, she faced starvation.

This was her life. It was becoming a burden to her mind. Who would miss her? She hadn't a friend in the world! She knew she was growing desperate. She was better out of the struggle. The struggle to live was not worth the mental anguish. Death, peace, the end of struggle, these became more pleasant to her mind. It was quite an easy thing to put an end to her existence. Just a little poison, then—the end. At last, summoning all her courage she walked boldly into a drug store and bought carbolic acid. Death—but the end of the struggle to live. Peace.

But she could not die in her rented room. This might cause the landlady trouble, and she had only recently taken the room. No, she must die in solitude, just like a dog without a home.

Having thus decided, she boarded a suburban car and travelled until she came to a secluded place. Then she left the car. No one was near. Calmly and deliberately she drank the poison. How it burned her throat! Never mind, the pain was nothing compared with her mental anguish! How long now before she died! She was losing consciousness—Was she dying?

COLD FACTS.

Ellen Kenealey was found in an unconscious condition. She was taken to the hospital. Here, after a treatment she regained consciousness. The hospital authorities notified the police. The police took her to the station, where she remained all night. To the police, she told her story of unemployment. "I cannot get work. I have no friends. I am better dead than alive."

Next day in the Women's Court she was charged with "attempted suicide" and ordered to the Reception Hospital for observation. But Ellen Kenealey was not to be observed for very long. The next day she died.

At the inquest, held three weeks later, all that was known of Ellen Kenealey was told. The hospital authorities claimed she fought against relief, she never complained of pains, and they doubted if she had taken poison.

The jury's verdict was, "We find that Ellen Kenealey came to her death on March 28, in the Reception Hospital as a result of carbolic acid, self-administered on March 26, while suffering from acute despondency on her inability to secure employment."

THE LESSON.

Ellen Kenealey's case was taken up by the Toronto Women's Labor League. The League protested through the press against what appeared to be neglect on the part of the authorities in not discovering how sick she was. The protest was not in vain. It brought to light the anguish of a hardworking, respectable woman worker who found herself unemployed.

It brought, too, a letter from one of her former employers who vouched for her respectability, industriousness, and good breeding.

Ellen Kenealey's case is but one of many hundreds. All do not act with the same deliberateness as she.

Life, under modern conditions of employment, only presents hopelessness when these conditions are not understood. The capitalist system of wage labor exploitation is ruthless with its victims. Workers are cheap these days. Their lives are of little importance.

If Ellen Kenealey had known these things she might have had another outlook. She might have been a member of a trade union, then she would not have felt so helpless and so lonely. The union not only is a wage protector, but it does concern itself in the welfare of its members.

Women workers, let the story of Ellen Kenealey impress itself upon you. Ask yourselves, shall it be the fate of Ellen Kenealey, or shall we join the union for protection? Into the union, and strengthen Labor's fight for unemployment insurance.

By permission of

("The Worker")

_____ Toronto.

THE STORY OF OUR FAMILY

(By Florence Custance)

(Synopsis of the two previous contributions published in the mimeographed issues.)

To understand the Story of Our Family it is necessary to accept the fact of the Law of Change—Evolution. Change takes place under our eyes, sometimes with great rapidity. Old things are discarded and new take their place. Yet, actually, nothing is entirely new, one thing develops from another. For example, all the great industrial processes of to-day depend upon a discovery made by our primitive forefathers—that discovery was Fire.

While some things change with great rapidity, the change in other things is so slow as to be imperceptible, and, in fact, the change can only be discovered through observations covering a long period of time.

Among the things that appear to be fixed are the groupings and relationships of people. The grouping we call "Our Family" is to us very dear; yet, even "Our Family" is not the same as the family of our primitive forefathers. Still they are linked up, and the family of to-day is but the outcome of the family groupings of long, long ago. It is the purpose of this story to unfold the reasons for the changes, and what those changes were, that have brought to us the present form of "Our Family."

(Continued)

THE ROOT OF SOCIAL PROGRESS

It may be asked "What is progress? And by what means has mankind progressed?" A great student and writer on this subject, Lewis Morgan, claims that mankind has advanced by means of, first, inventions and discoveries, and second, by means of institutions; that is, organizations of people themselves. He shows, too, in his book, "Ancient Society," that the urge was the preservation and security of Life. And, moreover, as people changed their methods of procuring and producing the needs of life, so their organizations (or institutions) changed accordingly. As we proceed with our story this will be very clear to us.

HOW MANKIND ADVANCED

We have already stated that fire was the important discovery which formed the foundation of many inventions. Fire, too, was a means of defense against wild animals, as well as a means of making food more pleasant to the taste.

Then there followed the invention of the "bow and arrow." This was used in procuring food and was also a weapon of warfare. Then came the making of pottery. Later came the domestication, or breeding, of animals for food, and along with this the cultivation of food plants, first for animals, and later for man himself. These were followed by the discovery of smelting iron and the invention of the iron tool. This last invention made it possible to clear lands of forests, build houses, and for man to have a settled habitation.

When settled habitation became possible the people living in this settled territory made further advancement; not alone of supplying the needs of the body, but attention could now be given to what is called Art (self expression) and to the study of the mysteries around them (the development of Science).

When the machine made its appearance, first used by the hand, then water power, later steam power and now electric power, progress went apace by leaps and bounds. To-day we find ourselves in an age which reveals constantly the fruits of man's ingenuity.

THE STAGES OF THE DEVELOPMENT OF MANKIND.

We are very fond of calling ourselves "civilized." This is more often than not said to distinguish us from others we desire to belittle. We are apt to think this name places us in the position of being "cultured."

But civilization has a deeper meaning, and is connected with a development upon which culture itself depends.

When tracing the stages of the development and progress of mankind, Lewis Morgan gives three main stages which are again divided into sub-stages, according to the degree of progress along the line of invention and discovery. These three main stages are: Savagery, Barbarism and Civilization.

(To be continued).

––––––––

SUCCESS TO THE "WOMAN WORKER."

"The Editor."

At last we have our magazine. Yes, and actually in print! This has been made possible because of the loyal support given our previous feeble mimeographed attempts. Many encouraging letters came from our Labor Leagues. Some of the Leagues bought sufficient copies for their membership; some sent in donations and paid for their next bundle in advance. By these means we have been able to get sufficient money together to pay for our first printed issue.

This is what can be called support. It makes one feel proud of our women and our movement. If this support continues, and we hope that our efforts will merit continued support, we shall have no need to fear for the success of the Woman Worker.

The Woman Worker is the voice of the Women's Labor League Movement. It will tell what our movement is doing to help raise the standard of life for women workers. It will deal with domestic, industrial and political problems affecting the lives of working women. It will tell about the struggles of the workers throughout the world and the status of women in the countries throughout the world. It will endeavor to speak truthfully about these struggles so that those who hear our voice will have confidence in it. And, lastly, it will breathe hope into our struggle for the happiness which we know is possible for the workers.

It will be seen that our magazine will be quite unlike other magazines which are published for the benefit of women. It will not contain fashions and patterns, and we are leaving recipes for cooking to the cook book. We shall not print sickly love stories, we are leaving these to the other magazines. Instead, we shall devote our attention to things that are overlooked by the other magazines. Everything that will be printed in our magazine will deal with life, real life, not imaginations. Its sole objective will be to champion Protection of Womanhood, and the Cause of the Workers generally.

Its columns will be open to all our readers. In fact, one of the main features of our magazine is "Correspondence from Working Women."

The Woman Worker should be in the hands of every working woman, no matter what her occupation. The women who are members of the Labor League Movement will accomplish a great work if they will undertake this for the Movement. Building our Labor League Movement depended upon OUR MAGAZINE. OUR MAGAZINE is here. All hands are wanted for its distribution. This alone will bring success to the Woman Worker.

REGISTERED NURSES HOLD FIRST MEETING

Recently the Registered Nurses Association of Ontario held their first meeting in Belleville, Ont. Some very important problems connected with their work were discussed. These were: supplying sufficient numbers of nurse teachers to meet the demand of training schools in the Province; the production of competent superintendents for small hospitals; supervision of the supply of student nurses; the bad practice of unsupervised nurses doing district work for insurance companies, and the danger of lowering the standards of nursing in Ontario through political influence.

These questions discussed by the nurses in convention are of sufficient importance to working women. Thousands of working women fill the hospitals, thousands depend upon nurses in childbirth. It is necessary that our working women shall support the effort of the nurses to keep the standard of nursing as high as possible.

TO OUR READERS

We want your letters. We want your opinions. We want your stories from life and of life. So write us.

WOMEN IN PROFESSIONS ORGANIZE AND DISCOVER THE ADVANTAGES OF ORGANIZATION

The women teachers in the Province of Ontario number about 14,000. Of this number 3,700 are organized in the Federation of Women Teachers' Associations. At the annual meeting, held in April, it was reported that one of the advantages derived through organization was that they had been able, to a certain degree, to combat unemployment. They were now in a position to place unemployed teachers in positions.

Through their organization they were demanding a higher standard of qualifications in order to reduce the numbers flocking into ranks already overcrowded. It was also reported that they had assisted, by means of voluntary contributions, the teachers who went out on strike in Blairmore, Alberta.

WHAT WORKING CLASS HOUSEWIVES AND OTHER WOMEN ARE DOING

Finnish Women Hold a Conference

The Finnish working women of Port Arthur, Fort William and the surrounding small towns held a conference during the month of May to discuss very important matters, both of organization and forms of activity. Among the things they proposed taking up and for which they will work are: Support Labor Defense, Fight Bootlegging and Drunkenness, especially among the Youth; Fight exploitation by the jobbing contractors which reduces the lumberworkers to a miserable state of slavery; Support cooperatives; To combat the Cadet system of military training of the school children; To take more interest in the forms of education of working class children.

Some of the delegates to the conference discussed joining the Women's Labor League Federation, but this was left over for further consideration at another conference to be held in the Fall.

BETH MIRIAM GIRLS DISCUSS "WHY THE POOR REMAIN POOR, AND HOW THE RICH OBTAIN THEIR RICHES"

Our Young Women Are Waking Up.

The Beth Miriam Girls' Club has about thirty members, all under twenty years of age. These girls organized for social purposes. They held sales of work and social affairs, the proceeds of which were turned over to the various charitable organizations.

Now they have discovered that this does not get them very far. They have decided that they will include "education" in the program of activity. Their first educational meeting took the form of a general discussion and Mrs. Custance of the Toronto Women's Labor League was asked to lead the discussion.

When asked by Mrs. Custance upon what subject they desired knowledge they said, "The problem of the workers in relation to the rich."

By the process of question and answer, thirty bright, intelligent girls discovered that the workers were poor because they received for their labors only a portion of the wealth which they produced. In Canada that portion was One-fifth, the class of employers got Four-fifths. The ever-increasing wealth of the rich was obtained from the workers because the workers, after working a portion of the time in which they produced enough wealth to cover their wages, were compelled to keep on working until they produced enough wealth or values, which covered rent, interest and profits for their employers. It was seen that the lower the employers kept the wages the more profits they would be able to keep for themselves.

This explained the reason for the existence of the rich. This was why the rich wanted to have a hold on the workers. This hold they had, because they had become the rulers, and in order to remain the rulers they spent much money and supported institutions which helped them to control the workers' minds. The result of all this was conflicts between the workers and the rich—those who produced and those who owned the products.

The Beth Miriam Girls decided that trade unionism was better than having a government board set a minimum wage. Some of them gave examples of how the employers evaded giving their workers the minimum wage.

We need a design for the cover of our magazine. It must of course, fit the name—Woman Worker. Who can supply this?

Subscribe for the
W o m a n   W o r k e r

10¢ a copy $1.00 a year

Women, Wage Work and the   1
Labour Movement

The problems faced on the job by women workers and the possibilities of organizing them into unions were arguably the most important issues at stake in the *Woman Worker*. Because of the Communist Party's attachment to Marxist-Leninism, the Party's Women's Department and paper editor Florence Custance saw the radicalization of women at the point of production as the most certain way of kindling their socialist consciousness. The incredible exploitation women faced as workers, all socialists and Communists of this era believed, would bring into sharp focus the oppressive nature of capitalism and lead women towards unions and political radicalism. Women, suffering the double exploitation of class and gender inequalities, faced job insecurity, lower pay than men, and humiliating harassment—conditions which Communists believed should stimulate their political awakening.

The mainstream labour movement had shown almost no interest in organizing women workers. The largest federation of trade unions, the Trades and Labour Congress (TLC), remained dominated by skilled workers whose craft unions by and large excluded women, with the notable exceptions of some garment workers' unions. Dedicated to the goal of securing for its members a "family wage"—a wage big enough for a male breadwinner to support his wife and children—the TLC worked primarily with an image of woman as helpmate and homemaker. As workers, women were seen as temporary, needing protection only while they laboured before marriage.

The Trades and Labour Congress was chastised in the *Woman Worker* for failing to organize women wage earners into unions, and the wives of working-class men into union guilds or auxiliaries. WLLS, while irritated by the TLC's treatment of women as well as by its overall conservatism, were still unwilling to give up on it entirely and they continually tried to influence it. After all, the organization had important historic connections to sections of the working class, and this was highly useful to Communists' united front policy. The Federation of WLLs had appealed unsuccessfully to the TLC for affiliation in 1924, and when Custance took up the editorship of the *Woman Worker* in 1926, she was still smarting from the rebuff—motivated mainly by the TLC's well known anti-communism. There was more cooperation at the local level, especially in Toronto and Regina, although in Toronto, the relationship was cut off abruptly in 1927 when the local WLL was expelled from the Toronto District Labour Council.

Communists were certainly more attuned than most trade unionists to the exploitation of women as earners and to the necessity of unionizing all women workers, skilled and unskilled. Yet despite their public rhetoric, the Communist Party had little interest in actually doing the difficult work of organizing women.

Operating with scarce resources, Communists often directed their primary attention to areas of production such as mining and heavy industry, giving only cursory attention to sectors employing female labour, such as the seasonal food industry, boot and shoe making, small manufacturing, textiles, and of course, domestic work. Domestic service still engaged between a quarter and a third of all women wage earners in Canada, and it was an organizer's nightmare since most domestics laboured by themselves, isolated within a single household. Many domestics were also recent immigrants. As the *Woman Worker* pointed out, an oversupply of such workers, encouraged by immigration agents and employers, kept wages and conditions poor, and led to both the abuse of child labour and difficulties in organizing adult workers.

Communists realized that the task of organizing women workers was fraught with logistical, structural barriers that were hard to overcome. In the 1920s the number of women working for wages (as well as the number of professional women workers) increased steadily in Canada. The percentage of women in the workforce went from 15.5 to almost 17 per cent by early in the next decade. While the vast majority of female workers were unmarried (and mostly young), between 18 and 19 per cent were either married, widowed or divorced. Women were also moving gradually into new areas of work, such as clerical, white collar, and retail. Despite this appearance of progress, women's workplace realities were hardly liberating. During the

1920s many workers were facing the onslaught of new attempts to streamline, rationalize and "speed up" work processes. Moreover, women were more likely to be responsible for domestic tasks, whether they worked for wages or not, and they were often portrayed in the mass media as temporary workers concerned with shopping and beauty, and of course in hot pursuit of a husband. Not least because of this ideological construction, women remained ghettoized within the workforce in areas of work considered unskilled, "feminine" and "domestic." These jobs were undervalued and certainly underpaid: women made, on average, 54-60 per cent of male wages. Seasonal, intermittent and part-time work was also common for women. As one *Woman Worker* reader pointed out in his letter about waitresses, the fracturing of their work day—along with intense employer opposition—inhibited their organization.

The 1920s were not necessarily an easy time to organize any workers in Canada, men or women. Despite talk of prosperity in the financial press, evidenced by increased production of consumer goods and a healthy stock market, the economy was actually depressed for the first half of the decade, and there was little sign of labour feeling confident and flexing its muscles. Radicalism was in retreat, chased down by employer and state offensives in the aftermath of the general strikes of 1919. More subtle barriers also existed, both to unionization and socialist action. Companies were experimenting with welfare and paternalist programs to induce workers to remain loyal and quiet. Many reform, charitable and religious organizations geared towards women, such as the YWCA, offered housing and recreational programs designed to develop moral and industrious women workers who would not be inclined to rebel against working conditions. While many middle-class reformers now accepted the reality of women working for wages before marriage, they did not see unions as a necessity and chose to focus their efforts on "suitable" leisure pursuits and on preserving the sexual morals of working women. As *Woman Worker* excerpts reprinted in the "Feminism and Social Reform" section make clear, WLLers struggled with the reactionary nature of many of these charitable and religious efforts.

Despite Communist women's aversion to middle-class moralism, it is revealing that similar concerns with the protection of women's virtue and morality creep into articles in the *Woman Worker*. As the story "The Modern Virgin" seems to say (see the "Women and the Sex Trade" section), one of the most devastating results of low wages for women might be the possibility of sexual seduction, the loss of virtue, and a life in prostitution. Writers in the

Woman Worker were also well aware of the temptations of mass culture and consumption in the 1920s: beauty contests and romantic fantasy, Custance worried, would certainly lure women away from socialism. There was some recognition that women's socialization as "sweeties and homemakers" had to be countered to create more outspoken, public, political "companions of men." Such language suggests that some WLL correspondents recognized the specific problems of women's oppression, and saw the emancipation of women as an integral part of the advent of socialism. Other correspondents placed the blame for political inaction squarely on the shoulders of fellow workers, whom they claimed did not take their wage work and the need to organize seriously enough and thus remained "contented" wage slaves.

The *Woman Worker* was an educational and agitational paper. Its first purpose was therefore to raise and sustain working-class women's anti-capitalist consciousness. At the most basic level, it did so by trying to explain, using Marxist analysis, the system of capitalist exploitation that workers faced, showing why "girls" were a source of extra profit to employers. Secondly, it pointed to the need to overcome divisions based on gender, ethnicity and race that served to separate workers from one another, limiting the possibilities for economic and political action. Gender and ethnicity were the most obvious barriers described and criticized, but occasionally the paper also protested the way in which racial divisions were manipulated by employers to prevent working-class solidarity. Articles like the one reprinted here on Asian labour (see "Foreign Powers and China," June 1927), were unusual and courageous for the time: in the 1920s, Canadian trade unions were still almost uniformly opposed to Asian immigration and labour, their vociferous opposition shaped by racism and fear of cheap labour.

Perhaps one of the most difficult issues the paper had to tackle was the question of married women workers. Most articles in the paper stressed the fact that married women were forced into wage labour to support their families. Like all workers, they should be encouraged to unionize. Contributors enjoyed taking on the social democrat and "labourite" politician, Walter Rollo, when he attacked married women for their presence in the labour force. But the overall perspective of the paper was somewhat contradictory, for it was still assumed that once married, women's work would be homemaking, not wage earning. A preference for the male breadwinner model of family life was clear, and the work of married women was always seen as an unfortunate burden, not a right.

Applauding women's attempts to unionize and their protests against working conditions, the *Woman Worker* tried to inspire other women to take similar paths. In the last resort, unions were seen as the best way of maintaining lasting organizations dedicated both to the improvement of working women's lives and to building a political critique of capitalism. The paper therefore advertised attempts to organize unions, and gave coverage to women's sporadic workplace protests. The latter were more predominant than the former in the 1920s. Often, correspondence from workers describing their workplace, conditions and problems were printed. These letters—from silk workers, domestics and garment workers—provide valuable and rare glimpses into the lives of working-class women in an era when few mainstream papers, even trade union papers, took the time to consider them.

A clear gap always remained between the Communist Party's rhetoric, calling for women's organization, and the reality of its lack of attention to the task. But for Communist women like Florence Custance and those who wrote for the *Woman Worker*, solutions to women's inequality *were* clearly important. Their intense condemnations of women's oppression and the indignities of wage work, and their desire to see women's lives improved, were real indeed. Moreover, given the barriers to organizing women into unions, the strategy of the paper, following that of the Communist Party, did make some sense.

First, the *Woman Worker* concentrated on reporting and correspondence from women in certain occupations and workplaces where they had at least a faint hope of attracting adherents. In the garment industry, for example, the presence of left-wing, Jewish workers provided some hope for future Communist organizing. The Communist Party's overall united front approach at this time called for active, but critical participation of Communists in existing unions and working-class organizations as a means of winning the working class to socialism. Second, given their own lack of resources, they focused on a few key issues for women, such as the minimum wage (see "Protective Legislation" section). Here they hoped to aid rank-and-file women in their fight for a decent wage, while still exposing the inadequacies of such reforms and the need for revolution. Finally, because the paper recognized that many women workers became full-time homemakers after marriage, they concentrated not only on women as workers, but also on women as full-time homemakers.

Further Reading:

- Joan Sangster, "The Communist Party and the Woman Question, 1922-29," *Labour/Le Travail*, 15 (Spring 1985), 25-56.

- Carolyn Strange, *Toronto's Girl Problem: The Perils and Pleasures of the City, 1880-1930* (Toronto: University of Toronto Press, 1995), chap. 7.

- Veronica Strong-Boag, "The Girl of the New Day: Canadian Working Women in the 1920s," *Labour/Le Travail*, 4 (1979), 131-164.

WHAT WILL THE TRADES AND LABOR CONGRESS DO FOR WORKING WOMEN?

[Editorial]

September 1926, pp. 1-2.

THERE are 400,000 women in Canada compelled to work for wages, according to official figures. About 100,000 of these work in factories. Of the 300,000 remaining, the greatest number are employed in the occupation of cleaning and the like. These work mostly by the day, are occasional workers, and continually change employers.

If, to this number, there is added the number of women who are engaged in home occupations, such as plain sewing, dressmaking, fancy-work of various kinds, artificial flower-making, etc., it will be seen that there are very few working women outside the circle of direct wage-earners.

How is it that women have been forced into this position? First of all must be stated, that this is the day of machine production, and this is at the root of changed home life. The advent of the machine has forced women outside the home, not only to maintain themselves, but also to maintain the home. In one report given by the Ontario Minimum Wage Board it is stated that "over 50% of the women working in the factories are married women." And those who work at home occupations and cleaning are either married women or widows.

The rapid entry of women into the field of wage-earning in Canada during recent years has left women at the mercy of their employers. Women are looked upon as "cheap labour." Minimum Wage Boards have done something to prevent sweated labor being disgracefully underpaid. But sweated labor exists despite Minimum Wage Boards. Also, the Boards have not been able to cope with the cunning of an employer bent on underpaying his women workers, in order that his business shall be a profitable one.

Who alone can solve the difficult problem of preventing women wage-earners being at the mercy of employers who care only for the profits they can wring from the labor of those they employ?

Those who can and must solve this problem are the Trade Unions. Will the Trades and Labor Congress of Canada at its convention during the third week in September in the city of Montreal discuss this matter seriously, or will it be content to pass resolutions only? If the Congress fails to discuss the vexed question of organizing women workers into trade unions then it fails in its duty.

Then, again, while it is very necessary that women wage-earners shall be organized according to their occupation, it is also necessary that the wives of the workers, especially those of the trade unionists, shall be organized, too. The work of the miners' wives on the picket line in Great Britain is something that should stir both men and women of the working class. Without such assistance and loyalty from their wives the men would have been forced back to work many weeks ago. It must be remembered that if the man earns the wage, it is the woman who has to eke it out for the family needs. Her efforts, her labors, are a necessary part of the process of production of to-day. Who has a right to say after witnessing what women can do, and the influence they can wield during a strike, that they should not be admitted into the Trade Union Movement? The organization of the wives of trade unionists into auxiliaries or guilds would be one of the simplest things the Trades and Labor Congress could undertake.

The only women's organizations that have taken up with real vigor the fight against low wages and unjust working conditions for women workers have been the Women's Labor Leagues throughout the country. In some cases their efforts have been recognized by certain Trades and Labor Councils, Toronto and Regina in particular. But, so far, they have for some reason or other, received rebuffs from the Trades and Labor Congress. And this despite the fact that they are doing splendid work under difficult conditions. The Labor Leagues have taken upon their shoulders the task of preparing the hard soil for trade unionism for working women in Canada. Will the Trades and Labor Congress of Canada, the central power of Trade Unionism in Canada, lend its assistance in actually building trade unions of women workers? We say it must.

September 1926, p. 6.

Dear Editor:—

I am working in a non-union shop, and a little while ago we had to work overtime every night in succession for about two weeks, and after so many nights of hard work we were well nigh exhausted.

When we complained, the foreman boldly announced, "Everybody must work till 9 o'clock." One girl who was not well said, "I am very sick, I must go to see the doctor." And when he heard this he came rushing like a wild beast and said, "Those who refuse to work overtime will be fired in the morning."

But none of us really thought this threat would be put into effect, especially when one had to stop work on account of sickness.

However, the next morning to our great surprise it did so happen. When the bell rang, the girl who had refused to work overtime, because she was too sick, and although she was not feeling much better even then, was called before the foreman. The foreman immediately started to insult her with vulgar remarks, and told her to clear out.

Imagine in what terrible circumstances this girl found herself when she was fired. It is hard enough to get on while we are employed, it is especially hard when sick and out of work.

This is the treatment we get under this present system of exploitation. Is it a wonder that prostitution is prevalent? Is it a wonder that women are often compelled to make terrible sacrifices in order to be able to exist?

This is all due to the economic system under which we live.

We must find a way out, but not by such degrading means. No, the only way to solve this problem of rotten conditions is through organized demands.

Working girls enter the trade unions and become active and let us fight for better conditions.

B.S.
Montreal.

WOMEN AS CHEAP LABOR

[Editorial]

October 1926, pp. 1-2.

IN the United States women who work in industry receive little more than half the wages paid to men, according to government report. This state of affairs is not merely true of the United States, it prevails in every country in which the profit system, known as capitalism, exists.

Woman is supposed only to need enough to provide her with food, clothing and shelter. She is supposed to have no other responsibility. Even if she has it makes no difference as to her wages. A man is supposed to be the person upon whom rests the responsibility of raising a family. Therefore, a man's wages are supposed to be not only for his own keep, but also for that of his family.

But the working-class housewife and mother knows how far her husband's wages will go round for the family needs. In many cases it simply will not go round. Rather than face debt, she puts her children into a public nursery and goes into the factory, or, out to work, as she calls it, herself. In some industries more than half the number of women employed are young married women, many having children under five years of age.

The nature of production today takes women more and more from the homes. Much of the work women are engaged in does not require skill, it is just a matter of speed. The nature of their work causes them to drift from one occupation to another. They are open to the worst forms of robbery by those who employ them as cheap labor.

The greatest trouble in this connection is that women, whether single or married, look upon their wage-earning efforts as a temporary need. Therefore, they make no attempt to improve their conditions. If one job does not suit they go to another, but more often than not they submit to conditions.

Woman as cheap labor is the worse kind of slave. If she is married and is compelled to work, she is doubly enslaved. Speeded to the limit of her strength in the factory, she works at her household duties until bed-time. She has no minutes of leisure, as her husband has, even to read the newspaper. It cannot be wondered at that these women grow old and worn out before their years.

Some may urge that we take a stand against the employment of married women. In face of the knowledge of the struggle of working class families to live, we cannot do this. We must, instead, urge that women, as well as men, become members of trade unions. This alone will prevent women being used merely as "Cheap Labor," and will aid in securing some measure of protection in this profit-getting age.

TRADE UNIONS
(By a Supporter)

October 1926, pp. 11-12.

It is surprising that today there should be working women who know either little or nothing about Trade Unions, yet such is the case. Those who have but a little knowledge of trade unions look upon these organizations of the workers as evil things. They claim that the unions cause strikes, that they cause disturbances in the country, and that they take men from their homes at night, when they could be doing something better than attending meetings.

It is plain that these views are impressions gained from newspapers that are published in the interests of those who either employ cheap labor or would like to employ such labor.

It is hard to convince women who have such impressions that, had it not been for trade unions, the workers who are living in what are called civilized countries, would be as badly off as are the workers in India and China today.

Trade unions have helped the workers to obtain a standard of life above that of a mere bread existence. Trade unions have been a means of securing a shorter work day. Trade unions have secured compensation for injured workmen and many other benefits.

The reason trade unions are not popular is because they are organizations of workers only, and they fight profits. They are not popular organizations, even among workers, because they are organizations of resistance.

Many workers prefer to belong to fraternal societies and orders of various kinds, because these do not compel one to fight. Sometimes the union compels this when workers' wages and hours of labor are attacked by the masters.

The masters do not fear benefit societies. In fact, sometimes they get into these themselves in order to use them for political reasons. The masters do fear, and even hate, trade unions, because they know that these stand between them and big profits on the one hand, and the workers and low wages on the other.

When workers grumble because their wages are low they really have themselves to blame. They have not helped to make the unions strong.

Union labor is always better paid than non-union labor. This is very clearly seen in the case of the garment trades in this country. The masters do not give more than they are compelled, and it is the union that tries to set the rate of wage.

Working class housewives should insist upon their husbands joining a trade union, in order to get a bigger pay envelope. Working women who are wage earners should join a union to get higher wages and better working conditions. The masters have their unions to protect their interests, so must the workers have theirs.

Into the Unions.

AN APPEAL TO WOMEN WAGE EARNERS
By Trade Union Supporter.

January 1927, pp. 8-9.

Women workers in shop, factory, mill and office, have you ever stopped to consider why you are forced to work—why you get wages for your work—and why you get only a wage that just keeps life within your body?

Have you ever wondered how it is your masters live—how it is they live in mansions—and why they are able to enjoy the luxuries of life?

If you have never thought of these things, it is time you did.

Do you suppose your master employs you because he likes you? You know when you go for a position, or a job, as it is most often called, you have to be able to satisfy your master or his staff that you are able to do good work, and you know you are not paid what you would like but what the master says he pays his workers.

Then you know when you work that you are speeded up so that production can be increased each day. You know you leave your work dead tired, all your energy is exhausted. But you may not know that this means cheaper production and more profits for your master.

You will have learned, that when you work, you are no longer counted human beings. Instead you become help, only hands, and are known by numbers.

This condition has become so common, and working girls and women have become so used to this treatment that they look upon all these things as matters of course. Is it any wonder that working girls and women are treated with indifference?

Girls Used for Profit.

It is time women workers in shop, factory, mill and office knew that their power to work or labor is used by their employers only for the sake of PROFITS, and that these employers can only live at their expense.

It must be clear to you that employers do not invest money in buildings, machinery, and materials, in order to give work to the poor. No, indeed, they invest their money so that it shall bring them profits.

But this is the method of production to-day. All the things we need are not made first because people need them, but instead because they are a good means of investment, because they bring profits.

It is time women wage earners learned that production depends upon the labor energy of the workers; when this energy is withheld, then see how the masters are fixed.

Wages for the Workers—but Profits for the Boss.

So we see that while production depends upon the workers, the workers get out of their labors a portion called wages, while the masters get the cream, called profits.

Workers' wages just mean poor clothing, poor food, poor shelter.

Masters' profits bring them the best of food, beautiful clothing, splendid mansions, and luxuries of every kind.

The masters love their portion. This is why they keep the workers down. This is why they cut wages. They always want more and more profits.

The masters do not care what becomes of working women and girls so long as they can get the means to provide their own women and children with wealth and luxury.

Want and hunger do not stare the women of the master class in the face, as it does the women of the working class.

It becomes necessary for working women to look after themselves, to talk about their lives, the conditions of work, and the problem of how to live.

Married or not, it makes no difference, women of the working class will have to be toilers. So it is time to lose indifference and to study and talk over your conditions of life.

Organize at once your study groups, talk about your workshop conditions, talk about your home conditions, talk about the conditions under which your husbands, or your fathers, or your brothers, work. These discussions will help you to understand why it is necessary to organize and struggle against the evil conditions forced upon the workers by the masters.

THE REAL BUILDERS—ARE THEY TREATED AS SUCH?

February 1927, p. 5.

Dr. Young, of the United Church of Canada, commenting on Canada's non-Anglo-Saxon population, tells us that:

"In this task (of developing our national resources) the non-Anglo-Saxon has had a worthy party. He has shouldered the burden as the Canadian man-of-all-work. He is doing seven-tenths of all the coal mining and 78 per cent. of all the work in the woollen mills. Eighty-five per cent. of all labor in slaughter-houses and meat-packing industries is non-British. He makes about nineteen-twentieths of all clothing, and four-fifths of all furniture. He turns out 80 per cent. of all its leather and one-half of the gloves, and refines almost all the sugar. Wherever he is, he is the backbone of industry. He engages in all the dangerous occupations, and he takes on the hard, unpleasant jobs which the Canadian workman is glad to relinquish. Without the contribution of the new Canadian in toil of brain and body the record of Canadian progress would have been impossible."

In spite of this, and it is a well-known fact, that many of these nation-builders have either the greatest difficulty in procuring citizenship rights, or are refused them, if it is found they have radical views. Who said Democracy?

THE JUNGLE
A Story of a Winnipeg Working Girl Lost in the Jungle of Master Class Duplicity.

February 1927, pp. 14-15.

Alice is a pale-faced girl of twenty years of age who is working at a mangle in a laundry, doing the small articles as follows, handkerchiefs, towels and toilet covers, for which she receives the munificent sum of nine dollars per week (or, rather, did). The other day, being pay day, the boss, when paying her, gave her eight dollars and seventy-five cents. When Alice protested he calmly told her in a sarcastic manner that she had been receiving good pay; she should only receive eight dollars and twenty-five cents, seeing that she does not commence working until Monday noon. Wonderful minimum wage for working girls and women in Manitoba! is it not?

Alice, like many other young girls, is being paid rotten wages because there is no one who bothers their heads about how working girls exist, or, for that matter, how the other fellow lives that has to work for lower wages, whether it be girl or boy, man or woman. As I write, my attention is being drawn to the "Coolie Wages in B.C." Lumber barons are offering twenty cents per hour for "husky young men." The struggle for the workers is so severe that most of them have no time to think of the other fellow.

Alice pours her story into the sympathetic ears of a fellow slave during the dinner hour. "Oh, what shall I do?" is her heart cry. "I've no father or mother, I have to pay six dollars per week for my board and room, and now I shall only have two dollars and twenty-five cents to dress on. I cannot do it. I have tried so hard, because since I left school I have believed that if we work hard and serve our employers well that we should be sure to rise higher, make our way in the world. I've been working hard for eight years and kept myself respectable." (By the way, Alice is clothed in the very poorest clothes that can be purchased, rotten, shoddy material that brings great profits.) "It seems endless. I wish I was dead. Is there no help for a poor working girl?"

Such is the cry in the dark of thousands of poor lost working girls, lost in the jungle of master-class hypocrisy and duplicity. Speed the day when all working girls and women will realize the lies that are being taught our children (our class) through the pulpit, the school and the press, as well as the mass of lying propaganda the masters and their henchmen are flooding the country with to fool the workers at every turn.

Yours for the Day of Freedom for the working class,
EDITH E. HANCOX,
Winnipeg.

WHAT A SALES GIRL WRITES

April 1927, p. 16.

Dear Comrade:

I am enclosing with this some writings of my experiences as a worker. It has been these experiences that have made me an agitator, and not as our rulers say, "the result of radical and Bolshevik propaganda." I had become this before I ever heard of such things.

You will not be surprised when I tell you I have become a little bitter towards my fellow workers. As the years pass on one becomes very weary waiting for them to advance.

The workers in the departmental stores are a breed all their own. Wherever I have been I have found myself isolated and alone. They have allowed me to put my hands in the fire and then take the benefits themselves. I am valued as a worker, but am turned down because I think and reason. So what with this and the depression in business through economic causes I am on the downhill grade financially. But I shall survive it somehow.

In spite of the fact that I have both a trade and a profession it is hard to make a living. Prices on labor here in Vancouver have been cut down by the large stores to such an extent that one cannot make a living.

Within the last few months I have known workers in my trade to be cut from $19.00 to $15.00 per week. One, a married woman, is supporting herself and a boy of six years on $15.00. She had one other child, which she was forced to give away; her husband had left her.

Seven years ago I was paid 50 cents per hour, working a 44-hour week. This was in the house furnishing trade. And now it is hard to make $15.00 a week.

In none of the stores are the workers allowed to organize. An "Association" is arranged for them by the heads of the firms, and the benefits derived from this are sports and a doctor if one happens to get sick. To most this means a deduction in pay. So the above mentioned woman really gets only $14.50 per week by the time fees of one kind and another are paid.

The women sales clerks are paid $12.75 per week. Anything more than this is an exception. And married men in the same line of work are supporting families on $15.00 per week. But they appear to be satisfied working till nine and ten o'clock at night without one cent for overtime.

I shall certainly attend the meetings of the League that has been organized here with a view to membership.

Comradely yours,
Shopgirl.

DOMESTIC WORKERS ORGANIZE

[Editorial]

May 1927, pp. 1-2.

AGAIN an attempt is being made to organize the domestic workers. The number of times this has been attempted in this country would be difficult to record. If the new organization lasts it will be a great achievement.

The Home Service Association, as the new organization is called, was launched a few weeks ago in Vancouver. The object of the Association is—to assist its members in their calling, to seek redress of grievances, to improve conditions of labor, hours, wages, weekly and yearly holidays; to keep a free registry to enable members to obtain positions; to obtain legislation to establish a minimum wage; to open a Hostel and a Training School. Sick benefits are another feature of the organization. The membership is open to men as well as women.

Taking the object altogether it is easy to see that there were some who helped in its preparation who were well aware of the difficulties of organizing working girls. The Hostel, Training School, Free Registry and Sick Benefits are, seemingly, attractions which must at the present time be used to induce working girls to organize for higher wages and better working conditions.

Up to the present time all such attractions have been entirely in the hands of the Y.W.C.A., church and religious societies. They are financed by governing bodies and the employing class. And this has not been without some purpose. These institutions have aided in supplying the employing class with wage workers who despise the labor movement and what that movement stands for. In other words, they have been the means of preventing working girls helping themselves by becoming members of trade unions. They have made the girls docile, patient, contented, cheap workers.

Why cannot Labor enter into competition with such organizations? Why should not Labor exercise its influence over working girls? Why should not Labor copy some of the methods of control used by the employing class?

The organization of working girls presents tremendous problems. But difficulties can be overcome. Workers want to see some benefits which organization will give them. The object of the Home Service Association offers something real to working girls.

The Association will do its members good service if it can procure redress of grievances, for these are many in domestic service. It should make an attempt to bring into its ranks the many hundreds of married women who work part time, and are a source of cheap labor.

At the present time domestic help does not come within the protection of the law. Yet fully 300,000 women in Canada are earning a living by working in domestic service in the cities and rural districts, that is, if we count in such help as office cleaning. Domestic workers are among the worst paid and worst treated workers in this country.

The Home Service Association appears to be an attempt to get these workers to help themselves. More of such efforts are wanted.

Foreign Powers and China, No. 2

June 1927, pp. 14-15.

[...]

The Yellow Peril.

The Yellow Peril bogey was a deliberate attempt to foster hatred against the Chinese. The Chinese were pictured as ignorant, dirty, opium-loving, cheap, pig-tailed people.

But to the workers of the western countries the Yellow Peril took the form of the fear of want. They became possessed of the idea that the Chinese would be able to put them all out of work, because Chinese Labor was so cheap they could not compete with it.

It did not occur to these workers to look a little deeper into the question. Had they done so they would have discovered that their own masters and the governments of their countries were growing rich at the expense of the Chinese as well as themselves.

Only of recent months, only since the Chinese workers proved by their strikes they would not be the cheap, underpaid tools of imperialist exploiters, have the workers of the western countries become convinced that there is not a YELLOW PERIL, but instead they have discovered a gigantic power of co-operation, a new force added to the brotherhood of workers, and one which is now in struggle assisting the emancipation of the workers of the world from capitalist slavery. [...]

WOMEN USED TO SMASH WORKERS' UNIONS

[Editorial]

July/August 1927, pp. 4-5.

THE greed of employers for profits knows no limit. Because of this workers have formed unions in order to protect themselves. Through these unions they have been able to get better wages and better conditions under which to labor.

In some cases trade union workers have obtained wages that are nearly double those of the unorganized workers. This is so in the clothing industry.

In Toronto at this time there are clothing manufacturers who have made up their minds to smash the needle trade unions. The reason for this is to get bigger profits out of their industry. To get bigger profits, they must pay their workers less wages. And since the unions will not allow the bosses to pay just what they like, the bosses are going to smash the unions.

And this is how they are doing it. They have told the organized workers they will not pay them the union rate of wages. This means they have shut out the organized workers. They have taken on in their places unorganized workers, and these UNORGANIZED WORKERS ARE WOMEN.

In addition to this, these bosses are setting worker against worker. It so happens that the greatest number of organized workers in the needle trades are Jewish workers. These workers know they have received good wages because they were organized, and they have been wise enough to stay loyal to the union.

It also happens that, in Toronto, the greater number of small clothing manufacturers are Jewish. So here we have a condition of affairs in which Jewish employers are fighting Jewish workers by employing English-speaking Gentile women, and paying them very much lower wages than they paid their Jewish workers.

A great number of these English-speaking women are new arrivals from Great Britain—Scotch and English girls who do not understand working conditions in the country to which they have just come. Others are the usual strike-breakers who allow themselves to be used because they dislike the foreigner.

In this way the employers are dividing the workers, in order to smash the unions so that they can bring down wages.

The bosses are organized. They do not question each other's nationality. The Canadian Manufacturers' Association is the bosses' organization.

On the other hand, the unions for the workers in the clothing industry are the International Ladies' Garment Workers' Union, the Amalgamated Clothing Workers' Union, the Fur Workers' Union, and the Hat, Cap and Millinery Workers' Union.

These unions are open to all workers in the needle trades. They are the workers' means of protection against low wages and unfair working conditions.

English-speaking girls should refuse to be used to smash unions that have cost so much to build. They should join the union and so help to keep up the wages that the unions have obtained for their members.

It is in the best interests of the employers to keep the workers divided. This helps to keep wages down.

All workers have one interest in common, that is, to get the most they can for the energy they expend in their employer's industry. The union protects this interest. Working women—into the union.

HELP WANTED—FEMALE

July/August 1927, pp. 6-7.

Women have been advised, admonished, and instructed as to their conduct, their costumes, and their consciences—that is—after we were granted a conscience—for, lo, these many years. And one is tempted to believe in the idea of a "special providence" though it's against all reason or justice—when one sees how unharmed we have been by all these attentions.

The fact that we have survived is because we've adapted ourselves; that is why anything survives.

We were just "sweeties" and "house-keepers" for ages—these are modern terms for toys and slaves of late; a few of us are learning to be companions. There is a growing demand among more civilized males for what they call "intelligent companionship." So here we are!

And this is not the last demand upon us—I am speaking now of the working woman—the parasite person has no social value. The world is now facing the possibility of another great war, in spite of the promises made us in 1914 that if we gave up our children then the world would be safe forever.

Enough has happened since then to prove that the "masters in all lands" have simply tricked the workers again—the horrors of poverty, because of low wages and unemployment, have increased mightily, and now looms this new misery—another and more hideous war.

Women have been called conservative, and it is partly true. Working men are still conservative, and the reasons are very clear if one takes the trouble to notice the daily workings of three very powerful forces—the press, the school, and the church. And all three are owned and operated by "the Boss Class," the small class in control—and naturally, through these channels we are taught to think and act, much as trained animals are taught, so that those who own us may make profit out of us.

We are taught to sit up and beg!

It is not entirely the fault of working women if we have been slow in taking our places beside our intelligent menfolk—our opportunities to learn truth as to conditions have been fewer than theirs—even the Trade Unions were not always hospitable to us.

But now our menfolks have been forced to the wall and are now calling for help. And just as we have answered the other calls and adapted ourselves to all the other needs, just so will we not fail our own class at this critical time.

We must organize as workers—we must protect our homes by refusing to help in any imperialist war—because we should have the understanding by this time that all such wars mean nothing to the workers but more poverty and greater degradation.

Surely the daily struggle for a chance to live decently for our share of the wealth which we alone produce, surely this is fight enough for us!

And we are in this struggle—we did not make it. But just as the workers have always had to fight wars with which they had nothing to do but lose their lives, so we working women must also wage this war—with this difference—it is our war, it does concern the safety of our children—it determines whether they shall have to sink to the black, hopeless poverty that is the lot of millions of little ones in the older lands at this moment, or whether they shall be saved from such a fate.

Let us not deceive ourselves, they cannot escape unless working women as well as working men have an understanding of the world process—unless we know what is happening to us—and why.

Some of the old Scots used to pray regularly this petition: "Oh, Lord, gie us a guid conceit o' 'oorsels." And never was there a more useful thing to desire and use at any time than a healthy sense of our own value.

Women who have been able to survive centuries of slavery, superstition, and many kinds of subjection ought to have sufficient "conceit" in themselves to realize their power, and sufficiently loyal to themselves to begin right now to use this power.

And a good way to begin is to read "The Woman Worker" and get someone else to read it—it helps us to understand things, and this will help to unite us for this greatest work of all—the gaining of freedom—not only for ourselves, but for workers all over the earth.

—H.D.P.

THE IMMIGRANT GIRL

[Editorial]

October 1927, pp. 1-2.

IMMIGRANT girls are working girls. Their voyage over the ocean to this country is not for sight-seeing, but for work.

Many of these girls are forced to be immigrants, either because they were inmates of what are known as "charitable homes or institutions" and the home would no longer support them, or because they were ambitious enough to want a better and more secure means of living than that which faced them in the "homeland."

And to these facts must be added the fact of inducements. Among these can be mentioned the assurances of employment and the possibilities of marriage and a home of their own.

The actual experiences of the immigrant girl often work out quite differently. The unfortunate "institution girl" may find herself bound hand and foot to the home where she is sent. She is the slave, the lackey, of the household, she has no rights. She mustn't complain, she becomes afraid to complain. A survey of the reformatories, houses of correction, and the like, could tell a sorry story of the experiences of these girls, that is, if they would.

The so-called "free immigrant girl," she who comes to this country on the assisted passages schemes, does not find herself in a very enviable position. Until she has met her obligation to the concern who "aided" her, her labor is nothing short of contract labor. Should she break contract because of disagreeable conditions of work as a domestic, she is hounded and rounded until she meets her debt and finishes her contract period. Should she refuse to go back to this she is deported. If the immigration department would, it, too, could tell a tale about this side of the troubles of the immigrant girl.

It is gratifying to find that the organized working women of Great Britain are taking up the question of "emigration" and talking over it very seriously.

We, on this side of the Atlantic, must do likewise.

Immigration agents and agencies, their method of work, and what they get out of the business of bringing working girls to this country must be exposed. The immigrant girl must be protected.

Married Women as Wage Earners

October 1927, pp. 7-8.

Often one hears when the Unemployment Question is being discussed that married women should not be allowed to work. But married women, working-class women, are forced to work, often out of sheer necessity, and not from choice! It cannot be for the fun of the thing that married women sit for hours in an employment bureau waiting for work, or make the round of visitation to factories day after day, or roam the streets looking for houses to clean.

It is reported that 50% of the women working in the factories of Ontario are married women, and we feel sure that all these have very sound reasons for becoming wage-earners.

Even the "golden west" is not so golden that the wives of working men can stay home, resting content that their husbands' wages will suffice for their families' needs.

The Labour Gazette for September gives some figures concerning conditions in British Columbia. On page 950, paragraph "Marital Status," the report reads:—

"The payroll returns of 1926 provided columns in which the employer recorded whether the employee was married, widowed, or single. In the fruit and vegetable industry the married women comprise a large proportion of the workers, due perhaps to the fact that the product they work in is very perishable and at the peak of the season all available help is pressed into service. In the laundry industry about 25 per cent. of the women recorded are married. Public housekeeping has a percentage of about 28.5 married women in its ranks. In the fishing industry, out of 26 reported, 16 are married or widowed. The telephone and telegraph occupation has the lowest percentage of married workers, namely, 4.7. In comparison with other occupations there are relatively few married women in office positions. Out of 3,756 employees reported in clerical work only 432 are classified as married."

It is certainly up to the Labour Movement to recognize that married women in industry—married women as wage earners—are a factor that has come to stay and must be dealt with accordingly.

Our demand is "ORGANIZE THEM." The fact that they are in some cases only part-time workers or seasonal workers should make no difference.

If the organized labour movement cannot adapt itself to new conditions as they arise, if it fails to contend with the organizational forms of industry, then it becomes like a stagnant pool, a breeding ground of dissension and dissatisfaction. The Labour Movement must be a FORWARD-LOOKING MOVEMENT.

Wage Slaves in Hotels

November 1927, pp. 8-9.

The railway companies of Canada reap such huge profits from their operations that they more than repay the shareholders for the risks they run in investing their capital in them. So, besides being transportation companies, they take their surplus investments into the hotel business.

The Canadian Pacific Railway is going to erect a huge, up-to-date hotel on the site of the old Queen's Hotel, just opposite Toronto's new Union Station.

If, when the hotel starts operating, it copies the plan prevailing in its Banff Hotel, for sure trouble will be in the brewing. Conditions are so bad in the Banff Hotel that even The Bisector, the organ of the Ku Klux Klan, cannot refrain from comment. The Bisector writes in its September (1927) issue: "Banff is a beautiful spot away in the heart of the Rocky Mountains. The hotel is a palatial building with home comforts, exquisite cuisine, and delightful entertainment, surrounded by gorgeous scenery, with facilities for all kinds of outdoor sport. Judging from the C.P.R. advertisements and the descriptions of tourists who are interested only in selfish enjoyment, it appears to be next door to heaven. But for those who are lured into that outlandish spot in a servile capacity, as the menials and slaves of the C.P.R. and the pleasure-seekers, it is only one short remove from the infernal regions.

"So much we glean from letters which some of these poor drudges have been writing to their friends in Vancouver. The work is real slavery; there can be no question of that. Few of the negroes in the cotton fields were driven so ceaselessly or so mercilessly. The girls have to be on duty daily at

6 a.m., and are on the run till 7, 8, or even 10 p.m. Taking one sample week recently, the hours worked were: Tuesday, 16 hours; Wednesday, 13; Thursday, 15; Friday, 11; Saturday, 14; Sunday, 14. In addition to this, the girls have to clean out their own rooms and do their own laundry. Though wearied out in body, they are wrought up to such a pitch of nervous tension that very often when most tired they cannot sleep at night, the inevitable result being physical collapse. Quite recently a girl in the dining-room with a tray in her hand, dropped from sheer exhaustion, and was in hospital for two weeks. There were at that time nineteen girls off sick owing to the working conditions. The distance from the top table in the dining-room to the cold meat and salad service in the kitchen is 637 feet, and the girls have to rush back and forth that distance in order to serve a guest.

"The feeding is on a par with the working conditions. The girls get a cup of tea at 6 a.m., and on that they have to labor for five hours, till 11 o'clock, which is the hour at which they get their breakfast. Their food is served in the scullery, and is such that they can take it or leave it—any of them, hungry as they are, preferring often to leave it. They 'pinch' the scraps of food left on the plates of guests, to eke out their scanty rations, and those of them who have friends in Vancouver get an occasional parcel of food sent to them, like the prisoners of war in Germany, to save them from starvation.

"And the wages—well, they are just of a piece with the rest. A cheque sent down recently by one girl to her family in Vancouver, for half a month's pay, was drawn out for the magnificent sum of twelve dollars and nine cents, showing that the company which can roll out the millions of dollars to its shareholders, can also reckon with its employees in such miserly fashion as to get back the odd cent of the odd dime. Yet, the girls do get tips, but there are a number of 'captains' in the dining-room, each in charge of so many tables, and every girl has to give her 'captain' half of all the tips she earns.

"Other and less creditable means of providing for themselves with money would appear also to be resorted to by some of the girls. It is against the rule to have men about their rooms, and there are detectives whose duty it is to see that the rules are observed; but men are to be found around at all hours, and the detectives appear either to wink at the practice, or to be powerless to put a stop to it. The girls are required to make themselves attractive looking, and with the thermometer in the kitchen, as it was on a day recently, registering 114 degrees, the traces of fatigue can only be hidden by a liberal use of powder and rouge. Unless a girl is painted up like Jezebel, she will be sent away to make herself presentable.

"Such a life does not tend to produce a high standard of ethics, and the only vent which the employees seem to find for their feelings is in a plentiful use of profane language. Any girl who cannot swear like a trooper finds herself very much out of place in these surroundings. This is perhaps scarcely to be wondered at in the circumstances."

We are compelled to ask, "What is organized labor doing?" "Is the Union asleep?" Things are coming to a sorry pass when the Ku Klux Klan has to come out in defense of working girls because organized labor is indifferent.

DO YOU WANT A 100 PER CENT. RAISE?

[Editorial]

January 1928, pp. 2-3.

DO you want a 100 per cent. raise? If you do, you women and girls who work in factories and stores, then you should know that there is only one way to get it, and this is by ORGANIZING.

If you do not believe us, then surely you will the government. We have before us the Labor Gazette, a monthly report issued by the Dominion Department of Labor, Ottawa. In this January's issue is a section dealing with the wages of male and female workers in New York. The following facts are given:

"Women's average wage, by industries, ranged in 1924-5 from $12.50 a week in the canneries to $24 in women's clothing.

"The averages for men started at about almost $26, in candy factories, and went up to $44.50 in women's clothing.

"Earnings as high as $40 or $45 a week for women were found in a few industries with strong organizations."

So the secret is out. Workers who build strong organizations can command HIGH WAGES. And this is the main reason why the bosses do all they can to smash the unions.

We have urged time and time again that women workers should organize. Only through organization, by means of a union, can you make your wage demands effective. So organize, then present your wage demands to your employer.

Another thing you will notice, and this is, how cheap women's labor is when compared with that of the men. The men's wages shown above are 100 per cent. higher than those of the women in similar industries. This is not because men are better producers, but it is because women are content to work for what the employers care to pay. Again we say, Organize. Then through your union demand—Equal pay for equal work. Don't be cheap labor to the boss.

CONDITIONS IN A SILK FACTORY IN ONTARIO

April 1928, pp. 5-6.

The hours of work in this Silk Factory in Southern Ontario are from 7.30 a.m. to 5 p.m. The girls do not work Saturday afternoon, but must work FIFTY-FOUR hours per week or they are not allowed a full week's pay. It is customary to work two or three nights a week overtime, but the girls are being paid only straight time for anything over 50 hours per week.

The nights worked are until 10 o'clock in the evening, and the girls say the work is tedious and under the conditions consider overtime an injury.

Some of the girls of necessity carry dinner, and there is no place to eat except right in the shop. Also the wash room is very unsanitary. When an inspector is known to be in town several girls are immediately put to cleaning up the wash room.

The company gets a permit to work the girls overtime for a period of three months, and after the permit expires the sweeper punches the girls' cards at six o'clock and the rest of the time is written on the back of the cards and eventually rubbed off to permit no detection, or violation of the permit.

Isn't it possible to get some of these conditions rectified?

Correspondent.

FIGHT THE SPEED-UP SYSTEM.

[Editorial]

June 1928, pp. 1-3.

EVERY girl who works in a factory knows that the "speed-up system" is the thing she is beginning to fear the most. This fear is expressed in the words of one girl who reported to us that "The speed-up system in our factory is getting terrible; we just have to work like slaves."

Only a short time ago we received word that working girls were not at all anxious that the Minimum Wage Rate should be increased, because it would mean more work for them, and it was felt that the factories already demanded from them all the energy they had to give from day to day.

Yet the general boast of the bosses is that the workers to-day are getting higher wages, and these for a shorter work-day. However, under the "speed-up system" these things mean nothing. To-day after a girl has worked eight hours at tip-top speed, she leaves work utterly exhausted. As a result the doctor and the hospital reap whatever benefit could be derived from better pay. But more often than not the girl neglects herself and has to pay for this neglect in after years.

To-day, the "speed-up system" and "piece-work" are the order in factory life. And in these we discover a most cruel practice. In order to get the most out of the energy of a working girl a standard weekly rate of wage is fixed, so also are piece-work rates, but the latter are fixed so low that a girl has to work at tip-top speed to make the weekly standard rate.

And a girl actually does put out her full energy to do this because she fears to be looked upon as a slow worker, for a slow worker is eventually fired.

Many girls admit that the standard weekly wage is gradually dropping. They are quite sure that the bosses are going to adopt the Minimum Wage as the Standard Wage. In one factory in Toronto the Standard Wage has dropped gradually from $22 to $19, to $16, to $14 per week. This condition prevails in many factories. So we can see that girls have good reason for making their assertions about the intentions of the bosses.

The "speed-up system" is the new process of "sweating labor." At one time the sweating process meant long hours and small pay. Now the sweating process means USING UP THE ENERGY OF A WORKER IN A SHORT PERIOD OF TIME so as to reduce the running expenses of a firm. Of course, this means factory efficiency and more profits for the boss.

It is useless for working girls to pine for a return of the old days when they could break from their work for a few moments to make a cup of tea, or to slacken up when the work was slack. It is foolish of them to think that the Minimum Wage is the cause of all their ills. They must know that the boss is in business not for the purpose of providing them with work so that they can live, but he is in business for himself so that he can live by means of profits, and profits are made out of the labor of those he employs.

So working girls must face the fact that the "speed-up system" is here as a result of competition between the bosses and as a means of bringing greater profits to them. Greater production is cheaper production. The energy of the worker, the health of the worker, the strength of the worker, matters not. To an employer of labor—business must pay, and no sentiment must enter into this process.

Instead of being indifferent to the indignities imposed upon them by the bosses, working girls must take heed of these things. To ignore the methods used by the bosses to wring profits out of their energy, working girls are ignoring the well-being of their very lives.

Working girls must have protection, they must fight for protection. And the means—well—first of all they must band themselves together in the factory itself. The workers of each floor or department of a factory should organize themselves as a factory committee, and as such take up grievances immediately. They must demand "rights," for these will never be given them.

In order to strengthen their cause they must belong to the broader movement which stands as a protector of the workers; this is the Union of their
industry.

The solution of the difficulties of working girls lies in organization.
So—organize factory committees—and join the Union.

OUR LETTER TO DOMESTIC SERVANTS.

[Editorial]

September 1928, pp. 2-3.

YOU know, sisters, that poor wages, an unlimited-hour work day, and often a seven-day week, are the usual things facing domestic servants. And
added to these are sometimes other hateful conditions connected with domestic employment, a nagging-never-satisfied mistress, poor food,
miserable sleeping quarters, and offensive behavior on the part of the men
folk of the house.

You are well aware of the fact that, when you apply for a position as maid,
you have to go well supplied with references that will satisfy the mistress of
the house that you are a good worker, that you are honest, clean, and of general good behavior. But you know that you dare not ask for a guarantee for
good treatment from her; if you did she would look at you in astonishment
and would consider you had lost your reason.

Of all the wage-earning occupations domestic service is the most humiliating. What makes the condition of work worse is the fact that there is not a
single remedy for any of the ills a domestic worker has to suffer.

There can be [no] disputing the fact that it is the non-English-speaking
immigrant girl who comes to this country as a domestic worker who is
treated the worst, she is almost entirely at the mercy of her mistress.

A letter The Woman Worker received recently from a domestic worker
gives one a little idea of the conditions existing in the towns of Northern
Ontario. The letter states: "The wages we receive are very poor, some of us
getting only fifteen and twenty dollars a month and yet have to pay for our
room. These are mostly those who cannot speak the English language. The
usual wages are twenty-five to thirty dollars a month, only a few get thirty-
five.

"The people we work for are not millionaires, but just those who call
themselves 'the upper class.'

"Some of the maids get one afternoon off each week and every other Sunday, but quite a number get only one afternoon off, and there are those who
don't get any.

"Then there is the staying in at nights. Some maids get out every night, but quite a number have to stay in two and three nights a week and then go home alone late at night.

"Nearly all are working eleven and twelve hours a day. The maids of this northern part don't get much sunshine for they have to stay in all day, they only just know the sunshine is there, the moon only is left for them to look at."

This letter speaks for itself. Practically the same conditions exist for maids in every other place.

Then what is to be done? Can you hope to get better treatment by begging this from the mistress who employs you? You know she will offer you a hundred reasons why she cannot give you the small things for which you ask. And always she will tell you that "her advice is for your good."

Yet what you want can be obtained. But you must go after it yourself. This must be done by putting up a fight for what you want. And how can this be done? The first step is TO ORGANIZE.

If you really want sunshine, and you should have this as well as your mistress, you must put out your organized demand, "A REGULAR WEEKLY AFTERNOON OFF, AND ONE DAY'S REST IN SEVEN." This is considered necessary and has been made the law for the benefit of factory workers, and the same should apply for domestic workers also.

Organization is not an easy thing we know, but we are ready to help you. Our Labor League Movement is organized for that purpose and you must come to us and use our organization for your protection. Get in touch with our local League women, they will assist you, they will tell you what to do. Until you have the strength to organize entirely on your own come into the Labor League Movement by joining our WAGE-EARNERS' SECTION.

ORGANIZE AND FIGHT FOR YOUR RIGHT TO GET SUNSHINE.

Send to us for advice, we will help you all we can.

THE WOMAN WORKER.

Dear Comrade Editor:

October 1928, p. 5.

I have just received the only magazine in Canada that takes an interest in the women of the working class, "The Woman Worker." Just a few lines on the task of organizing the women who work in hotels, restaurants and cafeterias. They are amongst the most exploited of women workers, working in unsanitary kitchens. The smell of cooking, steam and heat alone is enough to make anyone not working amongst it wonder how they stand it. Then there are the long hours on their feet, rushing here and there, putting up with abuse from the "guests" or customers.

Speaking recently to a girl waitress in a basement cafeteria of a big departmental store in Toronto, she told me her feet and ankles were swollen and ached so much after her day's work that it was agony to get home.

These are the trying conditions under which waitresses work. At this point it would be well to mention for the benefit of our readers not acquainted with this class of work that there are two kinds of waitresses—the steady waitress who does her job twelve months in the year for a living; the summer season waitress only does this for a change, also to make some extra money while on her holidays, away from her own job, such as high school students, domestic servants and school teachers. This helps to keep down wages of regular waitresses. They are expected to supplement their earnings of $20 to $25 per month with a bonus of $5 if they stay the season by gratuities from the guests for good service. This also helps to keep down wages, so away with the tipping system.

We should try whenever possible that when we have to eat or stay away from home to patronize only the best employers of women labor, thereby helping our movement to better the conditions and raise the wages of women workers in the catering business.

Yours fraternally,
(Mrs.) A.J.H.

THE CLOTHING WORKERS ORGANIZE

[Editorial]

December 1928, pp. 6-8.

THE establishment of the Industrial Union of Needle Trades Workers of Canada has provided already convincing evidence of the wonderful possibilities for organization work of a Trade Union nature among the thousands of workers employed in the clothing trades industry in Canada. In Montreal, Toronto and Winnipeg new local unions affiliated to the parent national organization have come into being and are growing rapidly. Perhaps the most gratifying feature of the work that is being done is the fact that practically all of the work is being carried on by very youthful workers, a majority of whom are young woman workers.

The reason for this, of course, is to be found in the conditions existing within the industry itself. Nationalization of production which has proceeded in practically all the industries of Canada and the U.S. during the past few years has been carried on in the clothing industry in a most ruthless way. Greater and greater sectionalization of the work, revolutionary improvements in machinery, and the collaboration of the trade union bureaucracy in the two largest centers of the industry (Toronto and Montreal) have combined to produce a tremendous increase in production per worker, at the same time making possible the introduction of an ever-increasing percentage of youthful and inexperienced workers into the shops.

Changing Conditions

While the production per worker has increased very rapidly the total increase in production has been so great that in spite of the more intense exploitation of workers the total number of workers employed in the industry has increased steadily during the past four or five years, and there are to-day approximately 30,000 workers directly employed in producing clothes.

While the industry has expanded, however, and the number of workers have increased the status of the workers as a group (which in the clothing trades was comparatively high), has degenerated terribly, as have also wages and working conditions. The chief reasons for this development are to be found in (1) a movement of the clothing manufacturers out of Toronto and Montreal to smaller towns, and (2) the deliberate refusal of the officialdom of the International Unions either to extend their organization along with the industry, or to put up serious resistance to the continual offensive of the bosses to reduce the wages and standard of living of the workers in the large centers to the same level that they are able to impose upon the raw, inexperienced workers who are drawn into their factories in the small towns to which the industry is expanding.

Demoralized Organizations

The natural result of the general situation in the industry which is briefly outlined above has been to produce a situation where, due to the drift of the industry "out of town," the center of gravity of the industry has shifted. Toronto and Montreal at one time embraced more than 85 per cent. of the factory-made clothing industry. To-day these two towns combined embrace only approximately 50 per cent. of the industry, while the rest is diffused through dozens of towns in Quebec and Ontario, extending right through Western Canada to the Pacific Coast. The effect upon the unions in Toronto and Montreal has been disastrous. Loss of conditions in shops and control of jobs has been met by the International officialdom with servile attempts to make the organizations valuable—not to the workers—but to the bosses, as thinly disguised efficiency departments. The stock argument that the officialdom of all these organizations depend upon when meeting employers to-day is that through their "standards of production" and similar schemes they can assure the employers of equally cheap production as can be secured by moving out of town. In other words, instead of fighting to organize the workers in new centers and raise their wages and standard of living, their policy is to make their unions acceptable to the bosses by making them the instruments through which the wages of the organized workers may be brought DOWN.

Organize the Organized

This, then, was the situation that confronted the thinking workers employed in the Needle Trades. Thirty thousand workers employed and the number growing year by year, less than five thousand organized and the number getting continually smaller. The industry spreading all over Canada, organization becoming more and more restricted to a few high-speed shops, where organization exists on the basis of agreement between the bureaucracy and the boss.

Clearly the only solution of the clothing workers' problem was in extension of organization "out of town." And because of the fact that the number of workers employed in the smaller centers is too small to allow of the maintenance of separate trade union apparatus in each of the sections of the industry, the only method of organization that offered any hope of success was organization by industry with the local unions of various sections of the industry (Cloakmakers, Capmakers, Furriers, Men's Clothing Workers etc.) all organized around one central body.

The bureaucracies of the International Unions would never permit such organizations, even if they were willing to attempt organization of the unorganized workers. In addition, of course, there existed the more fundamental reason for establishment of a Canadian Industrial Union, i.e., the fact that the bureaucracy of the A.F of L. is to-day openly an agent of American Imperialism, and is perverting the labor movement (at least that section of it under its control) into an instrument for capitalist exploitation of the working class. With these things in view the delegates from local unions who gathered together in a preliminary National Conference in August decided that the time had come for the establishment of an Industrial Union, open to every worker employed in the clothing industry, and organized on the basis of direct and complete control by the clothing trades workers of Canada.

The Union Grows

Thriving local unions and a steadily expanding membership show the correctness of their decision. The Dressmakers' Local of Toronto, for example, an organization already embracing three hundred young workers, mostly girls, is an inspiration. Very few of these workers have ever been members of a union before, but their enthusiasm and fighting spirit is convincing evidence of the rightness of these workers for organization; and their enthusiasm is contagious. Out of the enthusiasm of the Dressmakers there was generated an equally active interest among Raincoat and Waterproof workers which led to the rapid building of an active local union in this branch of the industry which also had never previously been organized. In Winnipeg and Montreal the same experiences have been the case.

The local organization in Toronto is now engaged in a bitter strike against the Durable Waterproof Company for recognition of the union. The boys and girls engaged in this fight are now, without exception, getting their first taste of trade union struggle. And to attend one of their strike meetings, to catch the spirit of lively, youthful enthusiasm, is certainly well worth while. It is more—it is a sign of the awakening consciousness of the masses of young boys and girls employed in this industry, and a beginning of a realization on their part of the need for organization and determined struggle. It is in this consciousness and the fact that it is fighting a militant struggle in the interests of the clothing workers of Canada as a whole that there lies the guarantee of success for the Industrial Union of Needle Trades Workers of Canada.

T.B.

WORKING CLASS MOTHERS CRITICIZED

[Editorial]

January 1929, pp. 5-6.

MR. W.R. ROLLO, former Minister of Labor under the Drury Government (Province of Ontario), now school attendance officer in Hamilton, Ontario, recently criticized working class mothers for being wage-earners. Mr. Rollo claimed that there was a tendency on the part of such mothers to shirk their maternal duties; that while such mothers could not be accused of starving their children, they did leave them to their own devices. He claimed, further, that there was no need for these women to go to work, because, in the majority of cases, the wages of the husband were sufficient to maintain the home. The fault lay with the workers. It was their craving for luxuries that compelled the women to go out to work to earn money to supply these.

The remedy, by the way, was supplied by Mr. Rollo. It was that a law should be made to prevent the employment of married women with small children.

Mr. Rollo, we believe, was at one time a working man, and as such was elected a member of the Provincial Parliament during the term of the Drury Government. Surely, he has forgotten the days he, too, worked for wages and faced the struggle of making both ends meet, otherwise he would argue differently.

The complaint of Mr. Rollo is as old as the wages system itself, and his remedy is just as old.

Always it has been claimed that when working class mothers worked it was because the family wanted luxuries. But who is to determine what are "luxuries," so far as the workers are concerned?

We are living in a period known as "civilization." It is "the machine age," and under this, life's necessities are not simple things—mere food, clothing and shelter. Cultural requirements and new standards make themselves felt and become parts of life's necessities.

If this is not seen, and Mr. Rollo evidently does not see it, then it is asylums and reformatories that should be advocated to cure the workers of their madness for luxuries.

But, let us come down to facts. In doing so, we are going to contradict Mr. Rollo. We know working class mothers do not wilfully neglect their children for the purpose of going to work to buy luxuries. When they become wage-earners it is because of necessity, and more often than not, for the purpose of buying the first necessities of life—food, clothing and shelter. Why this is necessary is clear to any who give it thought. It is because of the insufficiency of the husband's wages.

It is useless for people to moralize as Mr. Rollo has. It must be understood that the wages system and the purpose of production today lie at the root of the whole question. From this point only can we start, if we would get the proper viewpoint, and seek the right solution.

CHILD SLAVERY IN CANADA

March 1929, p. 7.

Ivy was a Home girl from London, England. She was brought to Canada by the Salvation Army and was given employment in a business gentleman's home. I would like to impress upon you, reader, that no employment agency would send a maid to this home on account of the lady of the house.

When I first met Ivy she was a nice, bright, red-cheeked girl, with fair hair, and she was fourteen years old.

Gradually I was able to learn from her what her duties were. Yes, she was a full-fledged housemaid at fourteen. She had to clean and look after five bedrooms, two bathrooms, sunroom, upstairs hall, and the stairs. Of course, Madam, the lady of the house was very particular, even to the way the corners of the sheets were folded on the bed, and often if these were not to her liking she would strip everything off the bed and make the little fourteen-year-old housemaid do it all over again, and in addition she would have to listen to a stern lecture about her behaviour.

Nor was the bedroom work her only work. She had to wait table four times a day, and when she should have had an hour's rest, as is usual for maids, she was asked to take the lady's three children out for fresh air. This was to give the nurse freedom to do dress-making for the family.

According to the terms of agreement, Ivy was to be paid $8.00 a month, and the lady was to supply her with the necessary clothes. But did it work out that way? For her clothes she was compelled to wear the left-off clothing of her mistress and she was given 50 cents now and then for pocket money, and was told the balance of her wages were being banked for her until she was sixteen years old, so that when she faced the world she would have a few dollars to her credit. I must mention, though, that the cast-off clothing provided her was placed against her wages.

Being sorry for the poor girl, I did all I could to persuade her to ask for a change of place. A great change had come over her, all her brightness was gone, and often she threw herself on her bed at night and cried from sheer exhaustion. So one day she consented to my proposal. She reported the conditions she was compelled to work under, and the officer promised to investigate, which he did. Thinking that it would help the girl, I called at the Army Lodge myself and explained what I knew about the case. At once they decided to take the girl away. This was done. Ivy is now Mother's Help in another situation. This has proved more satisfactory than the last.

I can only say that it is up to the girls working as domestic servants to organize for protection. So forward THE UNION FOR DOMESTIC SERVANTS!

Mrs. A.W.

ATTENTION WAITRESSES

March 1929, pp. 9-10.

From time to time efforts have been made to form a Waitresses' organization or union. Each attempt has so far failed miserably.

Possibly if we look the situation well over, study the conditions under which these girls work, and learn their outlook, we will be better able in further attempts to meet with success.

The first difficulty arises from the fact that this is unskilled labor—a job that almost anyone can do, provided they are quick enough in their movements.

Another obstacle is that a large percentage of the women thus employed are married women, who are working for extra money to eke out a husband's small wage, help educate the family beyond public school, get a few comforts for the home or perhaps to obtain a few of the good things of life for themselves.

These married women do what is termed extra work, (noon hour or banquets, etc.) The rates for this work are unbelievably small. For instance: The midday meal, luncheon, is paid at the rate of one dollar—never more. Banquet work: The call may be given for girls to be on the job at 5.30. They set up the tables and await the coming of the guests, very often hanging around an hour and a half to two hours before their arrival. They serve a meal of a few courses, each girl having around sixteen guests to wait on. Afterwards the tables have to be cleared of everything excepting table linen. Thus, four or more hours are put in for the princely sum of $1.25 or $1.50, according to the price per plate charged. Sometimes the girls are called for 10 p.m. or 11 p.m. to serve late dance supper. They finish up in the early hours of the morning, have to wait around for street cars for the rate of $1.50.

In one of the largest hotels in this city, Toronto, there is no possibility of getting anything to eat unless by stealth. An efficiency expert is on the job, to take care of this, although the food thrown out from each meal would feed dozens of families.

The bosses have these workers scared stiff by telling them that no union will be recognized. Most are afraid that if they attempted to organize their jobs would be lost and the extra money gone. Some take no account of the long hours put in for the small money, so long as they can figure on a few extra dollars a week. This is taken advantage of to the limit by the boss. Still the more intelligent and rebellious elements are disgruntled and dissatisfied and ready for organization and with them the weaker ones will come along.

Herein lies our task. We must make an effort to get these women together. Individual approach should be made to the most reliable girls and a group gathered around them first, so that a basis may be laid for the organization and a sentiment created inside for organization. Over and over again, calling public meetings has been tried, with little success. Most of the girls are really afraid to venture to these meetings before they feel they have some backing. The fear of the spotter and the loss of the job is sufficient to keep them away. There are the permanent girls, of course, and they must not be overlooked, but the majority are part or spare time workers.

Our Women's Labor League has been always ready and willing to assist and advise in any way possible. The task is difficult and much depends on the girls themselves. Avenues of approach must be discovered. Once the girls feel they are not alone, and through sympathetic contact, begin to appreciate the needs of the situation, there is no reason to believe the task or organization is much harder here than elsewhere. At least, it is worth while exerting effort in this direction.

B.S.

A WORD TO WAGE SLAVES

April 1929, p. 5.

A word to all you driven slaves,
Whose very souls are owned by knaves,
To you whose lives are nought but dread,
One ceaseless toil and fight for bread—
You mothers! whose hearts are torn to bleed
As you watch each day your children's need,
With faces wan and eyes that stare—
You scan the shelves of cupboards bare!

This is too oft the workers' lot
For wealth and power their masters got—
And we the slaves are gagged and bound
And left to grovel on the ground,
While robbers steal the wealth we make
And give us crusts for Jesus' sake—
They prate and chew about the pie
The crown and mansions in the sky.

And still another yarn you know
Is that we reap just what we sow—
The "Talent" story comes in sight
To prove to us that we've no right
To luxuries that they enjoy.
Perhaps we'll get some bye and bye!
And so you see with yarns galore
They have a salve for every sore!

Right now we know just where we stand
We wealth producers of the land.
Just all our wants we need but take
E'en though we know what is at stake.
So fall in line, for now's the time—
We need your help, then o'er the line—
A Life worth living for workers all—
United we're strong—divided we fall!

By A.C.

Protective Legislation   **2**

The Women's Labor League movement stood solidly behind the organization of working women as the best path to securing better working conditions under capitalism. Efforts at unionizing women workers, however, had not met with much success by the 1920s, and the WLLs recognized that other avenues were needed as well if conditions were to be changed. While never trusting legislative solutions on their own, the Women's Labor Leagues nonetheless pushed for the introduction of a range of protective labour laws and social welfare measures. Minimum Wages, Mothers' Allowances, Old Age Pensions, Workmen's Compensation—the Federation of WLLs and its Locals were ardent advocates of these and other provisions. But they were also staunch critics, keeping an eye on the limitations of legislative initiatives and, wherever they could, exposing violations. Nowhere was the Federation of Women's Labor Leagues more diligent in the watchdog role than in the case of minimum wages for women.

Protective labour legislation was introduced in Canada with the passage of the Ontario Factories Act in 1884. A few of the Act's provisions applied to men and women alike, but the statute was aimed most pointedly at female and child labour, imposing limitations and restrictions on their hours and conditions in the manufacturing sector. As industrial conditions received increasing public exposure, there was widespread alarm about the impact of employment on the health and morals of the newest and most vulnerable labour force participants, women and children. As the nation's future mothers, women were judged especially worthy of special protection. Racist and class-based fears about the declining white population and increasing presence of southern and eastern European immigrants led many Anglo middle-class Canadians to look to the state for the protection of "white" women's motherhood in particular. Self-interest was part of the motivation for some male unionists too who saw unorganized female and child workers—who were cheaper and were used by employers to undercut wages—as unwelcome competition in the workplace. Regulation of the terms of employment of this pool of labour was one way in which some male dominated trade unions hoped to preserve masculine privilege in the labour force and the home. At the same time, trade unionists believed in shielding women, the "weaker sex," from the exploitation of capitalism. Adhering to the ideal of the family wage, they also assumed that most women aspired to leave the work force for domestic life, not embrace life-long wage labour.

As more factory acts were introduced women and children continued to be the favoured target for state protection. By the 1920s the desirability of labour laws specifically aimed at women and girls was well accepted by most Canadians. This was not so in several other Western countries, however. The Federation of WLLs followed the debates in the United States and Great Britain. In both countries labour, with some exceptions, tended to stand behind gender-specific protective legislation. The issue was more divisive in the women's movement, especially in the United States where the "equality versus protection" debate caused some bitter splits. Two articles in the *Woman Worker*—one spilling over from January to February 1928 and the other appearing in January 1929—traced the dominant contours of this debate. The paper applauded labour's pro-protection position and harshly criticized British middle-class feminists, the majority of whom had lined up against special protection for women because they were afraid of the "backfire" potential of the legislation (employers could fire, or simply not hire, women to avoid the regulations), and because they were uneasy with the whole notion of women needing "special" protection. To Communist women, this dismissal of labour protection in favour of abstract arguments for "equal rights" smacked of bourgeois privilege.

Women's minimum wage laws, passed in most Canadian provinces between 1917 and 1920, were unique in their interference with wage scales. Governments, reformers, and certainly employers had long considered wages beyond the scope of the state's regulatory arm. The escalation of labour strikes and protests late in the war, however, softened much of this resistance and employers for the most part were resigned to the legislation as a necessary concession to keep the peace. The Women's Labor League in Winnipeg had been especially influential, along with labour, in the campaign for minimum wages for women in Manitoba. The actual legislation, however, fell far short of the League's expectations, and despite the fact that a WLL member was appointed to the Manitoba Minimum Wage Board, the President of the Winnipeg League, Helen Armstrong, was a fierce critic of the practices of the Board.

After the Ontario Board was established in 1920, the Communist Party newspaper, *The Worker*, printed scathing critiques of the rates themselves and the budgets upon which they were based. Some of these were penned by Rebecca Buhay, one of the most prominent women in the Communist Party, who argued the Board's cost of living budget was so inadequate that a reduction, not improvement, of living standards was the likely outcome. Buhay shared the concern sometimes heard in labour circles that the minimum wage could easily become the maximum wage, for what employer would want to pay more than what was absolutely required? She concluded in disgust that women's wage boards "under the guise of social reform" were actually accomplices in the capitalist assault on workers. The ruthlessness of employers who found ways around the legislation or ignored it altogether was exposed in the Communist press and the Board itself was portrayed as spineless by its reluctance to use its designated powers to prosecute, fine, and even imprison offending employers.

The *Woman Worker* kept up the pressure on the wage boards. In July 1926, in the first official issue of the paper, a writer (probably Custance) compared the prevailing wage rates of certain unionized women in Toronto with the minimum set by the Ontario Minimum Wage Board. (See "Girls Benefit by Belonging to the Boot and Shoe Workers' Union," in the issue reprinted at the beginning of this book.) The results showed how much more protection workers got from unions than they ever would from legislated minimums. Unfortunately, scores of women workers were not organized and had to depend on the wage rates set by the Board. Not quite as negative in her assessment of the wage legislation's potential as Buhay had been several years earlier, Custance insisted that the little protection the laws gave was better than none for the unorganized woman. But that was as generous as she got with the boards.

Hoping to influence the way the laws were designed and implemented, the *Woman Worker* made a mission out of exposing the inadequacy of the rates, as well as the limitations, loopholes, and violations of the existing legal minimums. By 1927 much of the energy of the Toronto Women's Labor League was going towards monitoring employers and the Ontario Minimum Wage Board itself, and their findings were well publicized by the *Woman Worker*. The Toronto WLL received many complaints from underpaid women, which were then passed on to the Board. Although some of these complaints resulted in back payments to the women, the Board was criticized harshly for its continued practice of quiet diplomacy in relation to employers. Fed up, the Canadian Federation of WLLs announced in the summer of 1927 that it was declaring "War" on violators of the minimum wage.

Custance reminded readers in an early editorial that the WLLs had always demanded a $15 flat rate minimum (much higher than the Ontario minimum rate of $12.50 per week for experienced women in large cities). They also called for the establishment of a national minimum for all workers regardless of sex. A woman's minimum wage, then, was just a step in the door to securing more decent wage floors for all workers on a national scale, without the wide provincial variations marking the current legislation. The labour movement, along with the Canadian Labour Party, was increasingly interested in legislating minimums for men too. Not all workers agreed, however, and one contributor to the *Woman Worker* expressed her own ambivalence. Florence Perry supported the demand for a male minimum wage on the chance that it might raise the general standard of living in workplaces and at the same time prevent employers from replacing women with unregulated male labour. But she could not help worrying that legal wage floors for men might actually deter workers from organizing and striking for wage improvements. The WLL Federation, while more confident in its demand for a national minimum for all, was absolutely in agreement with this comrade that the state was no replacement for the union.

The *Woman Worker's* battle with Minimum Wage Boards and employers was nowhere near done when publication stopped in 1929. Noticeably absent from their grumbling, however, was a critical appraisal of the basing of women's minimum wage budgets on a single woman with no dependents. Wage Boards were continuing this practice in spite of their increasing awareness that many women were supporting family members on their wage just as men were. The WLL's silence on this issue is a reflection of their lingering attachment to the male breadwinner, stay-at-home wife ideal known as the "family wage." Little wonder then that when the question of establishing male minimums came up Communist women, along with labour, politicians, and reformers, all assumed that the calculation would be based on a family, not an individual, wage.

The enormous amount of attention given by the *Woman Worker* to the minimum wage issue overshadowed commentary on other protective labour and social welfare measures affecting working-class women. Some attention was given, however, to the few income supplement policies in place in this early period of welfare state formation, most notably Workers' Compensation, called "Workman's" Compensation initially and enacted in many provinces by the 1920s; Mothers' Allowances, available throughout the West and in Ontario and aimed primarily at "deserving" widows; and Old Age Pensions, enabled by federal legislation in 1927 but available in just a few provinces by the end of the decade. The WLL movement also pushed for the establishment of unemployment and health insurance. In response to readers' confusion about how the existing laws worked from one province to another, the paper devoted a limited amount of space to answering common questions and concerns, as well as to highlighting the ever present gaps and evasions. Mother's Allowance laws were particularly confusing because of key differences between the provinces in eligibility rules, and the editor herself found them hard to sort out for she incorrectly told a Sointula, B.C., reader that mothers with only one child *should* be included but they were not. In fact, British Columbia's law, the most inclusive in the country, was the only one specifically allowing support for one-child families. The WLL paper championed some basic improvements in the laws and supported the creation of uniform Mothers' Allowance legislation that was federally designed but provincially administered. Yet while the trade union movement had protested the moralistic exclusion in almost all provinces of unwed and divorced mothers, the *Woman Worker* did not develop a sustained critique of the policies and their administration.

The slowly emerging Canadian welfare state offered generally better and more "entitlement-based" benefits to men through employment-related provisions such as Worker's Compensation than it did to women claiming support as single or widowed mothers through Mothers' Allowance. Still, the compensation given to male victims of workplace accidents were hardly generous, and the Women's Labor Leagues joined labour and "labourite" politicians like J. S. Woodsworth in highlighting the suffering of those whose benefits were not sufficient to allow the basic dignities of life for themselves and their families. The letter from a Cape Breton woman, Annie Whitfield, told the plight of two Glace Bay miners, both with wives and children, squeezed between the callousness of the mining company and the stinginess of government. As most WLL members were working-class housewives heavily dependent on a male breadwinner to feed their families, these accounts resonated strongly. While both men's and women's wages and benefits were scrutinized through the pages of the *Woman Worker*, there was no well developed effort to critique the gender biases underlying the different treatment of men and women by the state. There was one crucial exception. In early 1929 the paper published an extremely progressive editorial highlighting the hazards of domestic labour, the exclusion of domestic work from all protective labour laws, and endorsing the position that houseworkers, including both paid domestics and unpaid housewives, should be covered by Workmen's Compensation.

The WLL paper drove home its point again and again that the very best protection for working-class people under capitalism was the union, not the government. Communists dreamed of a Canada where workers' demands of good wages and secure futures were guaranteed by a socialist economy created and controlled by the working class. In the meantime, the WLLs for most of the 1920s fought to make legislative reforms more adequately protect workers in general, and working-class women in particular. Through its locals and its newspaper, the WLL Federation fought for and watched over measures promising women minimum wages, the elderly basic income support, and injured workers compensation. They also looked to a day when their demands for unemployment and health insurance might be met. Given the dire immediate circumstances of much of the working class, the state's protective arm, no matter how weak and ineffectual, could not be refused.

Further Reading:

- Linda Kealey, "Women and Labour during World War I: Women Workers and the Minimum Wage in Manitoba," in Mary Kinnear, ed. *First Days Fighting Days: Women in Manitoba History* (Regina: Canadian Plains Research Center, 1987).

- Margaret Hillyard Little, *'No Car, No Radio, No Liquor Permit': The Moral Regulation of Single Mothers in Ontario, 1920-1997* (Toronto: Oxford University Press, 1998).

- Margaret Hillyard Little, "Claiming a Unique Place: The Introduction of Mothers' Pensions in British Columbia," in Veronica Strong-Boag and Anita Clair Fellman, eds. *Rethinking Canada: The Promise of Women's History*, third edition (Toronto: Oxford University Press, 1997), 285-303.

- Margaret McCallum, "Keeping Women in Their Place: The Minimum Wage in Canada, 1910-25," *Labour/Le Travail*, 17 (Spring 1986), 29-56.

- Allan Moscovitch and Glenn Drover, "Social Expenditures and the Welfare State: The Canadian Experience in Historical Perspective," in Allan Moscovitch and Jim Albert, eds. *The Benevolent State: The Growth of Welfare in Canada* (Toronto: Garamond Press, 1987).

- Michael J. Piva, "The Workmen's Compensation Movement in Ontario," *Ontario History*, 67, 1 (March 1975), 39-56.

- James G. Snell, *The Citizen's Wage: The State and the Elderly in Canada, 1900-1951* (Toronto: University of Toronto Press, 1996).

- Veronica Strong-Boag, "The Girl of the New Day: Canadian Working Women in the 1920s," *Labour/Le Travailleur*, 4 (1979), 131-164.

- Veronica Strong-Boag, "'Wages for Housework': Mothers' Allowances and the Beginnings of Social Security in Canada," *Journal of Canadian Studies*, 14, 1 (1979).

- James Struthers, *The Limits of Affluence: Welfare in Ontario, 1920-1970* (Toronto: University of Toronto Press, 1994), chs. 1 and 2.

SASKATCHEWAN LEADS THE WAY—HIGHER MINIMUM WAGES FOR WOMEN AND GIRLS

[Editorial]

September 1926, pp. 3-4.

THE Saskatchewan Minimum Wage Board has issued new orders.

These raise the minimum rates of wages for women and girls employed in Saskatchewan shops and stores, laundries and factories, and mail order houses. These orders come into effect Sept. 21st.

The minimum wage for women employed in shops and stores is raised from $14 to $15 a week. Learners are to receive $10, $12 and $13.50 a week during the first, second and third periods of six months respectively. At present the rates are $7.50, $10 and $12 respectively.

A feature of the regulations is that seats must be supplied by employers in the proportion of at least one to every four employees engaged in shops and stores.

The minimum wage in laundries and factories is raised from $13 to $14, while the rates for learners are unchanged.

For all time worked beyond 48 hours, both experienced and inexperienced workers must be paid not less than the minimum rate.

The minimum wage for female employees in mail order houses is also raised from $13 to $14, while the rates for learners are set at $9 instead of $8 for the first six months, and $11 instead of $10 for the second six months.

It is gratifying to find that at least one province has moved in the right direction for bettering the standard of life for working women and girls. From what we can gather, it is evident that the progressive farm women and labor women have played some part in getting the minimum wage rates raised.

The Women's Labor Leagues have all along stood out for the $15 minimum. Now that Saskatchewan has moved, the fight must again be renewed with vigor by working women in the other provinces for similar wage rates.

Not so long ago the rates were lowered in Alberta. In Ontario the rates have remained unchanged. But so far as Quebec is concerned, the Minimum Wage Board of that province has not as yet issued a single wage order, although conditions of labor and rates of wages are perhaps worse in Quebec than in any other province.

The letter the Woman Worker received from a Montreal factory girl, and which is published in this issue, is just a sample of the treatment meted out to girls who have absolutely no medium for redress and shows the nature of the general conditions prevailing in that city.

Just now politicians are stumping the country telling us of Canada's prosperity. Government trade returns show that Canada ranks high in the list of the volume of trade done on the world's market. But who is profiting? Certainly not working girls who helped to produce the commodities, nor, for that matter, the workers in general. The results of that prosperity are seen in new factories, immense business buildings, and a greater display of wealth on the part of the owning and employing class. Some will say, "Why the working class are buying their cars!" This may be, but the cars the workers buy are Tin Lizzies and the discarded cars of the well-to-do.

It is time the workers realized they should receive some benefit from what is called Canada's prosperity. It will not come to them, they will have to go after it. There is really no excuse for the other provinces to remain behind Saskatchewan in giving a little more of the wealth produced by the workers to working women and girls. There is no reason why a minimum wage should not be granted to all workers throughout the country. A strong demand should be put forth for A NATIONAL MINIMUM WAGE for all workers.

MOTHERS' ALLOWANCES CLAIMED TO BE INADEQUATE

November 1926, p. 11.

Speaking before a public meeting of ratepayers in Toronto, Deputy Minister of Labor, J.H.H. Ballantyne, outlined the provisions of the Ontario Act dealing with Mothers' Allowances. He claimed the Act was very clear as to who was entitled to the allowance. He said there seemed to be a popular conception that the money was only to support a mother, whereas it was intended to support dependent children. The Act states that "Any widow with two or more children under sixteen is entitled to be considered for an allowance."

When asked what amount in cash would stop a widow from getting an allowance, Mr. Ballantyne replied, $500 in cash and $2,500 equity in a home.

That there is a growing dissatisfaction with the way some of the laws are being administered in the province of Ontario was shown when one of the ratepayers declared "That the Mothers' Allowance Board should not think they are the guardians of the public funds."

But it seems that the Government is more concerned with booze than bread at this time.

MISTRESS HOUSEWIFE, WHAT DOES YOUR HUSBAND GIVE YOU TO KEEP HOUSE?

By Trade Union Supporter

December 1926, pp. 7-9.

Mistress Housewife, on what do you run your house these days? Well, if your family is a family of five, and your husband's wage is $1,369.92 for the year, or $26.86 per week, please learn that you are running at what is called "A Minimum Subsistence Level," or, in other words, you and your family are just managing to keep bodies and souls together.

If, however, your husband is fortunate enough to earn $1,719.23 for the year, or $33.06 per week, and he gives you all this to run the house, you are supposed to be running your house at "A Minimum Health and Decency Level."

Now, we are mentioning these two kinds of budgets because they were discussed by a special committee of the Dominion Government. This special committee is trying to find out what it costs a working class family to live, so that it can fix what is called a National Minimum Wage for the workers of Canada.

It is pleasing to know that one union, the Canadian Brotherhood of Railroad Employees, has stated that the lowest figure on which a working class family can live in Health and Decency is $2,202.37 a year, or $42.35 per week.

So that the members of this special committee shall know our views on the subject, we class-conscious housewives address the following letter to them:

Gentlemen:

We wish to say a few words about the family budgets you have been discussing.

Now, we housewives know that figures are one thing and facts are another. We, who are wives of laborers, machinists, carpenters, etc., know very well that, owing to a number of conditions, we do not get even an average wage of $26.86 per week. Therefore it is pretty clear that the greatest number of working class families are living all the time from hand to mouth—they are on the border line of poverty and starvation.

We are not going to kick about a minimum wage; indeed no. But, for goodness' sake, let's have it every week. We want it understood that we can't live on AIR, and can't run a house on HOPES AND PROMISES, when our good men are thrown out of work through weather conditions or industrial depression. This is the thing that gets us. Because we do not get a regular wage, we either have to get into debt at the CREDIT STORES or go out to work ourselves.

If we are to do justice to our homes and our families and have minds free from the worry of debt, be able to send our children to High School, and start them on a career which will assure them bread and butter for life, we contend that this cannot be done on a budget less than the one proposed by the union which stated before your committee that $2,202.37 a year or $42.35 per week alone could provide a working class family with a standard of HEALTH AND DECENCY.

We know, of course, that we could subsist on dry bread and water, live in a hovel, and dress in rags. And we know, too, that if good profits for the masters could be made from the workers' energy by living this way, well, that is all we would get.

We may not know much, but we do know this, that modern industry requires a certain standard of energy, so the workers must be given a wage to keep that standard of energy in their bodies. We believe this is called the IRON LAW OF WAGES.

Really, it is most unfortunate for us who want a Decent Budget, that the greatest number of Canadian workers look upon their masters as good, kind bosses, who give them work because they love them. But this is because these workers have still the SLAVE MIND. We know that wages are only given as a means of renewing the energy of the workers, and only represent a very small part of the actual wealth they have created for their masters. And we know that the bosses only give what they are compelled to give. That is why, for Decency's Sake, and for Health's Sake, it becomes necessary for the Government to fix a MINIMUM WAGE.

Now, we agree that you are trying to do your best to help us poor, unfortunate beings of an unfortunate, "ignorant" class. But if you do not mind us saying it, we should like to point out that it has been the power of those workers organized in their unions which has raised wages from starvation level to the standard of Health and Decency, as well as struggled against those masters who would lower the Health and Decency level. And this is why the masters hate the Unions, why they try to smash them, why they try to belittle them. Of course, this is why we should support the Unions, and help to build them. Your Government may not like us to say such things, but, really, we do want to see the workers' unions as strong if not stronger, than the masters' organized institutions. This may be ambition, but it is Truth. For it means that we shall not then have to worry about a Minimum Family Budget.

Yours truly,
THE CLASS CONSCIOUS HOUSEWIVES OF CANADA,
Per Trade Union Supporter.

MOTHERS' ALLOWANCES AND WORKMEN'S COMPENSATION

January 1927, p. 4.

Labor's demand for more adequate allowances for mothers and a wider application of the working of the Workmen's Compensation Act, to bring better protection to those who are in unfortunate positions either by the death or accident to the breadwinner, should receive the fullest support of working class women.

The recent accidents in the mining districts of Canada, which have deprived women of their husbands and children of their fathers, make it imperative that the dependents shall not suffer.

The number of fatal cases during the month of November, for Ontario alone, (some 54 persons killed in industry), brings home to one the misery of desolate homes through the loss of the bread-winner. Surely every woman can see she must get right behind Labor's demands.

WHY ARE NOT DISHONEST MASTERS SENT TO PRISON?

[Editorial]

April 1927, pp. 1-2.

THE article in this issue of The Woman Worker dealing with Minimum Wage violations is of great importance to women wage earners.

The letters received by the Toronto Women's League from the Chairman of the Ontario Board, prove clearly that it is one thing for the Board to fix a Minimum Wage and quite another thing to know whether or not working girls receive it.

The Minimum Wage, as it name implies, is the lowest amount of money a girl can live on without starving. Or, as the Chairman often remarked at public meetings of the Board, the Minimum Wage just keeps body and soul together.

In spite of the fact that the Minimum Wage is only a step from starvation, there are employers who set themselves to rob working girls of that minimum. Often this is done in such a way that the Board cannot easily detect the deception.

No one disputes the fact that Minimum Wage Boards have brought some relief to those workers who were extremely underpaid, such as laundry workers. But the Board could have done a little more. They could have had those employers punished who deliberately robbed the girls who slaved for them. A few examples of this form of injustice would have benefited many women workers who have all along been the victims of fraud.

The Ontario Minimum Wage Act, for instance, makes provision for violations. This provision states "that these are punishable by fines from $50 to $500, and also imprisonment." Never once has the Board brought a robber employer to justice, although it has admitted that it has settled hundreds of cases of underpayment.

Shielding employers so that their business will not suffer, is no doubt an act of kindness on the part of the Board toward those employers. This may be called by some, Christian Charity. But what of the girls who have been robbed? What happens to them if they are forced on to the streets, or forced to steal? Christian Charity is lacking in their case. The stern hand of the law is brought in and the jail or prison is their lot.

The lesson, and the only lesson, working girls can learn from this is, they must stand up for their rights. They must learn that they must help themselves.

As individuals they can do little. As individuals they fear to offend their masters because they fear to lose their jobs, and this because their jobs mean bread.

But banded together working girls can protect themselves, not only to obtain their wage rights, but also to obtain higher wages and better working conditions. THE UNION IS THEIR BEST PROTECTOR.

Two things face working women and girls, UNIONISM, or CONTINUED ROBBERY by unscrupulous employers. We urge UNIONISM.

PENSIONS FOR CANADA'S AGED

April 1927, pp. 4-5.

Pensions now seem assured for Canadian aged workers. But by no means do the pensions measure up to the standard of wealth production of Canada, a standard for which the energy of the workers is responsible.

Twenty Dollars a month, that is, two hundred and forty dollars a year, is just a provision against starvation. It merely pays for food. This means that shelter and clothes must be items of charity.

But this is not all. There is a very obnoxious clause inserted in the Bill that victimizes those workers who were careful, frugal, and economic during the days of their wage-earning capacity. If an aged man or woman has become possessed of a little property, such as a house, this must be made over to the government, and the government will deduct from the sale of this property at the time of the pensioner's death, the amount of money received by the pensioner.

It certainly seems our master class government is not going to give something for nothing, as the saying goes. It is clear the government victimizes the aged worker for his thrift.

We can well ask here, "Are judges, senators, government officials penalized in the same way?" These would not be so insulted. But anything is good enough for workers, because workers are the lower order in society.

Some will argue that the action of the government is a step in advance, that it has committed the government to a recognition of the "pension right."

Be this as it may, we are going to insist that the aged shall have "maintenance pensions" and not a "pauper's dole."

A WORD ABOUT COMPENSATIONS

April 1927, pp. 15-16.

Dear Comrades:

In the January issue of The Woman Worker there was an item dealing with Workmen's Compensations. In my opinion this is something the workers should take more interest in. I wonder how many workers ever think of the small amount of compensation received by a permanently disabled worker.

Here, in Cape Breton, no matter how large a family a miner has, his family must exist on $12.69 per week compensation, and in some cases less than this; of course it depends upon the man's earnings during the last three months' work previous to his accident. But whatever he got in wages, he cannot get more than $12.69 per week for compensation allowance.

I will now tell you of two cases here in Glace Bay, as it may be of interest to the readers of The Woman Worker. Although I give only these two cases, it must be understood that these are not the only two cases of BROKEN SPINES in Glace Bay, there are more, and in most cases they are men with families.

About four years ago a miner here received severe injuries to his spine. About a year ago this man had to leave his home and go to a hospital in Halifax to undergo an operation, as his life was in danger. This meant great anxiety to his wife and family. But he pulled through. Now this man had a piece of bone taken from his shin bone and grafted to his spine. The bone was long enough to cover five joints in the spine. It has grown all right at the lower part, but not at the top; here it sticks out, and it is hard to say if it will ever knit with the rest of his spine. This man is middle-aged. A short time ago this man was informed by the Compensation Board that they again desired to operate. But he was not wanting to risk his life again and would not consent to be cut and sawed to pieces. So in a polite way he was made to understand that he must either consent or get work.

So now this man has got a job in one of Besco's mines. His job is trapping. This is opening and closing an air door. This is no light task to my thinking for a man with an injured spine. His wages are less than $3 per day, and the mines are on short time. He will not be able to bank very much to provide for old age.

The accident to this man was caused through a fall of stone, and he was buried under it. He has two boys going to school. His compensation amounted to about $12.69 per week.

Now, the other case happened three years ago, also in one of Besco's mines. This, too, was due to a fall of stone, and the man was buried underneath it. About a year and a half after the accident this man was able to sit in a wheel chair, and then of course he wanted to leave the hospital and go home. But he could not because his compensation did not allow for paying about $80.00 for a wheel chair. So the miners came to his rescue. They took up a collection at the mine and bought him a chair and he went home. He was not discharged from the hospital, so when the winter came he was obliged to go in the hospital again just to be kept warm. And this was a man who had spent all his life digging coal. When his wife asked for coal from Besco she was told that she must pay $3.60 per ton for the coal and $1.00 for hauling, and also she must pay cash on delivery. Because this could not be done the man was forced back into the hospital.

This man is paralyzed from the waist down. He has no other source of income but compensation allowance. He has three boys going to school. And this home must be kept going on $12.69 per week.

Once in a while the miners take up collections for such cases. But Besco, who is the cause of all this misery, never does a thing for these men. This is what the workers suffer for Besco's profits.

Annie Whitfield,
New Aberdeen, Cape Breton.

SHOULD MEN AND BOYS HAVE A MINIMUM WAGE?

May 1927, pp. 7-9.

The subject of a minimum wage for men and boys is one that has been brought to the attention of the Provincial Governments practically throughout the Dominion, and also to the Federal Government itself. The following resolution was introduced to Parliament by J.S. Woodsworth on March 15th of last year: "That in the opinion of this House a wage sufficient to provide for a reasonable standard of living should constitute a legal minimum wage." This resolution was referred to the standing committee on Industrial and International Relations for a report.

In its report the committee deals with the labor principles embodied in the Treaty of Versailles, and especially the one which reads "The payment of employees of a wage adequate to maintain a reasonable standard of living as this is understood in their time and country." The committee further recommended that a conference of Provincial and Dominion representatives intimately in touch with labor conditions throughout Canada be held in the near future to consult as to the best means to be employed of giving effect to the labor provisions of the Treaties of Peace.

We find in Alberta that an amendment has been made to the Minimum Wage Act, which provides that no male workers except indentured apprentices shall be employed in any class of work for a less wage than that fixed for female workers under the minimum wage regulations for the same class of work.

Ontario, Manitoba and British Columbia are also asking for amendments to their Acts, asking that the word minors be substituted for girls, to include boys under 18 years of age.

In British Columbia the Act has been extended to all male workers, this being the first legislation of its kind to be enacted in the Dominion, the first order issued under it being a minimum wage of 40 cents per hour to apply to the lumber industry. Perhaps some of you may know that the employers in the lumber industry in British Columbia got together and protested against this minimum wage. The case was tried in court, and again in a higher court, as to whether the Government had the right to fix the minimum wage, but a decision was given in favour of the Government in both cases.

There is still a great deal of controversy going on in British Columbia regarding the minimum wage. An article appeared in the Canadian Lumbermen's Journal (an employer's journal), Jan. 15th of this year, which read something like this: That as there is a duty of 25 to 30 per cent. on machinery being shipped in from the States to start a factory, it would cost more to construct than in a country where the duty is not so high, and that as a large proportion of the articles manufactured here must be exported they are unable to compete in the markets of other countries, where perhaps labor is cheaper than a minimum wage in Canada.

These are the kind of arguments we heard when the Minimum Wage Act for female workers was first organized, the merchants were all going to be put out of business, but they seem to be holding on very well. In my opinion the argument is a worthless one, for in many industries to-day the machinery is shipped from the States, and if the employees are well organized the rate of wages demanded is much higher than that set by a Minimum Wage Board. And still the employer is able to stay in business and make his profits, and if in the lumber industry or any other industry the employers are unable to pay a living wage then they have no right to be in business. I believe a minimum wage for male workers would strengthen the hands of the members of Minimum Wage Boards for female workers, as such arguments as this are continually being put up to the members: "If you set the wages too high and control the hours of the female workers, we shall employ men that we may work them longer and pay them whatever we may see fit to do."

The subject of a minimum wage for men and boys was discussed at great length by the Trades and Labor Congress of Canada according to its 1926 report, Regina and Edmonton both sending in resolutions asking for such legislation. The Resolutions Committee recommended that the Congress favour an adequate wage for male and female workers, which was adopted. All of us will agree, I am sure, that organization is the best method the workers have in demanding a living wage and decent working conditions. I am not sure in my own mind whether it might not deter organization if the workers were sure of a minimum wage. I have in mind the case of the laborers in Regina. Last winter we found that men were working for 25 and 30 cents per hour, but what do we find to-day? These men have organized, and they now have an organization 405 strong and asking for 60 cents per hour. While the agreement has not yet been signed, I doubt if such an organization would have been formed if these men had been getting a minimum wage of even 40 cents per hour.

Of course they may think the time opportune to organize, as the prospects for building this year are very good. But it is a hopeful sign that those men feel the need for an organization, and until the workers generally feel the need for organization it seems to me that the matter of a minimum wage should receive the sympathy and support of all organized groups in the Labor movement, as no doubt it will have a tendency to raise the standard of living for those employees which may be brought under it, and in this way assist organized Labor to maintain the standard of living which has been fought for for many years.

Florence Perry.

A BOSS PUNISHED FOR ROBBING A WORKING GIRL OF HER WAGES

[Editorial]

July/August 1927, pp. 3-4.

A FEW days ago a Toronto employer was fined $250.00 and costs for underpaying one of the girls who worked in his clothing factory. The case was taken up by the Ontario Minimum Wage Board, and was the first time the Board had taken a case to court.

The worker in question was a girl of sixteen. This girl was entitled as a be-ginner to $8.00 a week under the orders of the Board. She received less than this sum.

This employer is not by any means the only one who is guilty of robbing working girls. Time and time again has the Toronto Women's Labor League received complaints from working girls or their parents of under-payment. These complaints were always passed on to the Board for action. Until this last case the Board has acted the part of "arbiter" and has been satisfied if the employer paid the arrears or wages.

Only recently the Labor League reported a case to the Board. This girl re-covered $7.76 arrears of wages covering a period of two and a half weeks. This girl could not have been the only girl who was underpaid by the boss of this particular factory. This girl complained, so the case received attention. Many fear to complain because they fear to lose their jobs.

Because the Board has been easy with the employers the robbery of working girls went on unchallenged.

The minimum wage is, as its name shows, a wage only sufficient to pro-vide a girl with the barest needs of life. Yet even for this, working girls have to put out the fullest amount of energy, they are speeded up to the point of exhaustion.

The remedy for this treatment lies in the hands of working girls. They must organize themselves in the shops and factories. Through unions they must protect themselves against the greed and heartlessness of their em-ployers. Unions are not only protectors, but they are a means by which can be obtained a wage higher than the minium wage set by a government board.

Organized labor, too, must pay more attention to the laws that have been enacted for the protection of the workers. These are few and paltry enough. But even these must be preserved when we see how the employing class uses every means to deprive those who work for them of such small meas-ures of protection.

THE FEDERATION OF WOMEN'S LABOR LEAGUES DECLARES WAR ON VIOLATORS OF THE MINIMUM WAGE

July/August 1927, pp. 10-11.

During the past month the Federation Executive Committee has received complaints concerning conditions of work and wages that obtain in facto-ries operating in some of the larger cities. For instance, from Vancouver the complaint is as follows:

"In the cloak and dress factories in Vancouver the girls are working 90 hours a week; the machines do not stop running, even for lunch hour, and many girls are not receiving the Minimum Wage."

From Winnipeg as follows:

"There are laundries that are paying only $8.00 instead of $9.00 per week, which is the Minimum Rate for laundry workers here. Women and girls working in a certain brick factory get only 12 ½ c an hour. Girls working for the Central Press are receiving only $6.00 per week."

From Toronto as follows:

"That a girl working in a certain laundry got only $9.90 for a week's work, and this included overtime every night. The girl was working until 9 and 10 each night in the week. Girls are working in the white wear factories for the miserable wage of $4, $5 and $6 a week. Many of these girls are experienced workers who should be getting $12.50 a week. There are girls and women working in restaurants seven days a week in spite of the fact that the Factory Act calls for 'One Day's Rest in Seven.'"

It is evident that the exploitation and underpayment of women and girls working in industry is far more general than is supposed. The consequences, that is, the mental anguish and bodily harm which working girls suffer are such that the Federation Executive Committee declares *relentless war on those who rob working women and girls of the meagre protection of the Minimum Wage.*

The Federation Executive Committee calls upon its affiliated units to deal with every case that comes to their attention. Report these, not only to the Central Labor Bodies, but also to the respective Provincial Minimum Wage Boards.

The following letter was received by the Toronto Women's Labor League from the Ontario Minimum Wage Board. This letter shows that results can be obtained if we go after them:

Dear Mrs. Custance:

I am now able to inform you that we have secured for Miss E. Cooper the sum of $48.41 due her as arrears by the Exclusive Ladies' Wear Co. ...

We thank you for bringing this matter to our attention.

Yours faithfully,
J.W. Macmillan, Chairman.

Esther Cooper (the Esther who seeks the Right to Live in June's Shop and Factory Life), was robbed of the sum of $48.41. This amount only made up the Minimum Wage of $8.00 a week and in no way represents the actual values she created for her boss during the ten weeks she worked for him.

This girl found courage to complain. It can be left to the imagination what those girls suffer who fear to complain.

WE MUST WAGE A WAR AGAINST UNSCRUPULOUS BOSSES WHO MAKE BIG PROFITS AT THE EXPENSE OF THE ENERGY OF WORKING GIRLS.

CORRECTION

September 1927, p. 5.

In our last issue a report was printed concerning conditions in some industries in Winnipeg. The report on page 10 bottom of first column, reads: "There are laundries that are paying only $8.00 instead of $9.00 per week, which is the minimum wage for laundry workers here. Women and girls working in a certain brick factory get only 12 1/2 an hour."

The facts are as follows: The girls are getting only $8.00 per week in the laundries. The learners are entitled to $9.00, and the minimum wage is $12.00 per week.

The Alsips Co. no longer employ girls in their factory, but boys. This frees the company from the obligation of paying the minimum wage.

OLD AGE PENSIONS GRANTED IN BRITISH COLUMBIA

November 1927, p. 15.

British Columbia is the first of the provinces of Canada to meet the proposals contained in the Federal Old Age Pension Act and to put into operation the machinery through which Pensions will be granted the aged in British Columbia.

The rest of the provinces are tardy in their action. The workers of the provinces will have to urge their provincial governments into action.

The Old Age Pension scheme as it stands is a very meagre one. We cannot rest content with the present provisions. Agitation must be kept up in order that the age of the recipients shall be fixed at sixty, and that the aged shall be removed from a state of penury.

PROTECTIVE LEGISLATION AND WOMEN WORKERS
Restrictions on Employers Make for the Welfare of the Workers.
Statement by the Standing Joint Committee of Industrial Women's Organizations.

January 1928, pp. 13-16.

The Standing Joint Committee of Industrial Women's Organizations defines in the following statement their attitude on Protective Legislation for Women. This Committee speaks for organized working women in the United Kingdom. It represents over one million women organized in the political Labor, Trade Union, and Co-operative Movements. The views which it voices are those of women in these organizations. It is true that they are the same as the views of men who in some cases form the majority of the organizations represented, but as women the Committee has the special duty of securing what is in the best interests of women, and they have come to the conclusions set forth. These views are not new, they have been the views of the Labor Movement and the women within it ever since there has been organization to express their opinions, but it has become necessary to restate the position because of the attempts of certain groups of feminist organizations to oppose Protective Legislation for women on the ground that it is restrictive and injurious.

The Committee does not speak only for women who are themselves in industrial employment. It speaks also for the mothers of such workers.

The Standing Joint Committee is in favour of all legislation which improves conditions of employment for the worker, and is especially concerned in securing these for the worst paid and least organized sections; unfortunately women belong to this section. Moreover, the Committee is especially concerned in securing adequate care and protection for women exercising the function of maternity.

Special Difficulties of Women Workers

It is unnecessary to consider in detail the reason for the low wages and difficulty of organizing industrial women workers. In general, the employer regards women's work with favor because it can be obtained more cheaply than that of men, and in the whole history of their employment since the industrial revolution women have had to bear the worst burden of bad wages. It is true that in some occupations they actually do better work than men. But they have not had corresponding economic advantages. This in itself has made them more difficult to organize and, in addition, the fact that women normally leave employment on marriage has bad results in two ways: on the one hand, the age of the woman worker is lower, and she herself is less experienced than in the case of men, and on the other hand, she is apt to regard her employment as lasting only for a few years.

Speaking generally, women are less capable of violent muscular effort than men, and cannot undertake work entailing so heavy a physical strain. A few individual women may be able to do so, but broadly speaking this is not the case and it must be remembered that an employer considers the question on broad lines and does not select his workers after an athletic test.

Further, in addition to physical strain, under present social conditions, merging as we are from the dark ages in our attitude towards women, certain working conditions, such as night work and very late or very early hours (the two-shift system), are more disadvantageous for women than for men; whether that will always be so we cannot say, but we are regarding legislation from the point of view of facts as they are.

Three Forms of Protective Legislation

Yet in the present state of public opinion it is often easier to secure protection for women than for men, while conditions which men's stronger organization can gain for them can only be won for women by legislative enactment.

Protective legislation for women can be divided into three classes:

1. Provisions that would be good for men as well as women, but which can be obtained for women and not for men at the present time.

Legislation regarding hours of work comes under this heading. We can in factory legislation secure regulation of women's hours, and even the present Government (a year ago at least) was willing to enact a 48-hour week for women. Not all the efforts of Labor, and of agreements at International Labor Conferences, have been sufficient to secure 48-hour legislation for all workers. We prefer to take what regulation we can get rather than to delay it.

2. Regulations that are more needed for women than for men, because women are less fitted than men for certain dangerous and specially heavy muscular work.

Under this heading comes the exemption of women from all forms of active service, their prohibition in dangerous industrial processes such as work in underground mines, outside window-cleaning, the cleaning of dangerous machinery, also regulations as to the lifting of heavy weights, exposure to excessive heat, and the handling of poisonous substances which may be specially injurious to women. The prohibition of nightwork, in so far as night-work is necessary, may be placed in the same category. The experience in munition factories during the war brought once more into evidence the half-forgotten facts of unregulated nightwork—"deterioration in health caused by the difficulty of securing sufficient rest by day; disturbance of home life with its injurious effects upon the children; and diminished value of work done." (Report on Women's Employment by the Health of Munition Workers' Committee.) If women could be relieved of domestic duties, it may be that their resistance to industrial fatigue would approximate more nearly to that of men, but legislation has to deal with things as they are.

3. Some forms of protection are necessary for women because of their functions as mothers.

Under this heading come the provisions proposed by the Maternity Convention adopted by the International Labor Conference in 1919. This Convention, which has not yet been ratified by our country, declares that women workers should be prohibited from working for six weeks after childbirth, have the option of not doing so for six weeks before, and should have adequate maintenance during the whole period.

Our position, therefore, is that we take whatever we can get under all three heads, and if we cannot get it for men, or it is not necessary for them, we endeavor to secure it for women alone.

Effects of Part Legislation

Does such provision worsen the position of industrial women workers? In our opinion the facts all point in the other direction. The position of women in the industrial world during the last 100 years has been strengthened by every regulation for their protection which has been adopted.

We cannot believe it possible that anybody would desire to go back to the time when women were employed in coal mines, or when the hours of their work in factories were wholly unregulated. Without regulation those who are weakest get the worst jobs at the worst pay, and that means that women get them. It is, however, quite a mistake to think that when the hours in factories and workshops employing women are regulated, women are at a disadvantage in comparison with men.

An employer does not substitute men in such a case but all workers share in the improvement. As to the prohibition of night work, it has certainly not been injurious to women, and it has been an influence towards its abolition.

A comparison of the numbers of men and women employed in the engineering and metal trades is especially interesting. Allowing for slight differences in methods of compilation, the following numbers indicate the trend of women's employment in these trades:

Numbers

1881	38,000	(Census figures, Great Britain.)
1911	110,000	(Census figures, Great Britain.)
1926	252,000	(Ministry of Labor estimates, Great Britain and Northern Ireland— where the number is very small.)

Expressed in the form of an index number, there were 252 women employed in 1911 for every 100 employed in 1881, and 340 women employed in 1926 for every 100 in 1881.

On the other hand, the numbers of men have not increased so greatly. For every 100 employed in 1881 there were 189 in 1911, and there was no increase on these figures in 1926.

The worker who cannot be exploited at the employers' will because the law does not permit it, gains a stronger and not a weaker position in the industrial world. Legislation has had to step in to give women a chance of achieving a more equal footing with men. Without such protection it is not equality that the woman achieves, but far greater inequality.

Need to Examine All Legislation Proposed

At the same time the Committee does not believe that we should accept blindly all protective legislation; each proposal must be examined carefully, and we must feel that there is good reason for the provision to be made. The past history of the woman worker has shown that she has often been employed to break the wage-rate for all employees. That time has not yet passed, and there is a feeling that the introduction of women into employments where they are not accustomed to work endangers wages. The consequences of using women to break a wage-rate are so dangerous to both men and women of the working-class that some trade unions have taken a strong line against the extension of women's employment in occupations where they have not been previously employed. They have, however, never proposed that such restrictions should be made a matter of legislation.

Women and Lead-Poisoning

The restrictions, for example, of women employed in certain painting processes where lead is used are due, not to fear of the women, but to the definite medical belief that women are more subject to lead-poisoning than men.

The greater susceptibility of women to lead-poisoning has been the subject of very careful examination in the Potteries. The evidence of Dr. T.M. Legge, Medical Inspector of Factories, given before the Departmental Committee in 1908 was conclusively borne out by the figures of the greater incidence of lead-poisoning amongst women. His opinion is the opinion of the organized workers in the trade represented by the National Society of Pottery Workers, of whom the majority are women. At the present time the number of cases in that trade (which is the most important of those using lead in which women are employed) is about equal, but the rate per thousand is much higher for women than for men as there are at least one-third more men employed in the lead processes than women. During the war period a large number of women were introduced into the lead processes, but by agitation against their continued employment the numbers were reduced, but still are slightly higher than the pre-war level. We accept their view, based as it is upon definite first-hand experience, and welcome the fact that the protection of women in processes using lead has been increased, though we are whole heartedly in favor of a further protection which would include men as well.

The whole Labor Movement would prefer the abolition of lead in certain productions, but the present government has refused to adopt the proposals on these lines accepted by the International Labor Conference at Geneva. (Continued next issue).

PROTECTIVE LEGISLATION AND WOMEN WORKERS
(Continued).

February 1928, p. 12.

Restrictions on Employers Not Workers

The greatest evil in the industrial employment of women is low wages—whether of men or women. The low wages of men often compel married women who are already fully occupied at home, and who are bearing children, to compete for employment in industry. The low wages of women are an important factor in dragging down the wages of men. In our efforts through Trade Boards to abolish sweating, regulation affects both sexes—but the worst sweated trades are those which mainly employ women. The fixing of minima, both of wages and hours, which has, therefore, been of special benefit to women: would the feminist organizations regard it as "restrictive"? Would they prefer that the employer maintain his right to sweat his workers in the name of equality?

These considerations apply to industrial workers in factories and workshops. They do not apply to the professional and clerical workers. We are also entirely against prohibition of the employment of married women on the ground of marriage. It is because we believe in the emancipation of women, economic, social, and political, that we stand for the protection of industrial women workers against the ruthless exploitation which has marred their history in industry.

For industrial and professional women alike, we seek equal remuneration for the same job, and we desire that all professions should be equally open to persons of either sex.

Signed on behalf of the Committee,
Eleanor Hood, Chairman,
A. Susan Lawrence, L.C.C., M.P.,
M.J. Pidgeon, Julia Varley, Vice-Chairmen
Marion Phillips, Secretary.

—From the Labor Woman

MOTHERS—ARE YOUR GIRLS GETTING THE MINIMUM WAGE?

[Editorial]

May 1928, pp. 1-3.

HOW many mothers, whose daughters have become wage-earners, know that their girls have wage rights and protection by law? We fear very few.

And this is the reason why so many employers are able to get away with all sorts of things, or, in other words, are able to rob the girls of their wage rights.

For mothers who have not become acquainted with these wage protection laws, we will inform them that every Province of Canada, with one exception, New Brunswick, has a Minimum Wage Board. This Board fixes the rates of wages which employers must pay their female workers. These rates are fixed for girls according to age and experience. Let it not be forgotten that these rates are called the minimum or lowest rates the employers are allowed to pay. And, also, that the Minimum Wage Act of the various Provinces makes it a crime on the part of the employers if they violate the regulations of the Wage Boards. This crime is punishable by fine or imprisonment.

But, because employers are also the owners and controllers of the workshops, factories, etc., they are able to devise ways and means of getting around these minimum wage regulations.

One common practice is to move a girl from one department to another, and to keep her moving around the factory departments so that she remains always an inexperienced worker and never entitled to the full minimum rate.

Another practice is to fire girls who have worked in a factory long enough to be entitled to the full rate and to take on new hands—inexperienced younger girls at the lowest rate—only to fire these when their turn comes for the full rate.

Another, and an extremely vicious practice, is that connected with piece work. Employers, in order to get their pound of flesh for the wages they pay, fix piece-work rates so low that girls have to work at top speed to make the minimum wage rates. If they cannot then they are put on the list of slow workers.

The Ontario Minimum Wage Board allows the employers of Ontario a 20% exemption if they run their factories on a piece work basis. This means that so long as an employer pays 80 out of every hundred girls he employs the minimum wage rates, the other 20 girls don't count. The evil of this should be clear to all.

But do parents know of these things? Do they trouble to ask their girls questions about their work? Or are they only interested to the point that work provides the means whereby their girls keep themselves?

It is necessary that parents should become acquainted with the facts concerning factory work and wage conditions that prevail today. They should be made aware of the dangers of the speeding up system. And they should know that the speeding up process is getting worse as time goes on.

That the speeding up process has put fear into working girls can be seen when girls are compelled to say they hope people will not try to make the minimum rates higher because they will never be able to reach them. They feel they are being worked to the limit of endurance and can stand no more.

Thus we can see to what extent the speeding up process in industry is sapping up the life and energy of working girls.

We must tell those parents who allow their girls to work under such conditions that they are the friends of the employers and the enemies of their girls.

We must say to those parents who are indifferent to these conditions and think only of the few dollars their girls bring into the homes, that they have lost sight of their duty as parents, the protectors of their children.

Mothers in particular must heed the conditions under which their girls work to-day. They must not get rid of their responsibilities by saying, "I had worse than that in my day." We know many mothers are themselves wrecks because of the conditions they worked under during their wage-earning days.

It is the duty of all working-class parents to become acquainted with the Minimum Wage Act of their Province, also the wage rates that apply to the labor of their girls.

It is the duty of parents to help their girls obtain their wage rights, and to remember that these are only minimum rights and not all they should receive. Organization would bring them more. Unionism is the best form of protection.

For the moment, at least, they should show interest in their girls' welfare by seeing to it that they get the minimum wage rates.

And last, but not least, parents should see to it that their girls are acquainted with the minimum wage rates before they apply for work.

Only this interest and insistence on the part of parents will make employers of working girls think twice before they treat them in the ways already referred to.

Question of Equal Work and Equal Pay for Women

January 1929, pp. 10-11.

The question of special protective legislation for the benefit of women workers has been the subject of discussion in various countries during the past two years. References to this controversy have been made in recent issues of the Labour Gazette (December, 1927, page 1277; September, 1927, page 926; June, 1926, page 531, etc.)

The United States Women's Bureau of the Federal Department of Labour was called on in 1926 to mediate between the contending parties, and an advisory committee was appointed to investigate the effects of the special regulations on behalf of female employees. The report of this committee, recently published, is to the effect that the employment of women has not been restricted in consequence of such regulations.

The same question was debated last year in the British House of Commons, some of the women's representatives, including Miss Margaret Bondfield, opposing special regulations for women, and advocating instead policy of "equal pay for equal work." The same view is taken also by the Viscountess Rhondda, in a letter written from England to the New Republic (New York), November, 28, 1928, supporting the views of the National Women's party in the United States in opposition to distinctive laws for women. "Our own experience," she says, "has shown us that the only adequate protection of women lies in giving them equal conditions of work and equal pay. Under a system by which women wage-earners are 'protected' by a series of restrictions based not upon the nature of work, but on sex, women are still at the bottom of the wage market, the worse paid and, as you sir, acknowledge, the least organized section in the industrial community.

"In this country the more important professional women's organizations work for equal conditions of employment, such as the National Union of Women Teachers, the Federation of Women Civil Servants, the Women Engineers and the Women's Electrical Association, the Open Door Council, the Women's Freedom League, and St. John's Social and Political Alliance (the Roman Catholic women's organization) and this Society, have all taken a firm stand on this matter.

"This October, at York, the National Council of Women of Great Britain at its annual conference, at which 800 delegates represented women's societies of every kind and occupation, passed by an overwhelming majority a resolution demanding that in industrial legislation all regulations and restrictions in regard to conditions of work should apply equally to men and women.

"Englishwomen are realizing that without equal conditions of work equal pay is almost impossible. Low pay handicaps adequate organization, and ill-organized, low-paid labour will always be liable to exploitation. The only real protection for women lies in equal pay and improved organization, and we congratulate the National Women's Party on their championship of this principle."

HOUSEWORKER'S AND WORKMEN'S COMPENSATION

[Editorial]

February 1929, pp. 6-7.

IT is not generally known that considerably over fifty per cent. of women wage earners in Canada are houseworkers. And it is not often given thought that these houseworkers are the most neglected persons in the scheme of things. They are outside the pale of all forms of legislative protection. So quite truly they can be called the most unprivileged of the unprivileged class.

It is interesting to find that at last some thought is beginning to turn itself to the pitiful plight of houseworkers—the domestic servants and working class housewife.

Says the Victoria Colonist, in discussing the position of houseworkers in relation to accident insurance:

"Workmen's Compensation, if it is to be adequate in the expression of its needs, should cover housework. This is a phase of industry that, in the matter of insurance, has been far too neglected up to the present. The women who perform homely chores are as much entitled to compensation as any other class of the community, and no doubt would be prepared to contribute to the premiums of Workmen's Compensation. Under the present dispensation the housewife finds it difficult to get an accident policy. The belief exists, no doubt founded on statistics, that housework is the most dangerous of all occupations for women. As a consequence, insurance companies fight shy of the risk, or only accept it at much higher rates."

Also the Rochester Times Union has something to say on the same question. It gives the opinion that

"The high casualty list among women in the home 'is due to the housewife's own persistence in doing the day's work, even when weary from long hours, to her lack of proper tools or unfamiliarity with the tools she has.' There ought to be no such unfamiliarity in these days of domestic science in the schools, that is if the domestic science taught is practical and capable of application to the homes. Under Workmen's Compensation, in which an immense reserve fund has been accumulated—beyond present and immediately prospective needs—the housewives could be cared for without having to pay any higher rates of insurance than obtain in any average industry. This is a matter that should be of moment to women's organizations. The housewife is just as much entitled to protection as any workman."

What lesson can working class housewives and domestic servants learn from these statements? Surely this: That they, too, can obtain Workmen's Compensation if they will agitate for it.

Here is something the Women's Labor Leagues can take up, both on their own behalf, since they are for the most part working class housewives and in the interests of the domestic servants they are trying to organize.

Feminism and Social Reform 3

The history of socialism in Canada is marked by both partisan disagreements and cooperative partnerships with other movements for social justice, including the women's movement. Communist women in the 1920s were ambivalent in their attitudes towards women's organizations. On the one hand, they were deeply suspicious of middle-class feminists' tendency to define women's interests and needs based on their own privileged class location. On the other hand, cross-class alliances were not new to many women in the Labor Leagues, and the Comintern's united front strategy of 1920-1928 encouraged calculated efforts by the WLLs to influence the more progressive women's organizations. WLL women struggled throughout most of the 1920s to maintain their independent critique of reformism while also cautiously supporting some non-Communist women's organizations.

Allies were carefully chosen. Certainly there was no room for cooperation with rigidly conservative groups such as the International Order of the Daughters of the Empire (IODE), a favourite target for the *Woman Worker.* In the first issue of the paper (reproduced at the beginning of this book) the IODE came under fire in three separate contributions. Not only was this organization of wealthy British "ladies" a leading proponent of militarism and British-style imperialism, its members took reactionary positions on a range of other issues, perhaps most notably on unions. The editor predicted that "if an anti-strike movement develops in Canada the IODE will be the founders." Leftists outside the Communist Party agreed that the IODE was thoroughly *status quo,* and it was roundly criticized by peace activists, labour groups, and by the farmers' Member of Parliament in Ontario, Agnes Macphail.

Some other middle-class women's organizations were opposed and even ridiculed in the paper, although not with such vehemence as the IODE. The National Council of Women of Canada (NCWC), whose support for working-class women, when at all apparent, was notoriously patronizing, was dismissed rather politely when it advocated the appointment of women as Senators. It was not the Council's support of "sex equality" that was at issue here, one writer noted, but its investment in the Senate itself, which the WLLs, along with the Labour Party, steadfastly argued should be abolished. Characterizing the Senate as an organization of rich old men with strong ties to big business, the contributor worried that the addition of wealthy women would only strengthen the institution. The *Woman Worker* also took issue with the NCWC's support for censorship of "pernicious" and "demoralizing" literature, for radical publications such as *New Masses* were banned by Customs with this charge. Such actions confirmed that the NCWC agenda, no matter how apparently well meaning, was to shore up the *status quo*.

Communist women were also furious at the moralism that had so often fuelled middle-class women reformers' approach to the problems of working girls and women whose lives had been spotlighted since the 19th century by commissions and studies on industrial conditions. In the article, "How Well-To-Do Women Would Reform Wayward Girls," left-wing women's exasperation was directed at the Toronto and Ontario Councils of Women and at Judge Margaret Patterson of the Woman's Court, for offering "fallen women" moral platitudes and criminalization when material circumstances needed challenging. The author of this article also pointed to the double standard of morality and accountability that labelled the working class girl "wayward" for sexual behaviour that was covered up for the middle-class girl. Elsewhere in the paper, the Toronto Local Council of Women (LCW) was commended for its protest of beauty contests, with the qualification that the WLLs had taken this stand first. Communist women were fearful that preoccupation with personal beauty could be a frivolous distraction for working-class women from serious issues like the class struggle, and their opposition to beauty pageants can be read in this light. But the WLL analysis also challenged once again the middle-class tendency to moralize and blame the victim, in this case the women themselves who, in the minds of certain social reformers, were "exposing themselves" in beauty contests. The *Woman Worker* offered instead a critique of the capitalist commercialization of working-class women's bodies through such forums. This was similar to the materialist critique they developed of prostitution (see section on "Women and the Sex Trade").

The YWCA presented the Labor Leagues with a different case. For years the YWCA had offered young single working girls opportunities for social get-togethers along with programs and services like cheap "respectable" shelter, assistance in travelling to new communities, employment training, and advice for job seekers. As a great many working-class daughters were reached by the YWCA, the WLL responded with a mixture of support for some of its more realistic attempts to meet working girls' needs, but also nervousness at the competition they represented for the loyalties of these girls. The YWCA in Canada was, after all, still very much a reformist Christian organization which emphasized spiritual uplift and training for respectable womanhood over economic security. The WLL Federation was more encouraged by the actions of the Industrial section of the World YWCA which pushed its national counterparts to survey and improve factory laws and working conditions and promote the unionization of working women and girls. Custance promised the support of the WLLs should the Canadian YWCA pursue this line of work, but she doubted the organization would ever make that move since the wealthy conservative funders of the organization called the shots.

Women's organizations like the YWCA, the NCWC, and the Women's Christian Temperance Union (WCTU) were publicly identified with the women's movement—a movement which was not on the whole well received by Communist women. The middle-class basis of much of the women's movement was a constant source of tension for Communist women who, while supporting many feminist demands, did not call themselves "feminists." Communists could not forget that leading international feminists, such as Britain's Emily Pankhurst and Mrs. Flora Drummond, were viciously anti-labour, and the reputation of some Canadian feminist figures was not much better. Socialist women had also long been put off by feminists' unquestioned faith in legislative solutions, and they did not share their elation when progress was made at the end of the war on women's right to vote in federal and provincial elections. Individual women in the pre-war socialist parties had sometimes supported woman suffrage, but they were much more realistic than their liberal-minded sisters about what the vote could accomplish. While suffragists had regarded the vote as an important symbol of equality as well as a practical tool for promoting social change, socialist supporters had always seen it as one small step towards an equality that would only be fully realized after a class revolution. Suffrage reports in the *Woman Worker*, such as those concerning the continuing battle for the vote by Quebec women, were written with an eye to the bigger changes required before freedom would be possible for more than a select few.

In an editorial entitled "Which Freedom?" Custance offered a historical analysis of the growth of the feminist movement and the continuing class divisions between women. Industrial capitalism and machine production, she argued, created the preconditions for feminism. Middle-class women gained increased leisure and incentive to move into the male world of education and the professions. Finding advancement closed to them, they began to agitate for women's rights. Working-class women found themselves forced into factory production where they too were compelled to fight for their equality, although their struggle was shoulder to shoulder with the men of their class. Alluding to the sexism and discrimination faced by women in industry, Custance conceded that working women have had to struggle for equality and demand, for example, equal pay for equal work, but, she added, "this is a class question rather than a sex question, a condition of labor rather than of man's dominance." She was relying here on the traditional Marxist belief that women's emancipation would fall upon the heels of the revolution. Women in the meantime should not necessarily be silent about sexual inequality, but they should not be "led astray" by the liberal feminist "Slogan of Freedom." Nor should they be fooled, the *Woman Worker* warned, by rich women for whom "freedom" meant the right to trivialities like cigar smoking, held up by a new club of women in England as a "symbol of independence."

One feminist reformer gained more respect from the *Woman Worker* than any other non-Communist woman. Agnes Macphail, Canada's first woman MP, was elected in 1921 as a Progressive candidate and representative of Ontario's farming communities. If her unwavering hard line anti-militarist stance was the most attractive part of her platform to WLLers, her active support for workers and for the Labour Party platform won her considerable attention in the first year of the paper's publication. Macphail herself, although a strong advocate of feminist reforms, was not entirely comfortable with the label "feminist" and this too might have enhanced WLLers' trust in her judgement.

Conscious of the need to forge links between industrial women (socialists' usual focus) and farm women, the WLLs attempted to woo women in select farm organizations like the progressive United Farmers of Canada (UFC). Building such a bridge proved difficult. In 1928 Custance criticized the judgement of the women's section of the UFC in Saskatchewan when its leadership encouraged the affiliation of its members to the Saskatchewan Provincial Council of Women. Writing to defend the UFC women's position, the president exposed the urban bias of WLLers, explaining rural women's isolation and their need for connections with urban women in the province through such affiliations. Custance conceded the Labor Leagues' blindness to the full meaning of this isolation but held on to her point that conservative Councils of Women were hardly the appropriate allies for farm women who should be joining in the fight against capitalism.

With the Comintern Congress of 1928 and the triumph of Stalinism the united front strategy was called off by Soviet leaders increasingly mistrustful of western liberal politics and organizations. The WLLs now came under fire for pursuing the very alliances they had formerly been instructed to develop. A total turnaround was easier in theory than in practice, and the Women's Labor Leagues appear to have had more ambivalence than Canadian Communist Party leaders about the new policy line. It is true that a certain hardening of the WLL line on women's reform organizations appears in the *Woman Worker* in 1928 and 1929, with more pointed critique of the Councils of Women and liberal pacifists in particular (see "Peace and War" section). Yet this was only a difference in emphasis, not the about face expected by the Comintern directive. The reality was that the Federation of Women's Labor Leagues and its Locals had always approached coalition work with a critical edge. By the end of the *Woman Worker*'s publication in 1929, the Federation of Women's Labor Leagues was still approaching farm groups and it was still defending the feminist pacifist reformer Agnes Macphail against her conservative critics. The promise of coalition-building, for all its pitfalls, proved too compelling to be abandoned completely.

Further Reading:

- Carol Lee Bacchi, *Liberation Deferred? The Ideas of the English Canadian Suffragists, 1877-1918* (Toronto: University of Toronto Press, 1982).

- Terry Crowley, *Agnes Macphail and the Politics of Equality* (Toronto: James Lorimer, 1990).

- Wendy Mitchinson, "Early Women's Organizations and Social Reform: Prelude to the Welfare State," in Allan Moscovitch and Jim Albert, eds. *The Benevolent State: The Growth of Welfare in Canada* (Toronto: Garamond Press 1987).

- Diana Pedersen, "Providing a Woman's Conscience: the YWCA, Female Evangelicalism, and the Girl in the City, 1870-1930," in Wendy Mitchinson, Paula Bourne, *et. al.*, eds., *Canadian Women: A Reader* (Toronto: Harcourt Brace and Co., 1996).

- Wayne Roberts, "'Rocking the Cradle for the World': The New Woman and Maternal Feminism, Toronto, 1877-1914," in Linda Kealey, ed., *A Not Unreasonable Claim: Women and Reform in Canada 1880s-1920s* (Toronto: Women's Press, 1979), 15-46.

- Veronica Strong-Boag, "'Ever a Crusader': Nellie McClung, First Wave Feminist," in Strong-Boag and Anita Clair Fellman, eds., *Rethinking Canada: the Promise of Women's History*, 3rd edition (Toronto: Oxford University Press, 1997).

WORKING WOMEN AND THE LABOR PARTY PROGRAM

[Editorial]

August 1926, p. 1-2.

SEPTEMBER 14th has been named election day. From now on each of the political parties will be hard at work trying to convince the voters that it is the fittest party to be in power to represent the interests of the people of this country.

It must be understood, however, that political parties represent *certain interests* only, and never the interests of the whole community. The Conservative Party represents the interests of the banks, the big manufacturers, the speculators, and those who want trade protection against other countries. The Liberal Party represents the interests of small business, and those who want free trade. The Progressive Party represents the interests of the farmers. The Labor Party represents the interests of the workers.

The two most powerful parties are the Conservative and Liberal Parties. The farmers and the workers are only just realizing they must take a hand in government instead of only being used by the old-time parties.

For many years we have witnessed the stage fight between the Conservative and Liberal Parties, each strived for the reins of government by trying to discredit the other. In this election campaign we shall see the same thing. This does not mean we should be indifferent to the evil practices of evil doers in the government, but we must at least understand the nature of the fight between the Liberal and Conservative Parties, and we must not allow ourselves to be drawn into battle in their behalf.

These two parties, no matter what they may say to the contrary, represent the interests of the various groups of capitalists, and the interests of these, more often than not, conflict with the interests of workers and farmers. It is left to the workers and farmers to think of their interests in the same way, and although their parties are small, because they lack the wealth, yet, their interests are those of the great majority of the population of this country, therefore, these interests are of the greater importance.

It is not reasonable to expect, that those who work for wages and receive scant recognition in the factory and workshop should get more out of their masters by returning either them or their lawyers to Parliament. But it is necessary that the workers should get a greater measure of the wealth they produce, and to get this they must use pressure. This is why there is a Labor Party in the field. The program of this Party is of great importance to the workers, and must be supported by them.

No other party can be expected to give the workers, without pressure, such requirements as Old Age Pensions, Unemployment and Health Insurance, A National Minimum Wage, The Eight Hour Day and Five Day Week, Nationalization of the Natural Resources and their use for the cultural development of the people and not for speculation, and the repeal of laws which victimize the workers.

Experience has shown that the constitution of this country will not permit these benefits being granted the workers. At least this is the excuse given by the politicians of both Conservative and Liberal Parties. Therefore, it becomes necessary to call for the repeal of the British North America Act and the abolition of the Senate, which stand in the way of these benefits.

When all the issues which will come before the people at this election are boiled down, there will remain one thing only for the workers to do in order to get something out of this government turmoil, this is, vote for the candidates of the Labor Party—support the Labor Program—work for a government that will be free from speculation, graft and evil practices—a Workers' and Farmers' Government.

AGNES MacPHAIL, M.P.*

[Editorial]

August 1926, p. 3.

ELSEWHERE in this issue of The Woman Worker there is printed a poem dedicated to Agnes MacPhail, M.P. At this time it is fitting that we, too, should express our opinion on the actions of the only woman member of the Federal Parliament.

Miss MacPhail, a daughter of a farmer, a teacher by profession, has represented a farmers' constituency through two Parliaments. During these periods she worked consistently for the benefit of the electors. She also supported the most progressive measures brought before the House which would benefit the workers of this country. In fact, Miss MacPhail supported the Labor Platform.

Her fearlessness, her political independence, her deep interest and care for the well-being of the womanhood and childhood of Canada has endeared her to the working women of farm and city alike.

It is not surprising that the progressive electors of Grey County should send her forth again to battle in the elections for a seat in Parliament. This expression of confidence in Miss MacPhail by the farm men and women is a marked contrast to that afforded the women of the Conservative and Liberal Parties.

When a number of women, prominent in the ranks of these two parties, were questioned about contesting seats in Toronto, they declared that such a thing would be hopeless. Their opinions were, that a woman to brave the forthcoming political storms would have to possess cunning, brains, personal magnetism, pretty clothes, and a good bank account—and—would have to be approved by the men at convention. This last was the greatest difficulty, especially as a Federal campaign is looked upon as a man's business.

We can be thankful that the farmers of Canada have not such a viewpoint, otherwise we should not have known Miss MacPhail. It did not require all the qualities outlined by the Toronto women of the Liberal and Conservative Parties to convince the farmers that Miss MacPhail was fitted to represent them. Instead, it was the qualities of frankness, sincerity, sound judgment and forceful expression that convinced them of her fitness to be their representative. The organized farmers and advanced workers of Canada lead the way in the fullest understanding of "Sex Equality." Upon the shoulders of men and women alike must rest the responsibilities of work and duties. Those who do not understand this belong to the decaying system of privilege. When more women like Miss MacPhail are in the Federal House we shall know that the new social order is in sight.

WANTED—WOMEN M.P.'s*
(Dedicated to Agnes McPhail, M.P.)

August 1926, p. 6.

> O women—in our hours of ease,
> You are so good and kind, but, please,
> We want your sound and splendid sense
> Within that House of Sad Pretense.
> Is it enough? One lonely woman's zeal
> Fighting your battles for the Commonweal?
>
> Your country's heart is sick and sore
> Watching the capers of the party bore;
> His brainless squabbling for power and Gain
> While causes die for which you toiled in vain.
> Is it enough? One lonely woman's zeal
> Fighting your battles for the Commonweal?
>
> Was it for this your women pioneers
> Toiled for your rights in agony and tears
> To give you power to waste your precious vote

On venal partisans, creatures of wont and rote?
Is it enough? One lonely woman's zeal
Fighting your battles for the Commonweal?

One lonely woman in that squabbling throng,
Trembling, indignant, angry at the wrong
That murders pity for the aged poor
And pensions jobbery for the genial boor.
Is it enough? One lonely woman's zeal
Fighting your battles for the Commonweal?

Within your ranks are women brave and true,
Charged with the passion of their country's rue.
Call them to service in their country's need;
Your nation's heart is sick of graft and greed.
Is it enough? One lonely woman's zeal
Fighting your battles for the Commonweal?

Call them as women, free from party ties,
Which chill the heart and blind the seeing eyes.
We want their sound and splendid sense
To sweep that House of Sad Pretense.
Is it enough? One lonely woman's zeal
Fighting your battles for the Commonweal?

A.B.

*{Editors' Note: Macphail was spelt inconsistently in the original.}

BEAUTY CONTESTS

September 1926, p. 5.

The recent beauty contest in Toronto has brought forth condemnation from ministers of the church and artists. Both object to the display of feminine beauty in such a vulgar fashion. The onus of the responsibility for thus exposing themselves is placed upon the girls who take part.

We have an objection to beauty contests too, but not on the same grounds as the ministers and the artists. We like to see the daughters of the working class maintaining their beauty and physical fitness. Our objection to beauty contests is, that they are used merely as a means of advertising. In this particular case, not only did merchants advertise their wares, but the city of Toronto used the contest to advertise Sunnyside, to take trade to the refreshments booths, and to get revenue for the Transportation System.

WE VISIT THE MOUNTAIN
By A.D.A.

October 1926, pp. 7-11.

The Journey Started

"And what do you get for this, may I ask?" So questioned a woman at whose house I called canvassing for our labor candidate. Said I, "Well, madam, if you wish to know I can tell you. I get sore feet, a tired tongue, and a weary body, but I get no money, and this is what I think you refer to." The woman of the house seemed a little taken aback at the answer. Changing her tone of voice, she said. "I am a Conservative, our whole family have always been conservatives, so you know where my vote will go. But, I really think you should get pay for your work. Our Conservative men get paid for their work, but they think the women ought to work for the cause. The women are beginning to kick." This last comment was spoken half confidentially. "Well," I replied, "in the Labor Movement the men as well as the women [...] Our Party, the Labor Party, of wage workers [...] does not get financial aid from big business and people who own whiskey distilleries. We have to depend on the small contributions donated by wage workers. Of course, it is for the benefit of wage workers that the Labor Party exists." "Wage workers!" retorted the lady with a gesture of disgust; "most of those persons are idle, thriftless beings, the women waste their money on movies and the men on drink; they make no effort to get on, and grumble about the fellow who does." "That is a rather rash statement," said I. "Let us see who these wage workers are." I went through a list for her benefit. "There are the men who make the roads, clean the roads and look after the drains. Imagine what would happen if these cleaners refused to work! Then there are the men who build the railroads, the men who work the mines, and the men who run the trains, etc., etc. Not forgetting the women who have to work in factories and stores. In short, madam, the wage workers are the very people upon whom you depend for the necessities and comforts of life."

I discovered that our Conservative lady, while not living in a very pretentious house, was living off the interest on mortgages. This I discovered when I attacked those who lived by means of rent, interest and profit.

Seeing that it was impossible to convince her that Labor's cause was the only cause, I thought I would leave her with something to think about. So I said, "I must be moving on, but let me tell you that the people you despise because they are workers will one day be masters. The workers are beginning to learn how important and necessary they are; in fact, that all society depends on them. When the workers become masters, all will have to work, and those who do not work will not eat."

She looked at me quite angrily, and banged her door as if to show what she would have liked to have done to me were it possible.

I Meet a Harder Nut

I thought that this Conservative woman was a hard nut to crack, but presently I struck another even harder. Seated on her verandah in a rocking chair, was a plump contented-looking woman. I approached her and asked her the usual question: "Are you interested in the election?" "No, I don't bother my head about such things," she replied. "This is rather unusual," said I, "perhaps I can interest you in the program of the Labor Party, our labor candidate will have to support this program if he is elected." I went through the program, explaining the reason for Old Age Pensions, how the Senators had rejected the bill, and why we must get rid of the House of Senate. I told a vivid story of the misery of the unemployed, and explained why they were entitled to Unemployment Insurance.

She listened the whole time with a self-satisfied smile on her face, and when I concluded, she said, "I'm not interested." "Not interested," said I, in amazement, "not interested in the needs of others who are not as fortunately placed as yourself?"

"I'm not interested. I have nothing to worry about. Why should I worry?" she replied.

Said I again, "But is it nothing to you that the aged poor are sent to jail, that unemployed girls are jailed as vagrants, that some sell their bodies for bread, that little children starve for the necessities of life?" "These things do not concern me," she replied. I had never experienced such heartlessness. I felt disgusted with the woman, and thought I would take a chance at offending her so I said. "It may be that things won't always continue rosy with you, you may even stand in need of the things for which we are fighting."

"I do not think so; my husband has provided for my needs. I'm comfortably fixed. As for voting, I leave that always to him."

Such indifference, such contentment, such selfishness! I felt I wanted to shake that lump of inhumanity. I left her consoling myself with the thought that when she died no one would miss her.

Time Alone Will Change

I was yet to meet another immovable human. Going up to a woman who was taking it easy on her verandah, I said, "I suppose you are interested in the election?" "I should say I am. Who are you canvassing for?" "The Labor candidate," I replied. She laughed, saying at the same time, "Don't waste your time here, I'm a Conservative; I'm proud of it, and you couldn't change me in a thousand years, however hard you tried." "Very well," said I, "I'll not waste my breath on you; I leave you to Father Time."

An Old Trade Unionist

That day's work was very disappointing. But it could have been worse. I did meet one person who said, "Yes, my vote goes to the labor candidate." This person was an elderly man. He said, "I heard the labor candidate speak, he's a fighter. I belong to a trade union," he added. "Friend, you look as if you need a pension right now," said I. "Yes," he said, "I cannot work any more, I'm done for." "Cheer up," said I, "our man will fight for you." His eyes welled with tears as I shook his hand. Poor soul! His trade had ruined his health, he was hanging on to life by a thread.

Another Side of the Mountain

Fortunately, the following day I struck a different crowd of women. I discovered that the ages of women made quite a big difference. By this I mean, the majority of the women I met during my first day's work were elderly women—the grandmother age. Their families were off their hands and their minds were fixed on the past. They did not need Old Age Pensions.

The different crowd were women whose families were babies, or who were struggling along with children of school age or children preparing for a career. These women, finding a pair of sympathetic ears to talk to, did not hesitate to tell their stories of daily struggles; the small wages their husbands earned; what each had to do with that wage to make ends meet; how they denied themselves pleasure so that their children should have a chance to make good. And when I said, "Well, what are you going to do about it? How do you intend to help yourself at this election?" "Oh! I don't know," often came the answer, "my husband always advises me." "But cannot you think for yourself, you have the vote, this is for your own expression of opinion, not your husband's," I would say. Nearly always the answer would be, "I haven't time to read. I know nothing about politics."

It required a lot of patience to tell each woman in turn what was at the root of her grievances, and why the workers must stand together.

Most of these women thought "politics" was something quite outside their homes. They had no idea that hours of labor, even wages, the cost of living, the education of their children, the school cadets, were bound up with politics.

When I explained these things to one young mother, she said, "How glad I am you came to tell me this, we women need educating so much."

Privation

Some of the tales of suffering in working class homes were heartrending. One mother asked me to step inside, so we could talk at ease. This woman was raising a family of six children. Her husband had been off work for nearly six months through illness. The result was she was struggling under a burden of debt; the biggest worry was the six months arrears of rent. In addition to this her eldest daughter, a girl of fifteen, was in ill-health. Her husband had just managed to get work, but his wages were very low, just forty cents an hour. She had tried to get work herself, but the wages offered her were so low that it would not pay her to go out and to leave the children to look after themselves.

It was lunch hour and the children came in from school. Their meal was bread and peanut butter. "Tell me how my husband can get more wages; tell me how I can get work; these are the things we need most," the poor woman exclaimed, half crying.

We talked about the Labor Movement. I explained how she and her husband must interest themselves in this, as this is the movement that provides the means through which the workers can struggle for the things they need. Also, that they must support the Labor candidate as an expression of trust in the Labor Movement. Each vote for the labor candidate strengthened the cause of labor.

With the promise that she would talk the matter over with her husband, I left this poor mother with her family and her burdens.

Crude Notions

And what notions, strange notions, our working class housewife had of Miss Agnes MacPhail! Our working woman is just as ignorant of the forward march of her sex into the field of political activity as she is of politics in general.

"Miss McPhail! That woman! She's a disgrace to us women! No decent woman would sit among all those men!" was but one of the comments of disapproval.

So it fell to me to champion our only lady member of the Federal House of Commons. "Miss MacPhail is one of our most courageous and best women," I would reply. "She is not in Parliament for herself, but for a cause. She has to fight for this cause and she displeases many of those men in Parliament. This needs courage. She fights against war, the wrong education of our children, and many other things which hurt us, as well as for things which benefit us. Miss MacPhail urges other women to join her, to help her. She does not like being there alone, but it is due to our backwardness that she is. We have yet to wake up."

(Forgive our sisters, Miss MacPhail, for they know not why they think these things.)

I Meet the First Woman Rebel

It was the day before the election. I had just a few more houses to visit. My rebel woman was sweeping her verandah. I wondered, as I approached her, whether she would be another hard nut to crack. "Are you interested in the election?" I asked. "Indeed I am," she said, "and I'm going to vote for the man who can help the workers." This was like balm to sore ears. Then, as if to give vent to her pent-up indignation, the result of the struggle with poverty, she denounced the conditions of toil for the workers, the long hours they worked, the low wages they received, how workers felt themselves forced to join certain organizations to secure jobs for themselves. She stormed against the newspapers which printed one thing one day and the opposite to the same subject the next. Finally, she wound up by saying "In Russia the workers were compelled to take drastic action. I tell you, that is what will happen in Canada one of these days, and it may not be so very far off. Do not misunderstand me. I love Canada. I am not unpatriotic. I have heard that you people in the Labor Movement want to destroy our country, that you have no use for it."

Here was a real rebel. I told her her words made me glad, and that she was the most intelligent woman I had struck during my canvassing expedition. I assured her that she was figuring out things pretty correctly. But it was necessary to correct her wrong impression of Labor's attitude toward Canada. I told her that we in the Labor Movement liked Canada so much that we wanted Canada for the only useful people, the workers and the farmers, the producers of life's necessities. Now Canada was in the hands of speculators, profiteers, sharks of every kind, who bled her of her wonderful wealth as well as robbed the workers of the fruits of their labors. In fact, we wanted the World for the Workers.

I left my rebel woman, knowing she was on the right track and knowing that two votes from that house would be cast for the labor candidate.

The Mountain

What was the mountain I visited? Not a summer resort! Oh, dear, no! It was the mountain of ignorance, apathy, prejudice, mainly the result of maleducation. *And what a Mountain!* A mountain of slaves, caressing and hugging and worshipping the chains of bondage. As I reflect upon my visit to this mountain, I feel I want to bore, bore and bore, into its very bowels. I want to make it a seething volcano of working class activity and consciousness. I want to make it a live force struggling against injustice and for freedom.

Will this mountain, now under the control of the dark forces of a master class, ever be won to fight for freedom? Of course it will! Of course it must! But, Oh! for the tools! Certainly those we have will have to be adjusted to this task. Those we have not, we must make.

But go to the mountain—the masses—the workers!

DRINK NOT THE CAUSE OF THE CLASS POVERTY OF THE WORKERS

December 1926, p. 5.

At a recent meeting of the Toronto pastors of the United Church, it is reported that thirty-three pastors stood up and declared that in the last year they had not been called upon to assist a single family which had become destitute through DRINK.

From this statement we must conclude that they had been called upon to assist some destitute families. If this is so, then we must ask, Are there other reasons for poverty and destitution besides drink? Then, as this must be so, we must ask, Are these not as bad as drink?

The preachers of the Gospel must know that there is one great CAUSE for the poverty of the workers. They must know that a certain condition prevails which keeps the workers on the border line of destitution despite the hours they toil and the economy they practise. Why cannot they be frank and declare: The poverty of the workers lies at the door of the master class, the exploiters of the labor of the workers?

And as exploiters, the Liquor Interests care not about the misery their commodity brings. They only laugh when they see the foolish workers pouring liquor down their throats, getting befuddled, and losing their senses. This means profit to them; why should they worry?

Workers will continue to be between the devil and the deep sea until they see that their interests lie in getting rid of the profit system.

WHAT SOME WOMEN CALL FREEDOM

December 1926, pp. 5-6.

Wives and daughters of some wealthy business men in a place called Wallasey, Cheshire, Eng., have formed a Club. Their object for so doing is to make cigar smoking popular for women. They regard this as a symbol of independence, as up to the present cigar smoking has been only a privilege for the men.

Leaving the habits of the Indian women; who are supposed to be barbarians, out of the question for the moment, we will agree that rich women, like all other women, have certain bonds to break. But, unfortunately, cigar smoking will not break them. The bonds that tie them are linked to a social system which has private property as its foundation. The bonds that enslave rich women will break, only when certain other bonds which tie the wage workers to the same system, break first.

To help break their bonds these women would do well to help the workers in their struggle. But will they? Oh, no! They would much prefer smoking cigars, because it is the least trouble, and certainly the least disagreeable.

Working women in this case will not worry themselves about the habits of their rich sisters. They are wiser if they take the path with the men of their class, in the direction of working class independence and freedom. This will mean the end of the wage slave system, and all else will follow in its train.

CONSERVATIVE WOMEN MAKE DEMAND FOR EQUAL REPRESENTATION

January 1927, p. 4.

Women members of the Conservative party are demanding a 50-50 basis in representation at the forthcoming national convention of their party.

This speaks for itself. Conservative women have received a raw deal during the past few years at the hands of their men. But, really, what else could be expected when Conservative men look upon their women, not as political equals, but as merely society entertainers.

The women of the Labor Movement are more fortunately placed. Sex equality from the political standpoint is not questioned. This is because men and women alike in the Labor Movement must go forward together in the struggle for economic freedom.

TORONTO LOCAL COUNCIL OF WOMEN PROTEST AGAINST BEAUTY CONTESTS

February 1927, p. 6.

The Toronto Local Council of Women have done right in protesting against commercializing the beauty of young women. We have protested right along against this. We welcome this addition to our protest.

HOW WELL-TO-DO WOMEN WOULD REFORM WAYWARD GIRLS
By A.I.

March 1927, pp. 12-13.

Who are wayward girls? Why a certain type of girl who belongs to the working class.

Are there, then, no rich wayward girls? Well, this is a funny question. But, between you and me, in confidence, you know, it can be said that when a daughter of the rich class happens to do an act similar to that of some of the daughters of the poor, few hear about it. She is sick and is sent away for a rest cure. Wealth, you know, covers a multitude of sins. It is said, too, that one is guilty only when found out.

Wealth cloaks the moral "turpitudes" of the rich. The poverty of the workers makes them "social lepers" when they happen to follow the conduct of No Man's Land.

The unfortunate poor girl cannot hide the results of her wanderings from the path of moral convention of to-day. Once discovered she knows no peace. She must live. But she is a leper. She cannot find work. She becomes hardened. She loses all sense of responsibility. She knows only that of her body. She spurns sympathy. She feels everyone's hand is against her. She pursues her path, takes chances with her life, limb and freedom.

But surely the surroundings in which these girls lived in their young days, their bringing up, the kind of homes they lived in, their associates, their education, their experiences on the street, their whole environment—have something to do with their fall from the present-day standard of morals?

Well, you, dear reader, who ask this question, may think this way, but Dr. Margaret Patterson, of the Toronto Women's Court, the Ontario Provincial Council of Women, and the Toronto Local Council of Women evidently think otherwise.

If press reports are true, then the women who belong to the before-mentioned organizations must look upon these so-called wayward girls in the light of being criminals, that their actions are the result of real inborn badness and wickedness of heart, or that they are feeble-minded. For were this not so they would not have presented to the Ontario Government the demand—that the terms of imprisonment for wayward girls be increased from the present two-year maximum to that of five years.

Social Safety First

These ladies may, of course, put forward the claim that these wayward girls are a social menace, and that social safety demands their isolation.

If these wayward girls are a social menace there must be something wrong with society to have produced this menace. Things do not come of themselves; everything has a cause. This means that our wayward girls are merely the result of a cause. And what do Social Service organizations declare about this. They state that broken homes, poverty-stricken homes are the cause of ninety per cent. of the wayward girls.

Then society is to blame. These girls are not criminals, but victims of a vicious social order, one that condemns ninety per cent. of the people to lives of poverty, and gives the ten per cent. the privileges of wealth and luxury and ease.

It is not imprisonment that these girls should have, with guards, military discipline, cells, hard work, and all the conditions that go with hard labor. They deserve a better fate, because of the things they lacked during childhood. They should have hospital homes, sunshiny and bright, with doctors and nurses in attendance. They should live in artistic surroundings and experience a taste of real culture. They are condemned to short lives anyway, so why not give them a little taste of heaven while they are on earth.

These girls are human beings with warm blood running through their veins. They have feelings; they long after the things of life, and long more for these things when they are absolutely denied them.

Our good women sing in church, "As pants the hart for cooling stream," yet they do not think that the poor, wayward girl in the first place panted for a little sunshine, a little kindness, a little happiness, a little joy, as well as often for a little food. And this because she was human.

And what of the men who buy? Ah, he is privileged to a certain extent. But some of these, too, are social victims. Their poverty will not allow them to marry. But they do not lose their freedom, as do the wayward girls.

Oh, the cruelty of the poverty of the workers!

Oh, why cannot the workers see and feel more keenly the insults the present system levels at their class!

Arouse yourselves, working women! The wayward girls are your sisters—the victims of the social conditions of to-day. The wayward girls are daughters of the workers. We cannot allow this stigma to remain. We must fight against the evil, prostitution, by fighting the conditions that make the prostitute.

WAR IS DECLARED ON "DEMORALIZING LITERATURE"

April 1927, pp. 5-6.

The National Council of Women, in its recent meeting, went on record favouring a Board of Censors who shall determine what we shall read. This is because it is thought that a great deal of harmful literature is being devoured by Canadian readers. The terms "pernicious" and "demoralizing" applied to literature can cover a vast field. And these women, whose interests are bound up with the present order of things, can claim that anything which criticizes this order is "pernicious" and "demoralizing."

Recently, a magazine called "New Masses" was declared "Unfit" by the Customs Department of the government. There is only one reason why such a magazine should be refused the privilege of the Canadian mails, and this is that it is "progressive." Unlike the Tabloid Press, "New Masses" is strictly educational.

But no doubt it is the way "New Masses" teaches that does not find favor in the eyes of "some persons near the government." It is inclined to ridicule the present order of things, to shock mock modesty, to call a spade a spade.

If "New Masses" is to come back to Canada again it will have to wrap all its thoughts in heavy bandages of cotton wool, so that only very deep thinkers can peer through for truth. Such is hypocrisy!

THE Y.W.C.A. IN CANADA

[Editorial]

October 1927, pp. 2-3.

WITHOUT a doubt the Young Women's Christian Association can claim to be the most popular of young women's organizations at this time. The thing that has helped to make it popular is the protection it offers.

Time and experience have made even this organization face a few facts, and if the reports we have received are any proof of this, then it can be said that, at least, the World Committee is trying to cope with some of the conditions.

The Industrial Section of the World Committee is putting some very pointed questions to its national bodies. To us Nos. 3 and 4 are interesting questions. These questions ask what the Associations are doing to promote improvement of factory law, a higher standard of life, and if they are encouraging the organization of women engaged in industry, this means, into trade unions?

We wonder how the Dominion Council in Canada will answer these questions. Indeed we would like to see the answers. So far as we can gather the Y.W.C.A. here has not done much, if anything, along this line. There has been no visible sign that they have helped the girls of their organization to help themselves by forming trade unions to keep up the wage standard.

We are aware they (the official and honorary members) have interested their Y.W.C.A. membership in sport, culture (literary and deportmental), but this is only individual improvement and not the collective improvement of working girls at the seat of production where their labor power is exploited.

In this country the Y.W.C.A. institutions are big and expensive. The maintenance of these cannot possibly be borne by the membership. Campaigns are put on for financial assistance. And herein lies the root of the trouble. It is a case here of "those who pay the piper calling the tune."

When the Dominion Council of the Y.W.C.A. sees fit to start work along the lines wanted by the Industrial Section of the World Committee of the Y.W.C.A. they will find the organized labor women of Canada ready to help them.

WOMEN FOR THE SENATE

October 1927, pp. 12-13.

The National Council of Women, the national body that represents the many and varied organized groups of women in this country, other than the groups of working-class women, holds its annual meeting in Stratford during the early days of October.

Among the resolutions which will engage the attention of this meeting will be one which will request the Dominion Government to grant to women the right to be appointed members of the Senate. If there should be clauses in the British North America Act which forbid women to be so appointed, the Dominion Government will be asked to urge the Imperial Government to amend the Act so that equal rights may be granted to women to be members of the Senate.

While we support "sex equality" there are circumstances which alter cases. If working women support sex equality in this matter they will be acting against their "class interests." We have not yet found any difference between the men and women of the rich class, both equally exploit the working class.

Organized labor in Canada is opposed to the Senate. It has declared it to be a useless instrument. It has always acted the part of an enemy to the workers. It opposed Old Age Pensions. It is against Unemployment Insurance.

Yet its members are old men, persons who have served their day in the House of Commons. These men receive an annual salary of $4,000, and they get this until they die. Their pension is secure. In addition, most of them are on the boards of directors of the Big Houses of Finance and Big Business Concerns. If women of a similar class are appointed to the House of Senate, and this is what would happen, the workers might have to fight a stronger foe. We do not want the Senate strengthened—we want it out of the way.

Working women cannot possibly lend support to such a resolution. Instead, we must support the demand of the Canadian Labor Party, which is "Abolish the Senate."

WOMEN OF QUEBEC REFUSED THE VOTE

[Editorial]

March 1928, pp. 2-3.

THAT the women in Quebec must attend to the needs of their homes and families and not bother about elections, is the decree of the Legislative Assembly of the Province of Quebec, Canada.

After a heated debate, the bill for Women's Suffrage which was introduced into the House by Mr. Tremblay, member of a Montreal riding, was defeated by 39-11 votes.

It is reported that it was the members of the rural ridings of Quebec who opposed the bill. These rural overlords gave as their opinion that "women should not go canvassing votes and running for public office when there was the home and the children to look after." And so, it might be commented, disturb the comforts and personal attention the women must give to their good rural husbands.

Perhaps, too, they had in mind that their women might ask for Birth Control rights. This surely would grieve those good rural husbands who delight in having their wives surrounded by their flocks of babies.

However, it can be left to Mr. Tremblay to state the case so far as the good men of Quebec are concerned. It is evident he knows. In reply to those who opposed the bill, he said: "I think it would be better for married men to stay at home with their wives and discuss political matters instead of drinking around town. In this way discord in family circles would be in a large measure done away with."—Toronto Star, Feb. 28th.

It is absurd to refuse to grant the right of the vote to the women of Quebec. They have the right to vote in Federal elections, why not then the right to vote in provincial and municipal elections? Without doubt these men fear the forward march of women, and that this spells the doom of their dictatorship over, at least, their own immediate females.

So far, very little has been done in the Province of Quebec by those women who are interested in obtaining suffrage, and this little has been confined to the process of lobbying. This is a somewhat feeble way to tackle the question. It is not enough to go to the Provincial House and corner the members and try to coax them into supporting Women's Suffrage. What is wanted is a provincial campaign in order to make the demand for suffrage as wide as possible. The women of Quebec need this for themselves, that is, if we are to believe reports. This campaign could disclose the fact that the French-Canadian woman is more exploited than her sisters of the other provinces—as a wage worker she works for less and under worse conditions than the women elsewhere in Canada—as a mother she is classed in the list of those having the highest death rate.

The Women's Labor Leagues of Montreal will not waste time if they help to push forward such a campaign. They can stir the unions into action for this cause. They can help to put a little life into the Quebec Section of the Canadian Labor Party by urging this Section to take a prominent part in such a campaign.

Forward to the task of waking up the Province of Quebec from its medieval sleep!

UNITY BETWEEN WORKING WOMEN OF CITY AND FARM

[Editorial]

March 1928, pp. 3-5.

IN this issue of The Women Worker there is published a letter received from the President of the Women's Section of the United Farmers of Canada (Saskatchewan Section).

This letter, as our readers will gather, is sent in answer to our criticism of the action of the officers of the Union in urging their Women's Section to affiliate with the Saskatchewan Provincial Council of Women.

The reason advanced by the President, Mrs. Hollis, is that they considered this affiliation necessary because they felt the need of contact with the city and urban women. This is a feasible reason. Perhaps we who live in the crowded cities where life and activity are continual cannot fully realize what isolation means to our sisters living on the farms in the vast prairie provinces of this country.

We would like to make clear that our criticism was not directed against the Saskatchewan Provincial Council of Women in particular. We are aware that there are many well-intentioned women, even working women, working with the various provincial councils; in this connection can be mentioned the Regina Women's Labor League, a unit of the Federation of Labor Leagues.

But this fact does not make the Women's Council Movement, as it might be called, a movement best suited to the needs of the working women of farm and city.

'Tis true, this movement takes all forms of social welfare work under its wing; it interests itself in women's right; it endeavors to lift the standard of citizenship onto a high level, etc., but its attitude towards the workers is one of "patronage" and "sympathy"—an attitude which is obnoxious to working women who know only too well the source of all wealth, the reason for poverty, and why one class is enslaved and another class privileged and enriched.

Naturally, this very fundamental fact makes them view everything of a social nature with different eyes, as, for instance, instead of advocating that jails and reformatories should be made more comfortable for the delinquent girl, we say, give a working girl an adequate wage, and thus enable her to live a respectable life. Again, we do not consider such a girl as being born "bad," but we say instead, that she is the victim of the social system of today, and in some cases have to show our well-to-do sisters who are connected with Council Movement, that they are not altogether guiltless in contributing to the delinquency of working girls through their support of low wages.

It can be seen that there is little in common between working women and women of leisure who spend a part of their time in social uplift work.

On the other hand, we are heartily in agreement with Mrs. Hollis' statement that she considers "the problems of Agriculture and Industry as practically the same."

It is because these are the same that we claim that industrial workers and farmers must get together to solve the big problem of their enslavement to CAPITAL. This is why we want to establish closer relations with our sisters of the farm. And, too, this is why we must show the limitations of the Women's Council Movement.

ANSWER TO OUR CRITICISM

Saskatoon, Feb. 8, 1928

March 1928, pp. 15-16.

Mrs. Florence Custance,
    Editor Woman Worker,
    211 Milverton Blvd.,
    Toronto (6).

Dear Madam:

Having always been interested in social and economic questions and feeling personally that the problems of Agriculture and Industry are practically the same, I brought your paper before our Executive Board and got them to subscribe for it for use in our Central Office.

The first number received, October, 1927, contains a criticism of our organization, or rather the officers, for advising our women members "to co-operate and work in harmony with the Provincial Council of Women." Your reasons for adverse criticism of the above action are stated very clearly, and the chief seems to be that the P.C.W. is "anti-labor." You also fear that the farm women of Saskatchewan are being persuaded into affiliation with an organization that is trying to undermine the political influence of Miss Macphail.

The Women's Section of the Saskatchewan Grain Growers' Association was for many years affiliated with the Provincial Council of Women; the question as to the advisability of affiliation was frequently discussed, chiefly because we wondered if the farm women were receiving much benefit from such affiliation. The conclusion arrived at was that this was practically our only bond of connection with the city and urban women, and only in this way could the viewpoint of the rural women be placed before them.

It may be news to you that the Labour Women of Regina (one of the most active labour organizations in our Province) are also affiliated with the P.C.W. The Council thus gives us a direct means of contact with the labour women, and altogether we think this has been of great benefit to the women citizens of Saskatchewan.

Members of the Council of Women have worked on the Minimum Wage Board and have generally been very sympathetic with labour.

Miss Macphail's action with regard to Cadet Training and Peace Propaganda has received very enthusiastic support from Western farm organizations of which our women are active members.

In affiliating with the P.C.W. it is distinctly stipulated that we have full freedom of independent action, as Article II of the Constitution shows. Article II reads:

"The aim of this Provincial Council is to bring the various organizations of women in Saskatchewan into closer relation, through an organized union, but no society entering the Provincial Council shall thereby lose its independence in aim or method, or be committed to any principle or method of any other society in the Council, the object of which is to serve as a medium of communication and a means of prosecuting any work of common interest."

Our aim in this affiliation, if it takes place, is to work with other women citizens in every possible way to improve social and economic conditions, whether in city, town or rural communities. As members of our own farm organization we have equal status with the men, and very often are able to interest them in reforms being asked for by the women citizens of the province. Thus, by co-operation with other women, as far as possible, and with our own men, we can help in accomplishing many needed reforms.

I thought you would be interested to know our general attitude in these respects.

Wishing you every success in your work.

Sincerely yours,
(Mrs.) A.L. Hollis,
President Women's Section, United Farmers of Canada,
Saskatchewan Section, Ltd.

THE FAILURE OF THE SUFFRAGE MOVEMENT TO BRING FREEDOM TO WOMAN

December 1928, pp. 12-14.

The great activity shown when occasion demands by political parties in their efforts to get the woman vote, brings to mind many of the promises and prophesies which were made by friends and foes in those not distant days when it required a little courage to wear a "votes for women" button.

Of course the "Antis" sounded their usual alarm—the home would be destroyed—and one admits that many suffragists also showed their ignorance of the "world process" by their optimistic arguments along opposite lines: And after it was all over what happened?

In the first place, the anti-suffragists who were loudest in proclaiming that "woman's place is the home" were the very first to step out and seek political and other offices. And of all the others who fought so well for this right of self-expression, only one or two, here and there over the whole country, saw that this was not the end of the struggle, but only a very small beginning.

To be sure, it was not a working class movement. The majority in it were middle class and fairly satisfied with conditions—as one well known club woman said to me "It seems so absurd that my gardener can vote and I can't." It was just a matter of status with her.

They were the sort who used to get up in meetings and enquire anxiously—"but who will do the menial work," when one was trying to picture a better social order. Evidently, if it meant work and responsibility for all, they were not going to stand for it. But they were mostly nice, kind ladies, and they often meant well, as on the occasion when one of them undertook to investigate conditions in a certain workshop, she brought back an excellent report, and when asked from whom she got her information, she said, "Oh, I went right to the manager!" And how they wanted to supervise the spending of working class housewives at the beginning of the war. It seems that some of these wasteful creatures were discovered buying oranges and pickles—and later on it was gramophones and pianos!

But when election time came these same fine ladies were very busy calling on women in various working class districts, and acting so "perfectly lovely," that many a foolish woman voted against her own interests and against her family and her class, because she was so flattered she was easily deceived.

In the U.S.A. a group of influential ones, called "The Women's National Party," are now going before Congress—supported by members of the employer's association—and opposing legislation that would aid great numbers of women to an approach to economic equality with men. They call it, asking for "equal rights." If, for instance, men are working ten hours a day in certain places, women employed there must also have the "right" to work ten hours a day. If successful, they will nullify the work of years done by trade unions and labor groups for the betterment and relief of working women. It may be that they do not grasp the serious problems of the woman worker, but, anyway, they are proving again that the business of fair play for all who work for wages is the worker's own task.

Another reason why the vote has been of so little use to us is the fact that hundreds of thousands are always disfranchised.

The law requires certain conditions and the worker following his job or moving about in search of employment is thus automatically off the voters' list.

And the working class generally is suffering today in "mind, body, and estate" because we've been too confiding, too good natured, too patient. We have failed to see that whatever value there was in the vote was lost entirely unless used for ourselves. And if this be intelligent selfishness there's little to argue about.

Certainly the so-called "dignity of labor" is only an election phrase, but there are enough workers to give it real meaning. We could very well take a lesson from the conduct of those in authority over us. They realize what class loyalty means, even though they may not like or in any way approve of each other individually. Yet they are rarely so silly as to be caught voting or acting in any way against their class interests. They stick together.

And since we have in Canada such a high class paper as "The Woman Worker" it must be now much easier to get together in great numbers with one common denominator—working class freedom.

If we meet just as working women, with no handicaps because of race, creed or color, it will speed up the day when voting will not be the farce it now is, when governments will not be something remote and threatening, when the ruling of peoples will give place to the administration of things "for the well-being of all."

October 30, 1928   H.D.P.

FARM AND RURAL WOMEN

[Editorial]

January 1929, pp. 3-4.

TWO conventions were held recently, which are of interest to working women. One was that of the Women's Institutes of Ontario, and the other was that of the United Farm Women of Ontario. Both are organizations of farm and rural women.

The former organization is a well established one, and the convention was its twenty-seventh annual meeting. One of the delegates claimed that the organization was "a factor to be reckoned with" since it had now 1,100 Institutes established in Ontario with a membership of 40,000.

Perhaps one reason why the organization has had such progress and met with success is that it has received grants from the Provincial Government. This has also resulted in the organization becoming a political football, although the great bulk of the women may not realize it. That this is so, can be seen from the fact that last year one woman who was eligible to stand for the position of president was passed over, and it is claimed, simply because she supported Liberalism.

It is clear that the Women's Institutes have a long way to go yet.

The United Farm Women of Ontario, on the other hand, are, on the whole, far more advanced from the political standpoint, since they are a definite part of the farmers' organization. As such, of course, they do not receive a government grant, nor do they get special privileges, such as lecturers supplied by the government. They should not regret this as was done in their convention.

Naturally, because the United Farm Women of Ontario is a more advanced organization it is not as strong from the standpoint of numbers. There are at present 78 clubs, with a membership of 1,925.

Among the subjects discussed at the convention of the United Farm Women were, "Maternal Mortality," which, it was claimed, must receive more attention, and plans devised to prevent the deaths of mothers through child-birth. Opposition was expressed to the proposed Ontario Divorce Court on the ground that it would lead to more divorces and greater domestic misery. Agreement was expressed to the proposal that women should sit in the Senate. One resolution was passed which demanded that at least one woman should sit on the Township Boards of Education. Equality of Property Rights was also demanded, as expressed in a resolution which claimed that a wife should receive half interest in the property, money, etc., belonging to the man.

The secretary of the U.F.W. of O. reported that their organization was affiliated with the Provincial Council of Women, and this action had been taken to make women's efforts more effective.

We doubt very much if this was a wise step. Evidently, the farm women have forgotten the treatment meted out to Miss Agnes Macphail because of her letter to the school boy who wanted information about China, when that country was in the turmoil of war and revolution.

Apart from the many shortcomings of the organizations of the farm and rural women, they can teach the working women of the towns and cities a lesson on organization. If our working women were organized as well a great deal more could be accomplished, and a stronger and more effective labor movement would be the result.

Let us take this lesson to ourselves and bend more energy to the task or organization.

Peace and War 4

During the 1920s the *Woman Worker* joined a number of new Canadian peace and disarmament groups in voicing a commitment to world peace. Drawing inspiration and ideas from socialist, and to a lesser extent feminist, traditions, the Women's Labor Leagues promoted a distinctive analysis of peace and war that was influential in shaping the politics of later generations of socialist feminists.

The pacifist tradition in Canada extends back to the 19th century and includes individuals and organizations with widely divergent viewpoints. Women's most visible peace work in the pre-war years was undertaken in the context of the middle-class women's movement, where pacifism was often promoted hand-in-hand with the demand for the vote and a host of other social reforms. Prominent Canadian suffragists like Nellie McClung assumed that once women won the right to vote they would use it to clean up the corruption and the warfare that men had historically created. Men and women were fundamentally different, feminists argued, usually linking those differences to a combination of biology and socialization. As mothers who gave life and nurtured children (and husbands), women were believed to be "natural" peacemakers.

If pacifism was not an exceptional stance in the decades before World War I, to call oneself a pacifist in the midst of the patriotic fervour of war was risky business. Anti-war activists in Canada, as elsewhere, experienced harassment, intimidation, and threats of physical violence from intolerant pro-war zealots. In addition, Canadian governments and law enforcers anxious to stifle dissent shut down radical and pacifist presses, raided the offices of left-wing organizations, and jailed many socialists and pacifists, especially non-British immigrants, under the charge of sedition.

Many prominent feminists in North America and Europe, including Canada's Nellie McClung, became leaders in the movement for war preparedness, often taking the "maternal" ideology of their former pacifism and re-directing it to justify women's support for war. Labour's initial opposition to the war was undermined as workers enlisted in greater numbers. Even the established socialist parties were seriously divided by the war. Opposition to conscription generated more unity in left and labour circles, despite the Trades and Labour Congress's eventual support for the government's conscription bill.

A small minority of Canadian women held strong to their pacifist principles during World War I, and most still held some "maternalist" ideas about women's special connection to peace, despite the highly visible female role in war support activities. But wartime feminist pacifists also made a variety of socialist or social democratic economic critiques of war as a capitalist and imperialist venture. One concrete result of their efforts was the establishment in 1915 of the first all women's peace group in Canada, the Canadian Women's Peace Party, later known as the Canadian branch of the Women's International League for Peace and Freedom (WILPF).

After the war, pacifism, and the new talk of internationalism among peace activists, still raised hackles for several years. The peace movement would regain something of its pre-war stature and a new respectability, but not until the mid-1920s when eyes were lifted from the immediate demands of personal recovery and economic, social, and political reconstruction. The peace movement, however, lost the radical edge it had developed during the war. Socialists and feminists still offered their economic and gender analyses, but they were overshadowed in the 1920s and 1930s by new coalitions of liberal and conservative men and women focused on achieving peace and disarmament through new post-war institutional channels such as the League of Nations. As in the pre-war years, women were prominent contributors defining a new role for Canada in international peace politics through such groups as the WILPF, the National Council of Women of Canada, the League of Nations Society, and the United Church.

The Communist Women's Labor Leagues were set apart ideologically from this new coalition and they had no patience with the new star on the international block, the League of Nations. The articles reprinted here on peace and war from the *Woman Worker* reveal an analysis indebted first and foremost to a Marxist and Leninist critique of imperialism. Warfare had not ended with the armistice; it had merely taken new forms as the "new master class" trampled on workers at home and seized upon new imperialist ventures abroad. American and European aggression in China was particularly disturbing to Communists and the WLL paper continually applauded the fight of millions of workers and peasants for independence in the 1925-27 Chinese revolution. The League of Nations was accused of being a "League of favoured nations" that turned a blind eye to imperialist encroachments. It was established as a ploy of the rulers intended to distract workers everywhere from their fight for freedom from wage slavery. The *Woman Worker* demanded an end to the economic root of all conflict: the capitalist drive for profit. Only when socialism replaced capitalism, and international cooperation replaced nationalism, was peace possible. In the meantime, WLLers put their faith in "fighting" for peace through the organization and resistance of working class men and women who bore the fullest brunt of capitalist wars. State-initiated violence was condemned, but violence used by workers to resist capitalist oppression and pursue the revolutionary dream was never ruled out as a necessary part of revolutionary struggle. After all, the Russian Revolution, a tremendous inspiration to Communists everywhere, had been accomplished through violent class conflict. The absolute pacifism and non-resistance advocated by some in the peace movement found no sympathy among Communist women.

If these views in many ways isolated the WLLs from the mainstream peace workers, Communist directives for a united front strategy encouraged some attempts at forging alliances during much of the 1920s. There was some basis for unity, especially with some of the more progressive left-leaning women peace activists. Pacifist groups since the pre-war years had opposed the militarization of children in the schools through cadet training and the glorification of war in the curriculum. The WLLs stood solidly behind this de-militarization campaign and gave it high visibility from the start. The first full issue of the paper featured several slams to the IODE (especially for their donation of military pictures to schools), and a contribution by Agnes Macphail explaining the extent of the military presence in the schools and appealing to women to tell the Department of National Defence to get out of their children's schools. (See reprint of July/August 1926 issue.) Macphail's call to women as mothers, "Where are you mothers? This is your great task," was sometimes echoed by Communist women and their sympathizers. Indeed, the criticism of "parents" for indifference was aimed most pointedly at women, and the paper featured a long "Open Letter" to working-class mothers, written by Custance on behalf of the Canadian Federation of WLLs, and urging women to

oppose cadet training, the Boy Scouts, the Girl Guides, and to provide children at home with "the correct viewpoint on War." The
mothers in the WLL imagery, however, were class-conscious militant working-class mothers, not the generic and "naturally pacifist"
mothers of the pre-war maternal liberal feminist rhetoric.

By the late 1920s the Canadian Communist Party and its WLLs
were affected by changes taking place in Russian communism. As
Stalin took power in 1928 the united front approach was discredited
and the WLLs, already under suspicion for their housewife composition and for cozying up to bourgeois pacifists, were pressured to take
a harder line. Although Canadian Party officials complained that the
WLLs were not fully embracing the changed politics, the paper did
increasingly adopt a more critical assessment of feminist pacifists.
In 1927, for example, the paper printed approvingly parts of the
Toronto WILPF pamphlet on cadet training; it had worked coopera-
tively with that organization on more than one occasion. But one
year later the editor ripped into the American founder of the WILPF,
Jane Addams, criticizing her belief in human nature and her calls
for peace as naive at best and dangerously supportive of capitalism
at worst. In the spring of 1929 the Canadian feminist pacifist Alice
Chown was subjected to similar criticism for her "prayers and good
will bunk," after Chown spoke at a meeting of the WLL in Toronto.
Distancing the Leagues from even the label "pacifist" the Federation's "Open Letter" to mothers warned working class women
against the increasing popularity of pacifists, those "Non-Resisters"
and supporters of the League of Nations. Macphail herself, however,
seems to have escaped their fire, suggesting perhaps that her political value as an ally was still recognized.

A good example of the shift taken by the WLLs as communism
entered its "third period" occurred in Toronto in the winter of 1928-
29. The Toronto WLL had been represented at a reformist peace
meeting organized by the Women's Church Committee of the League
of Nations in November 1928, but early in the new year they had
withdrawn their involvement. Apparently feeling the need to justify
their actions to readers and respond to critics who thought they
could have stayed for some of the educational work, Custance explained they had learned that "there is a big difference between
wishing for Peace and getting Peace; wishing—only requires feeling;
getting—requires action." An important part of the action missing in
this and other peace meetings was a commitment to fighting imperialism, and of particular concern among Communists by 1929 was a
belief that the imperialist nations were actively conspiring in war
plans against Russia. Consequently, more attention was given in

the paper to shoring up support for a beleaguered Soviet Union. (See "Women and the Next War" and "Ourselves and the War Danger.")

Through the pages of the *Woman Worker*, the Women's Labor Leagues promoted an analysis of war and peace that drew primarily upon the pre-war socialist critique of war as driven by the forces of capitalism and imperialism. Feminist influences played a role in shaping some of the appeal to women as mothers, but contributors to the paper never lost sight of their belief that women's perspectives were defined more by their class than their gender. While allying themselves selectively with pacifists throughout much of the 1920s, especially on educational issues such as the militarization of schools, total non-violence was seen as an untenable position for the working class. Absolute pacifism was associated by the end of the decade rather dismissively with the lofty idealism of middle-class pacifist reformers and feminists who were by then lumped together as empty talkers and pawns of big finance. The class-first analysis of the WLLs provided a much needed corrective to the mainstream women's peace movement in the 1920s, with its wide-eyed hope for the League of Nations and its historical blindness to women's potential as aggressors. But the narrowness of their class consciousness also limited their ability to develop a more complex understanding of war as a phenomenon that is structured by class, race, and gender interests.

Further Reading:

- Barbara Roberts, "Women's Peace Activism in Canada," in Linda Kealey and Joan Sangster, eds., *Beyond the Vote: Canadian Women and Politics* (Toronto: University of Toronto Press, 1989), 276-308.

- Barbara Roberts, *A Reconstructed World: A Feminist Biography of Gertrude Richardson* (Montréal: McGill-Queen's University Press, 1996).

- Thomas Socknat, *Witness Against War: Pacifism in Canada, 1900-1945* (Toronto: University of Toronto Press, 1987).

- Janice Williamson, and Deborah Gorham, eds., *Up and Doing: Canadian Women and Peace* (Toronto: Women's Press, 1993).

- Veronica Strong-Boag, "Peace-Making Women: Canada 1919-1939," in Ruth Roach Pierson, ed., *Women and Peace: Theoretical, Historical and Practical Perspectives* (London: Croom Helm, 1987), 170-191.

ARMISTICE — AND SINCE

[Editorial]

November 1926, pp. 1-2.

NOVEMBER 11th, Armistice Day, will recall the four years of the Great War. It will recall the anguish and suffering those four years brought to many millions of people. It will recall promises made and broken. It will recall the dreams that many had of happy families, home fires, and the gratitude of a grateful country to those who sacrificed their lives to make "the world safe for democracy."

Casting our minds back over the years which have followed Armistice Day, we are forced to the conclusion that this day did not usher in PEACE; instead, it was the day on which was declared the collapse of the war conducted by the militarists.

But War did not cease with the signing of the Armistice. The only thing that happened was a change in the methods of warfare. What machine guns, bombs, poison gas, and trained soldiers did not succeed in doing, financial trickery, cunning, and starvation accomplished. Victors and Vanquished alike have gone down, and a newer master class force has come out on top. The American Dollar is the new god and the new force.

Since Armistice Day thousands have lost their lives. The victims have been workers. These were bound to feel the pinch of the new warfare, even as they were made the food for the guns. Those who protested against starvation were shot in cold blood. Those who endured starvation became its victims. To-day, there is mingled with the hatred of nations towards each other, that of the more bitter hatred of the classes within the nations. The struggle of the miners in Great Britain is proving how bitter this hatred can become. Armistice could be arranged between rival commercial nations, but no truce is allowed the miners, who ask that their wages shall not be decreased. And these miners are the men who fought to protect the soil of the landowners from which they draw their royalties from the coal the miners dig.

We ask for Peace, but upon what does Peace depend? Surely it is the end of conflicts. The conflicts which make for WAR are those connected with acquiring wealth. These conflicts must end before we can expect war to end.

The horrors of the GREAT "MILITARY" WAR were not terrible enough to frighten people from another. Greater and more fearful preparations are being made for the next war. This preparation is going on under the very nose of the League of Nations, which body claims it is striving to bring peace to the world through disarmament. At the same time this League of Nations wipes its hands off China. It refuses to interfere in the civil war going on in that country—a war whose real, but hidden aggressors, are the imperialists of Britain, France, United States and Japan.

Many and various ways are suggested for the ending of WAR, but there is one force alone capable of dealing with WAR—and that force is the WORKERS OF ALL LANDS. This force alone can end the conflicts over wealth-getting for the sake of profits; first, by refusing to fight for master class interests; second, by substituting the system of co-operation for the present system of competition. This road will not be an easy road, but it is the only road to take if we are really sincere in wanting peace.

WAR CLOUDS

[Editorial]

February 1927, pp. 2-3.

HAS WAR been declared on China? While no formal notice has been given to this effect it would seem that such is the case. Else why send warships, regiments of soldiers? Why should some of the newspapers do all in their power to inflame the minds of their readers against China? If war machinery is being sent by Great Britain to China to protect the British residents in China, why should not China send warships to protect Chinese residents, let us say in Canada, where many Chinese reside, if war machinery is a sign of peace?

Those who have followed events in China know well enough that the British Government has allowed all kinds of acts which were intended to provoke the Chinese people. Workers and students have been shot down, the city of Wanhsien bombarded for three hours killing over 500 civilian Chinese, wounding 1,000, destroying nearly 2,000 houses, and damaging property to the extent of ten million dollars. Many more things could be cited.

China is no longer a backward country. She is no longer self-contained. She wants to enter into world affairs as an equal and not a subject nation. For one hundred years after a British robber trading company broke through her walls she has been the prey of Western exploiters. Now, she refuses to sign unfair treaties which would sell her people into slavery, and place her natural wealth in the control of foreign hands. THIS IS THE REASON FOR THE WAR ON CHINA. Ships, guns, and armies are for the purpose of forcing concessions and trading privileges from the Chinese.

China has pleaded for her independence. Now she is prepared to fight for it. The Nationalist Government of China desires to deal fairly with those who will trade with her, but it must be on equal terms, and not as a slave colony. The new national spirit of China refuses to be degraded. It will not give in to the greed of financial interests of Great Britain or any other country. It will not stand for Imperialism, the power of great nations.

Working women more than any others know the misery that war brings. We hold out our hands in sisterly greetings to our sisters in China. We will aid them to the best of our ability. At all times and in all places we will demand "Hands off China."

WE CAN HAVE NO FAITH IN THE LEAGUE OF NATIONS

By Mrs. Burt, President Toronto Women's Labor League.

March 1927, p. 9.

Is it not strange that some people have an unquestioning faith in the League of Nations? Stranger still is the fact that a great number of people, even those who call themselves good socialists, should have faith in the state of the capitalists and its powers of coercion?

From what angle shall we discuss this monster that has stood quietly by and allowed Europe to drift into further economic chaos and war?

Ostensibly the League was formed to make war impossible, or at least that is what the founders pretended, and yet we have the glaring inconsistency of allowing each nation to build or make armaments. Further, they believed in national sovereignty. That alone doomed or damned the League. A society of supreme nations is as impossible as a society of supreme individuals if we wish peace in the world. We wish our humbugging, hypocritical diplomats and statesmen would cease trying to make us believe we can have peace based on their nationalist principle.

Some time ago one of the delegates to the League told the truth when he said: "National sovereignty means war." Fifty-one governments have joined themselves together with the avowed object of abolishing war, and apparently they have agreed not to touch or deal with the causes of war. Do they presume to tell us that the causes of war are ETERNAL? The causes of all wars are economic. Thus the founders of the League (if they are sincere) should have aimed at the prohibition of economic frontiers.

Therefore let us have no illusions about what the League can do. Let us understand instead that it is a dangerous organization, where scheming politicians vie with each other at the game of international intrigue.

The so-called League of Nations is not a League of Nations, it is only a League of favored Nations. One thing is certain, they never intended it to be a League of Nations in the fullest sense, or they would have allowed every nation to join it. Some one may ask: Is it possible to reform the League of

Nations? No, because article 26 of the covenant makes any amendment in practice impossible. Besides, how could those tricky, anaemic old-world diplomats do anything? The only thing accomplished by the League is to expose to public gaze the depravity and bankruptcy of the old traditional diplomatic abuses.

What has the League of Nations done for China? China is part of the problem of the Far East and cannot be studied in isolation. The foreign powers control so much of China that it is impossible for the Chinese to free themselves except by revolting against their oppressors. It is said by competent writers that if China controlled her customs, her treaty ports, had financial control of her railways and mines that China could soon be master of her own house.

The League of Nations is bankrupt. International Unity of the Workers is what is wanted to end misery and bring World Peace.

WORKING WOMEN! FIGHT THE WAR MENACE

[Editorial]

July/August 1927, pp. 1-2.

ON August 4th, 1914, the Great War broke out. In four years over ten millions of men lost their lives and millions are living who are disabled for life. The war was a trade war, but it was called the war to "Save Democracy" and the "War to End War."

It is now 1927 and the germs of war are more vicious and more widespread than in 1914.

In 1914 Germany and the Kaiser were the foes. In 1927 war forces are being organized for action against the United Socialist Soviet Republics.

The promises made by those in authority during the Great War fell flat as we all know. The workers everywhere suffered the most, women were deprived of their husbands and sons, children of their fathers. Breadwinners were slaughtered, while the war-lords and the bankers received the gains.

The fearful sufferings of the workers and peasants of Russia during the first two years of the war, sufferings caused by the loss of seven millions of men, caused them to make the first break in the war, they refused to be used simply as cannon fodder. Later, they showed the rest of the workers of the world how "Real Peace" and "True Freedom" for those most enslaved could be obtained. They took power into their own hands. For this act the war-lords and banking profiteers have never forgiven the workers and peasants of Russia. They see in this act their own power over the wage-workers, the wage slaves they exploit, threatened. This is why they have declared that the U.S.S.R. is the world menace of to-day.

We know, however, that the U.S.S.R. has proved itself, and is still proving itself, the great peace force of the world. It has successfully resisted being drawn into wars in spite of the insults and outrages that have been inflicted on those who represented its government.

We must know, too, that British, French, Japanese, and United States troops are now in China not only to fight the Chinese Freedom Movement, but to gain a ground in the East from which to attack the U.S.S.R. Plans have been laid already by these powers for attack in the West. The governments of Poland, Bulgaria, and Roumania are only the tools of the great powers for this end.

So the plan of war is prepared already by the war makers. They have now one task left, that is to prepare the minds of the workers for this new world war in which the power of the workers and peasants of the U.S.S.R. is to be crushed.

But the workers must not allow themselves to fall into the trap of the war makers.

We of the working class must not allow ourselves to be led by the nose by the profiteers who use our class for their own ends, then, when that end is served, cast us on one side like dogs.

We, as workers, have no quarrel with the workers and peasants of the U.S.S.R., they are our brothers—the working women and the farm women are our sisters—they feel as we feel—they suffer as we suffer. They call to the workers and farmers everywhere—Help us to maintain Peace.

It is our duty to reply—We will combat the War Cry by demanding Peace. We have nothing to gain by aiding the war makers. We will fight war by refusing to aid the war makers. We have everything to gain by uniting for Peace.

OUR BOYS FOR "SOLDIERS"

October 1927, pp. 11-12.

It is well to know that Dr. Hardy, the secretary of the Canadian Teachers' Federation, is "whole-heartedly for cadet training." To what extent he will try to influence the few teachers in Canada who do not approve the training remains to be seen.

It is evident that our public schools, the schools to which the workers' children are sent, are becoming more and more the instruments through which the militaristic spirit is being developed.

So far the parents seem to be quite indifferent to this. The parents are leaving their children's education entirely to outside forces. Presently they will receive the "shock of their lives." They will wake up to find a war upon them. The shock will not be overwhelming until they find that their sons are called to the colors. Then these good fathers and mothers will begin to squirm and fret, to plead and cry that their sons should be excused from military duties. Of course the war should be fought, but their sons, oh, no! Never mind the sons of other parents! And, of course, they will make promises to give other service for the good of the country. Who can recall the "pleadings" of parents before the military tribunals during the last war?

The school boys of to-day will be the conscripts of to-morrow; just a few years separates the school boy from his youth, and now is the time to think of these things. And, especially now, when war clouds are hanging heavily over the world. Now is the time for every parent to ask himself or herself. "Do I want my boy to be a soldier?" and "Am I doing what is right to my boy by letting him be trained for WAR?"

If the answers are "No," then now is the time to act. Start right away by telling your boy the purpose of the Cadets. Then you must protest against your boy being forced into the Cadet Corps. Then you must lend your aid to fight against Cadet Training during school hours. And, to make your protest more effective, you should join the Home and School Association of your district, and there use your influence to combat the supporters of War and Cadet Training. Start now, don't wait and then cry later after the milk has been spilt.

—A Taxpayer.

MY COUNTRY
By Robert Whitaker.

December 1927, p. 8.

My country is the world; I count
No son of man my foe,
Whether the warm life-currents mount
And mantle brows like snow
Or red or yellow, brown or black,
The face that into mine looks back.

My birthplace is no spot apart,
I claim no town nor State;
Love hath a shrine in every heart,
And whereso'er men mate
To do the right and say the truth,
Love evermore renews her youth.

My party is all human-kind,
My platform brotherhood;
I count all men of honest mind
Who work for human good,
And for the hope that gleams afar,
My comrades in this holy war.

My heroes are the great and good
Of every age and clime,
Too often mocked, misunderstood,
And murdered in their time,
But spite of ignorance and hate
Known and exalted soon or late.

My country is the world; I scorn
No lesser love than mine,
But calmly wait that happy morn
When all shall own this sign,
And love of country as of clan,
Shall yield to world-wide love of man.

THIS WOULD KILL SENATOR BEAUBIEN

April 1928, p. 5.

We are trying to get a picture for the cover of The Woman Worker. Our regular readers know this, of course.

Recently we received two fine drawings, one of which will, no doubt, be chosen.

I cannot begin to imagine what poor old Senator Beaubien would say were he to see one of the drawings. For sure he would have forty fits. He is nearly beside himself now over what he calls the "menace of communism in the schools." But this drawing would finish him.

The drawing shows a working woman dressed as a soldier— with gun in hand—ready for action.

Of course, our Rebel Woman sent it to us, just to show us how she feels about things and what she is ready for apparently.

But since we are not allowed to send pictures which depict violence through the mail, we shall be compelled to keep the picture in storage for the time being. It is far too good to be destroyed.

It should be stated, though, that while pictures depicting violence cannot be sent through His Majesty's Mail Service, our children are allowed to gaze every day at the horrible war pictures which hang on the walls of the school rooms. However, we know it is a question of circumstances altering cases.

THE WAR DANGER

An Open Letter Addressed to Working-class Mothers.

[Editorial]

July/August 1928, pp. 2-5.

WORKING-CLASS MOTHERS:

Are we merely bringing children into the world to be slaughtered when they grow older in wars that are waged in the interests of the privileged few? Or—

Are we going to prepare the children we bring into the world to struggle against such wars and to struggle in the interests of their class and for the Freedom and Peace which will come out of this struggle? It is the one thing or the other, and it is for you, working-class mothers, to decide.

The Last War

The months of July and August recall to many of us the events which led to the World War of 1914-18.

We can recall the loud cry that was made when an Austrian prince was killed in Serbia; then followed quickly the declaration of war by the Allies and Central Powers against each other; then the excitement of the call to arms of fighting men; then the recruiting of new fighters; then the campaigns in the interests of Democracy, and so on.

The years that have followed the World War have been years of enlightenment. We have had time to read, to learn, to think.

We have learned that the killing of an Austrian prince was but the match which set fire to and brought to a head the quarrels of rival nations that had been brewing for many years. And this war, we have learned, was not a surprise war; it had been planned for many years; armies had been trained, navies had been brought up to date, and many new war devices prepared for its coming. And the reason for the war was to decide who should have the remaining world markets and spheres of influence (territory) to exploit.

We know that the people who were not prepared for the war were the working class. Not knowing of the things that were going on behind the scenes of government, most of them really thought the war was for a righteous cause; that it was to save Democracy—if they were of the Allied nations, or it was to save the Fatherland—if they were of the opposite camp.

All thought it was going to be the very last war of civilization—the war to end war.

We know now that we of the working-class were deliberately fooled, and perhaps we women of the working-class were fooled the most. While it may be true we parted with our fathers, husbands, and sons in tears and with fear in our hearts, we did, however, permit our men to go without protest on our side, because we were frightened into thinking that very terrible things would happen to us if we refused. And, when fear was not enough, bribery played its part; we were promised food, clothing and shelter all the time our men were at the war, and afterwards, if they did not return.

And we have had time to ponder over the results of the war, to ask ourselves who suffered, and who profited, and if the profits which fell into the hands of a few were worth the sacrifice of the lives of over ten millions of working-class men.

We know as workers we are in the same position as we were before the war—but with the feeling of greater insecurity—we do not know what is going to happen next.

Security Impossible

Europe has not recovered from the shock of the War. To-day nation is set against nation more bitterly than ever before. The conditions of life for the workers are so insecure and wretched that they are forced to protest against their misery by demonstrations, by strikes, and even by revolts. The governments keep the workers down by special laws and the use of terror, as well as by buying over the leaders of workers' organizations.

Even America, which was supposed to have profited most by the War, is not unaffected. The American Dollars which were loaned the governments of Europe to help them re-establish themselves and to reconstruct their industry, etc., have to be repaid. This means that European goods must be sold in the United States and in Canada. So European cheap goods are throwing hundreds of thousands of workers out of work even in the Land of the Almighty Dollar.

Those who profited by the War, and who at this time hold nearly the whole world in their hands, are the Big Financiers—the Banking Interests. These control both nations and governments, and this for the purpose of exploiting both the natural resources and the energy of the workers of these countries.

Can such a condition produce Peace, Security, Contentment?

The truth is that to-day there is more jealousy, rivalry and discord between nations than there was in 1914. And also there is a greater preparation for war than there was before 1914; more men are being trained to kill; more men are actually under arms; more and very modern and dreadful war devices are invented and made.

There is to be another war, working-class mothers, that is certain—otherwise these costly preparations would not be made!

This Next War

And you may be wondering why the Big Financiers do not make war now since there are more conflicts than ever before. Actually war has never ceased. There have been wars ever since 1918, the only difference being that these were not between civilized Christian nations themselves. Only a few months ago United States gunboats fired upon the peaceful people of Nicaragua. And the gunboats of all the Christian civilized nations were sent up the rivers of China to fire on the Chinese people in the interests of Big Finance.

But the thing that holds the greed and mastery of the Big Financiers in check is the fact that they are uncertain as to the outcome of another war. The last war saw the workers and peasants of Russia revolt against the war that was forced upon them; they refused to fight; then later they took up arms in their own defence and as masters of Soviet Russia.

Now the Big Capitalists find themselves up against another menace to their power, so, while struggling amongst themselves for power they are faced with a new government, a government of the workers and peasants which has set an example to the workers of the world and has shown them how to end the War Danger.

So the thing that makes the Capitalists fear another war is the fact that the workers of the other countries may do as the workers of Russia did in 1917. We can be sure they will not start another World War until they are somewhat sure of their ground.

Even at this time they are asking themselves: Which is the greater menace to ourselves, the one among us who is striving to be all-powerful, or this anti-capitalist country, the Soviet Union?

And we can see that while these Big Financial Interests are watching and preparing war upon one another, at the same time they are all directing their war plans against the Soviet Union and its Workers' and Peasants' Government.

Not Enough to Preach Peace

Only a few were brave enough during the War to raise their voices against it, and most of them were punished for their pains.

But the awfulness of the War has increased the forces of those who want Peace. Peace Movements and Societies are becoming more popular as a result. The Non-Resisters or Pacifists place their faith in the League of Nations, and are the strongest supporters of the League. How they can continue to have this faith in an organization that has proven itself useless and incapable of bringing peace is a puzzle to one who is able to reason. While the great struggle was going on in China the League of Nations refused to interfere. And at the Disarmament Conference held recently at Geneva the Disarmament Proposals of Soviet Russia were turned down with ridicule by this same League of Nations.

To-day the League of Nations stands openly as the tool of Big Finance, the instrument that was erected for the purpose of turning the revolutionary thoughts of the workers into other channels.

The League of Nations is the bluff of Big Finance calling Peace! Peace! while the munition makers, etc., are working top speed preparing for war.

Peace Societies talk of the horrors of War and the stupidity of people in killing those they have never seen before. But shock and appealing to reason will not solve the problems bound up with War. At the root of War is the possession of the means of life, the sources of wealth, and all that these things mean in terms of power, pleasure and the fullness of life. These things will never be given up without a struggle by the class owning them. In face of this the workers, the exploited class, cannot afford to be non-resisters. Working-class mothers cannot and must not be pacifists. Instead we must be militants, active fighters against the war danger in all its aspects.

Our Preparation

While the forces of Big Finance (Imperialism) are preparing for War, we working-class mothers must prepare, too. Right at home our duty faces us. Our first steps must be taken with our children. Our children must know of the War Danger. They must understand why wars are fought and who are forced to fight in these wars. And they must know who profits by War. The correct information they will not get from the teaching they receive in the schools, because here War is glorified, war heroes are the best heroes, and patriotism is the only virtue. So it becomes the duty of every working-class mother to give her children the correct viewpoint on War. After all the experiences we have gone through for fourteen years it must not be said that it was through ignorance our sons and our husbands entered the wars that are to come, and unknowingly to preserve for the privileged few the wealth that has been taken by stealth or force from the working masses of the world.

War does indeed face the workers. And they will be forced to choose between two sets of interests when issues reach a breaking point and War starts in all its awfulness. These interests will be those of the Banking Interests (Imperialism) on the one hand, and those of the working-class who want Class Emancipation (Freedom from Exploitation) on the other hand. The first means a continuation of the Old Order of things. The second means the beginning of a New Order.

The issues before us are clear. Thoughtful mothers must take heed. Now is the time to prepare. To wait until the Dogs of War break loose will be too late. Many things can be done right now. What are these? We must combat the false teaching of history which our children receive in the schools.

We must oppose the Cadets, the Boy Scouts and Girl Guide Movements and refuse to let our children take part in them, because they are the tools of Big Business and Big Finance and are organized in the name of Patriotism to serve their ends.

We must expose the fallacy called the League of Nations and denounce it for what it is—the League of Big Finance. And we must instruct our children how to oppose it in the schools.

This is work that can be done right now. And in doing this a working-class mother is doing her bit to fight the Imperialist War Danger and helping to serve the best interests of her children and her class.

Oppose Imperialist Wars, as these serve but the interests of the few and crush and annihilate the best of the working-class masses.

Support and Help forward the Struggle for the Freedom of the Workers and All Oppressed People, for this means the end of War and the oppression of men by men.

—Issued by Executive Committee,
Canadian Federation of Women's Labor Leagues.

JANE ADDAMS, PACIFIST, SUPPORTS LAW-MAKERS

September 1928, pp. 9-11.

Jane Addams, the well-known pacifist, did not get entirely away with the "peace talk" she delivered in Los Angeles a few weeks ago. Her support of the United States Government and the Kellogg treaty brought her audience to their feet and she was showered with questions to which she gave answers that showed either how little she knew or understood of the forces at work in this age of Giant Capital, or that she was not inclined to tell the truth, the whole truth, and nothing but the truth about King Capital. The following questions and Jane Addams' answers to the same gives one an idea how the president of the world organization known as the Women's International League of Peace views most important political issues:

"How many wars were caused by selfish capitalism?" Some, perhaps, but not many. There are many causes of war. So replied Miss Addams.

"Would the Kellogg treaty lead to total disarmament?" Not for some time to come. But it provides a sense of security, after which armaments will gradually be dispensed with, and other methods of settling disputes will be devised.

"What of Russia's offer of disarmament and the abolition of war materials?" The nations felt that to accept it would have been a "mere gesture" that could not be put into effect.

"What of military training in the schools?" This is gradually passing. Miss Addams named colleges that are dropping it.

"What about American Marines in China and Nicaragua?" Our marines are legally in China to protect American citizens. As for Nicaragua, the administration said that the Nicaragua government had asked the United States to send marines to supervise the election. The United States tried to disarm both sides, but Sandino resisted disarmament. It would now be necessary for the marines to remain until after the election in October and perhaps afterwards to sustain the election. Miss Addams felt the government is acting in all sincerity.

"Are patriotism and nationalism detrimental to world peace?" They should not be. Men find it possible to be loyal to their families, to organizations, to many interests, as well as to their country. She felt the loyalty of patriotism can include all loyalties.

"Can there be peace without political equality among nations?" Oh, yes, she felt so. She cited the instance of a small central African nation bringing a complaint against Britain at the League of Nations. Three English statesmen, including Lord Balfour, rose to agree with the small nation, to explain the circumstances and promise the desired improvement.

"Do not surplus wealth and foreign investment incite war?" No, it need not lead to war. Other methods are being found. A measure is already suggested in Congress declaring that no citizen could call upon the United States Army to defend his investments in foreign countries.

—Taken from Alma Whitaker's Report.

It can be seen from the answers Jane Addams gave to the questions put to her that she has founded her understanding merely on faith and belief in human nature. One would certainly think the world is growing better and better every day if one were to believe what the Pacifist leader has to say. We have good reasons to know that it is not so. And how can it when there exists a social system based upon wage-slavery, when there exists exploitation of the weak by the strong, when there is competition of every kind among the most powerful for world supremacy?

Something more than faith and belief in capitalist governments are necessary if exploitation is to be overcome: something more than calling "peace, peace," will have to be done. Since we have nothing to lose and everything to gain by telling the truth, we say that we know that the oppressed and the exploited, upon whose backs rest the powerful exploiters —that these will have to throw the capitalist parasites from their backs and erect a new system based upon co-operative effort. With the incentive to amass private wealth gone, man will organize and work for the common good. Thus, and thus only, will peace be made possible. Then, and then only, will "mediation and persuasion" enter into the settlement of human disputes as useful tools.

But how would you answer the questions put to Jane Addams, our reader may ask? These, then, are the answers. For the last four hundred years all wars have been trade wars, that is, war either for the conquest of lands and peoples, for markets for products, or for investments, or for obtaining raw materials.

The Kellogg treaty is another "peace bluff." It happened that the other United States piece of bluff, the League of Nations, fell under the control of the British, and this was not to the liking of the new world power, the United States. So the United States boycotts the League of Nations and sets up her own demands, which are called "peace" demands. The real motive behind the Kellogg Treaty is to give power to the United States to determine who shall be the aggressor in the next war, and where and when the next war shall be. Such is "diplomacy."

Soviet Russia, knowing only too well the nature of the nations of to-day, presented her peace proposals for a number of reasons, first of all because she really wants peace; secondly, because she wanted to test the sincerity of those who were always talking peace; and thirdly, to show the workers of the world that capitalist interests are bound up with "war," and all the "peace talk" of capitalist nations is but "bluff" after all.

And, too, Militarism is extending itself more and more into the ranks of the youth. Cadet training is increasing, not diminishing, even though a few colleges may have banished it from their midst. Armies and navies will have to be maintained to do the kind of work the United States marines are doing in China and Nicaragua. The Cadets pave the way for the building of these as necessity arises. At this time American marines are in China and Nicaragua for the purpose of protecting the investments and the interests of U.S. investors. Our own commonsense will tell us that the natives of Nicaragua did not request the U.S. Government to send marines to help them with their elections. Those who asked for this were investors and exploiters of the natives of Nicaragua. Would not Sandino, the native leader, be a downright fool to lay down his arms under such a condition?

And as for "patriotism and nationalism," these are but means to an end, and this end is the protection of the interests of the wealthy of each and every capitalist country. And, of course, political equality is necessary between nations; this is so in the Union of Socialist Soviets Republics. But this can be built only upon economic co-operation between nations, and the Soviet Union is the only place where such a condition prevails.

The last question is answered by the first.

Those who would be sincere about "peace" must first of all face the facts of the workings of present day society, otherwise there will be many wanderings from the right track.

F.C

A CALL FOR PEACE

[Editorial]

November 1928, pp. 2-3.

A MASS meeting, to urge the renunciation of war as an instrument of national policy will be held in Convocation Hall on November 22 under the auspices of several Toronto societies working for the Women's Church Committee of the League of Nations Society. Delegates Mrs. Morton and Mrs. Campbell attended this meeting to find out if the Women's Labor League could participate in this effort of the women of Toronto to urge peace. Discussion was shut off several times as our delegates attempted to ask if a speaker could be had who would be courageous enough to condemn military training in the schools (which, after all, is a kindergarten for future soldiers). Mrs. J.H. Wickett, who was acting secretary of the meeting, made a splendid plea on behalf of the boys and said that they were even debarred from rugby and other sports as a means to force them into military training. The speaker stated that boys were attracted by brass buttons, uniforms and trumpets and were all primed ready for bloodshed when war came. The chairman said that, while we all knew wars were fought for economic reasons, the question of military training could not be discussed at the mass meeting, at least it would not be wise. The Women's Labor League delegate pointed out that if they were sincere in their call for peace, they must have a speaker who would tell the truth about causes of war, that raw materials and control of world markets were responsible, that it was the working class who had to fight the battles and the same working class who had to pay for the war after we had won it. Needless to say, this will not be done at the coming mass meeting. Women's church committees do not speak in our language, and once again the people of Toronto will listen to the warbling and prattling of the "Peace Doves." They will ask us to pray for world disarmament, and while the ever-trusting workers are praying, the War Lords or (Defence Ministers) shall have declared war, and once more our youth shall be demanded for a bloody sacrifice to the God of Capitalism. Wake up women of Canada, the time for praying is long past, this is the time to organize and act, there can be no peace under this cursed system of degradation and poverty for the working class and ease and luxury for the idle rich. Educate your fellow worker, abolish capitalism and wage slavery and fight to make the world safe for the workers. The Women's Church Committee do not seem to realize that in spite of "League of Nations Societies," "Peace Pacts" and all the other National Banquets, that preparation for war is going on and is greater today than it was in 1913. The Women's Labor Leagues must continue to enlighten working class women and girls. If the Women's Church Committee is decided on praying for unity and peace, the Women's Labor League is more determined than ever to carry on the great struggle of educating and organizing the workers, and with a loud voice we shout: "Workers of the world unite, you have nothing to lose but your chains and a world to gain."

A.C.

"PEACE, PEACE, WHEN THERE IS NO PEACE" (JEREMIAH)

November 1928, pp. 7-9.

There never was a time when Pacifists were more active or when peace plans were more varied and fantastic than right now, and so, while it is our business as workers to make war at least difficult, if not impossible for the Imperialists, still we must keep in mind that there are no grounds for the hopes that are held out by the Pacifists, that if we are safe from wars we are also safe from other dangers that are equally threatening to the lives and comfort of most people.

Apart from the well known fact that more workers are killed and maimed every year in industry than have ever been destroyed by war, let us look for a moment at the ghastly farce of a peace without justice.

Do we not remember the years between 1911 and 1914? when we were soaked in peace movements—fairly drenched and dripping with peace! even the munition makers offering peace prizes and giving them to the Czar of Russia, the German Kaiser and Theodore Roosevelt!! Yes—they all got peace prizes—then we got war. Now we seen an even more dangerous array of peace-making agencies—the League of Nations and the Kellogg peace pact. Both are so full of "reservations" that whenever it suits any of the powers to bring on a war, they have all sorts of excuses, explanations, and other devices, handy and ready for use.

Mr. Kellogg took his precious peace pact to Europe in a battleship! and actually cabled the U.S. Government to hurry up their program of fifteen battleships. Incidentally—the amount now spent yearly by the U.S.A. for militarism is seven hundred million dollars—it makes the Kellogg pact look very like a smoke screen for war.

But, suppose that by a miracle we could bring an end of war under capitalism—suppose the Imperialists of Asia, Europe and America were able to arrange their interests without bloodshed—would that mean peace on earth? Every worker who has a grain of spirit or an atom of pride left must answer NO.

Man has always refused to accept his fate—he has always reached out determined to conquer conditions. This fight for a "square deal," which intelligent men and women recognize as the class struggle, has gone on for uncounted years, and must go on until there is freedom and possibilities of happiness for all.

That is—unless we are willing to accept charity and become mere "beings"—there is plenty of charity if you are willing to "trade in" your self-respect for a "hand-out."

No—the struggling and cheated farmers and the exploited men, women and children in the towns do not want war—nor have they ever caused a war—but neither can they any longer have faith in or patience with peace talk which brings with it no assurance of security or comfort for those who produce the world's wealth.

Because the workers of this continent have been so exploited, we have now the richest land on earth—but our people grow old long before middle age because of the everlasting struggle against that three-headed monster, unemployment, sickness, old age.

And we cannot kill this monster by hoping—or praying—or wishing —our Pacifists and our Social Democrats to the contrary notwithstanding.

These misleaders of the workers would have us believe that industry may be "humanized" under capitalism, that capital and labor may be "harmonized" under a system that gives us child labor and constant unemployment —that it is only a matter of "better understanding," etc., etc. Surely we have had enough of these false arguments and this doubly false leadership!

Surely we are ready to fight for ourselves—first for our immediate demands, that our homes may be saved to us and the children fed, and always with the knowledge that the only hope for civilization is complete working class control—and this excludes no human being who is willing to give service of hand or brain.

As one has said elsewhere, it is possible now for us all to know a good deal about the rest of the world, and there is one spot that should stir the curiosity and interest of every worker at this time—we should be asking why is it that in Russia—a country that is poor, compared with us, because it is lacking, as yet, in machinery and equipment for producing wealth and comforts—why is it that Russia can and does care for her old, her unemployed, her expectant mothers and her little children? Why is she the only nation that dares to tell her soldiers the truth about war? Why is everything so different with us. Is it not that here we have a country ruled by organized wealth, and there is a land ruled by organized workers. What these workers have done under unfavorable and often terrible conditions should help us all to think straight—and act accordingly, by organizing in trade unions and labor leagues—especially by helping the young workers to see and understand the splendid task before them—the task that only they can perform —to help them to know the value and the need of discipline.

And all this, in order that we may develop a true working class democracy of farmers and city workers.

Then only will peace really mean freedom from war or strife.

H.D.P.

WOMEN AND THE NEXT WAR

January 1929, pp. 13-14.

The war danger and the organized attack on the U.S.S.R. is only obvious to class conscious workers. In Canada, the official labor movement refuses to recognize the immediate war danger and its consequences to the working class, while champions of the League of Nations and Pacifists content themselves with pious denunciations.

Canada has definitely committed herself on the question of the coming war against the U.S.S.R. Premier King has signed two documents: 1, The famous Peace Pact, to outlaw War; and, 2, to build two cruisers. Canada, a partner to British Imperialism, will see to it when the war signal is sounded, that the Canadian workers will be plunged into another war.

Despite the fact that war preparations are going on at full speed, despite the fact that the capitalist class are creating a war psychology while talking peace, the misleaders of labor, the officialdom, are also talking about peace and co-operation with the capitalist class. In the coming war the Social democracy of Canada will act in the same way as did their colleagues when they committed the workers the world over to be slaughtered for the profit system. Prior to the World War, the social democrats talked about a general strike in the event of a war, but no sooner was war declared, when they acted like Judas. While eleven years in history is a very short time, nevertheless, the working class have learned a great deal as a result of struggles, defeats and betrayals. In brief, I want to deal with woman's role in the coming war. As far back as 1916, Lenin said: "Today the Imperialistic bourgeoisie is not only mobilizing the whole of the nation, but also the youth of the nation. Tomorrow, it will also take in hand the militarizing of the women." The above quotation is timely, as we see that the capitalist class believe and are definitely working towards the militarization of women.

We see that as far back as 1925, the American ministry of war devised a plan to mobilize the women, not only for the factories, but also for active service. In France there is a law for arming the nation, including the women. We can cite practically every capitalist country as conclusive proof of the systematic work that is being carried on to mobilize the women in the coming war. Athletic clubs are organized where shooting is considered as a sport, yet in time of war, these organizations serve as a recruiting ground. There is a "League of Defense" in Finland, which embraces 45,000 women ready for active service. In Latvia, there is a defense organization that trains women for auxiliary service in the army. Every capitalist country is definitely preparing and mobilizing women for the coming war. Aviation in the past was not practised by women; today women have entered that field for the purpose of being able to serve on all fronts when war breaks out. Women of the working class are today occupying a strategic position as they are engaged in industrial establishments, that in time of war will be turned into ammunition factories, such as the automobile industry, aluminum factories, chemical factories, etc. In view of the fact that only one per cent of women workers in Canada are organized in trade unions, the task of organizing the unorganized women falls on the militant section of the labor movement. We find where working women are organized that they are co-workers with their men comrades, and partake in the struggle that confronts our class. The class-conscious women recognize but one enemy, and that is the Capitalist class.

The heroic deeds of our women comrades and the part they played in the French Revolution, in the Russian Revolution of 1905 and 1917, and in the Chinese Revolution just recently is an inspiration to the workers the world over. The women of the working class have gladly given their lives so that a great cause may live. The duty of our working women in Canada is to defend the Workers' Republic, the only fatherland that the workers have. Soviet Russia is the only country where women have gained their freedom and are today the builders of a new social order. The Russian Revolution has been the means of emancipating the women, and gave them that long sought-for freedom. The working class of Canada must do their class duty and stand shoulder to shoulder with the Russian workers and peasants. So long as the Capitalist system lasts there can be no peace. The contradictions of the present social order make war inevitable. Since 1918, when war was officially called off, unofficial wars have been going on. In 1919-21 Poland against Soviet Russia; 1920, Greek-Turkish war, the Spanish war in the Rif, war on China, war in Nicaragua. And throughout all this endless chain of war social democracy did not raise its voice against war and intervention. The workers must not allow the betrayers of Labor to once more defeat our cause. The defence of the Soviet Union expressed in the struggle against the war plans of the Imperialists and their agents in the ranks of the working class will mean the ultimate victory for the working class.

Annie Buller.

OURSELVES AND THE WAR DANGER

February 1929, pp. 2-3.

FROM several sources criticisms have come concerning the attitude of the Toronto Women's Labor League toward the Peace Conference recently organized in Toronto.

The November issue of The Woman Worker contained an article which stated very clearly the position of the Labor League delegates who attended the first meeting of the conference.

If the women of the Labor League Movement are choosing more carefully the organizations with which they are willing to associate for the purpose of fighting for Peace, it is because they have learned that there is a big difference between wishing for Peace and getting Peace; wishing— only requires feeling; getting—requires action.

But on no account can our Labor League women be charged with "insincerity" in their strivings for Peace. We can recall that it was the co-operation of the Women's Labor League with the League for Peace and Freedom, a few years ago, that helped to make the only real public demonstration in Toronto against war a big success. We know, also, that the Women's Labor League did its part in welcoming the "unpopular Pax Special" delegates to Toronto. And, too, it can be stated, that the meeting arranged by the Women's Labor League was the only meeting of working women addressed by delegates of the Pax Special during the whole of their tour throughout the United States and Canada. There are those who still remember the delight of some of the Pax Special delegates in finding that at least they had come in contact with the "real stuff" that was to be found in the ranks of working women.

Every effort that was worth while has not been turned down by the women of the Labor League Movement. But a line must be drawn when it comes to co-operating with those who will not face facts. And this was the case when the Labor League could not continue to work with the Peace Conference organized by the Women's Church Committees of the League of Nations.

It may be argued by some that our women should have stayed to have helped along the educational work that the Conference is organizing. But when we know that the educators they will bring to their meetings are of the Norman Angell type, what good can come out of such education?

Even the more thinking who went to hear Norman Angell's address on January 22nd, left the meeting disappointed, for in his address no mention was made of the great role played by Soviet Russia in world affairs today. In just such a manner he left out of his calculation, when writing his book, "The Great Illusion," the significance of the great struggles between capitalist nations and the role of the workers in capitalist wars. He built all his arguments upon the dependence of capitalist nations upon each other and that this dependence made "War" an illusion as a method of settling their disputes. He went so far, then stopped. No, Norman Angell cannot be taken as an expert on the question of Peace. He cannot be followed.

The women of the Labor League Movement take a very definite stand on the question of Peace. This stand is, that if we want Peace we must look the facts of War right in the face since the two are bound together, for only in this way will the right path for our efforts be found.

And when we examine all the factors of War existing right in our midst what do we find we must do if we want Peace? We find that we must wage a struggle against those who provoke War—these are the Imperialists and War-mongers. We find we must support the cause of the victims of the designs of the Imperialists and the War-mongers, and this means we must support Soviet Russia in her struggle against her imperialist foes, as well as support the Freedom Movements of the colonial peoples, such as those of India and China. We find we must expose the character of the so-called instruments of Peace, such as the League of Nations and the score of Peace Pacts and Treaties. This, too, means denouncing those who support such means while knowing them to be but "Red Herrings," intended to keep people talking Peace while the imperialists and war-mongers further their plans for war.

We know that to do these things requires courage, because they are among the most unpopular actions of today. But since facing facts brings these duties to the front, the women of the Labor League Movement will not shirk their tasks, and they will, on all occasions, make their position clear on the question of Peace and show its relation to the ever-present War Danger.

WAR—SHAM AND REAL

February 1929, pp. 15-16.

To the Woman Worker,
  Toronto, Ont.

Dear Comrade:
  Often do I wonder, looking at the pictures on the screen, that "Why always war!" Certainly, war pictures are thrilling, particularly war in the air,

as we mostly see it screened now. But isn't there some other meaning? Do not the capitalists mean to fill the hearts of the workers with patriotism? Do they not, with these heroic war-pictures, make the Canadian youth look forward to war as a step-ladder to fame, glory? They know that a great war-time is drawing near, therefore, they must prepare the workers to meet it as they wish workers to meet it. Isn't that really the reason why theatre after theatre screens pictures of war?

But, workers! When seeing those pictures, the uniformed officers, the delicate ladies who give their all and win the victory for the whole army—does it really convince you that war can be only that. Of course, it does not! On the screen you never witness the stark cruelty to workers that war can be. No, because that wouldn't be romantic! It would be too true to be alluring. In screen-war we only see officers and lovely ladies who always escape death and bombs.

And to think that any young worker dreams of climbing to such heights! Futile hopes! Workers' parts in wars are to kill and get killed—to suffer—but not to enjoy fame.

Yet how many young workers dream of being an air-hero in the coming war. How many forget that while they could achieve heroism, millions of helpless children would die—millions of happy homes be wrecked. O, young worker, stay your mind from imagination and realize that war is not only an adventurous game.

Yet, to the movies we flock, to get more patriotism into us? And I think that at last we will have enough of it—at least, when another mighty imperialistic war has rocked the earth.

With Comradely greetings,
ALI MALM
Sointula, B.C.

MISS CHOWN AND THE WAR DANGER

April 1929, pp. 11-12.

Is there a War Danger? This was the subject of the February educational meeting of the Toronto League, which, by the way, is an open meeting. Miss Alice Chown was the speaker.

President B. MacDonald in her opening remarks called the attention of the audience to the great preparations for war that were going on to-day all over the world, and urged working class women to take heed of these things and to help educate workers against helping capitalist wars.

Miss Chown started off by stating that she had regretted ever having accepted the invitation to speak to the League, because she thought it would be difficult to tell the women of the League anything about War and its Dangers.

As the speaker proceeded, the talk developed into a history of the League of Nations Society and some of the things it had accomplished. To show how difficult it was to do anything among uneducated people she referred to the word 'evolution' and said that how, after sixty years, this conflict in thought was still going on, which showed the very slow progress of the world. The League of Nations we were told was the miracle of the ages. (Perhaps it would have been better to have termed it the MUDDLE of the ages). It had now fifty-five nations on the roll and all these agreed on this miracle. One of the great things it had done was to put Austria on a sound economic basis (for capitalism of course). Another great miracle was a demand introduced by the Italian delegate to curtail the growing of opium. (One can see the logic in this request since there is enough dope created in Rome to chloroform millions of minds the world over). Miss Chown also told that the League of Nations was slowly but surely gaining the confidence of the people and she still had hopes of the League of Nations creating the spirit among nations that would make war impossible. The abolition of War depended on how quickly we could educate the people to this feeling of love and goodwill.

During the discussion, Comrade Florence Custance showed that the League never was and never could be an instrument of Peace, that it was formed in those days of bitter class conflict to offset the revolutionary wave that was sweeping across Europe after the war and when the workers of the whole world were in ferment. She pointed out that the spirit of domination was still rife and warned the speaker that it was something more than goodwill that was needed to ensure peace. To prove that the Imperialists use other means than words for their purpose, our comrade referred to America's contribution to the Peace Pact—namely 15 cruisers. She said that war would only be postponed until the powers could mobilise enough force.

Referring to Canada's position in the next war she said that there was the likelihood of Canada being another Belgium—that is—in the event of the war being between United States and Great Britain.

Other comrades voiced their opinion in this matter. It was made very clear to Miss Chown that the Labor League women could not be fooled by prayers and goodwill bunk, and that we were more determined than ever to carry our message of organization to working women.

This meeting was well attended. It is the intention of our League to carry on with this propaganda on the War Danger.

A. CAMPBELL, Secretary.
Toronto League

Women and the Sex Trade   **5**

Among the issues troubling both reformers and radicals during the early 20th century, prostitution was high on the list. To middle-class women concerned with the abuse of women by men, the commercial sale of women's bodies was an evil demanding the immediate attention of the national and international community. Feminist reformers, as well as many Protestant Churches, were especially horrified by sensational press reports depicting the forceable removal and trafficking in young girls under the rubric of what was called the "White Slave Trade." Prostitution was a central concern of the powerful social purity campaigns of the pre-World War I period, which warned of moral decay and physical degeneration if sex education, chastity and purity for men and women alike, were not embraced by all citizens.

Working-class and radical left commentators often had a different interpretation of prostitution, but they too could respond to the issue with moral revulsion and calls for a complete end to the sex trade. Contributors to the *Woman Worker* shared in the alarm about prostitution and the white slave trade, while remaining suspicious of the motives and methods behind middle-class reformers' attempts to stamp out these "social evils." (See also "Feminism and Social Reform" section.) In its wholesale acceptance of the League of Nations report the Women's Labor League seemed to accept without question that the trade was very extensive, and Communist women condemned it in the same moralistic style as many of the reformers.

Also like the moral reformers, the WLLs did not question an underlying fear which fuelled the international discussion on white slavery: the claims that white, European girls were being tricked or coerced into the business, sent to Latin America or Mediterranean countries to be used, and cast off, by men there. Racist imagery and ideology fed the panic about white slavery—indeed the very term spoke to visions of endangered white womanhood yet ignored the ongoing sexual exploitation of women of colour. This racist ideology was used by Canadians like Magistrate Emily Murphy whose alarmist book, *The Black Candle*, published in 1922, linked the increase in prostitution to the presence of male, Asian immigrants and their promotion of narcotic use.

Even if the *Woman Worker* evidenced some of the prevailing ethnocentrism and racism which focused public concern narrowly on white women being pushed into prostitution, the WLL paper was a far cry from *The Black Candle*. For one thing, the WLLs refused to blame the victim. Ever present in the discussions of prostitution was the insistence that its root cause was capitalist-induced poverty. Popular narratives in Communist women's circles featured respectable working-class girls who were anxious to lead moral lives but were driven into prostitution by unemployment or insufficient wages. Sometimes innocent girls were duped by "vicious men" (and even women) promising decent employment (a ruse of immigrant agents/procurers) or a "little joy." Who could blame the poor girl portrayed in one article who had known only hardship and struggle and whose final downfall was precipitated by a quest for pleasure? (See "A London Girl.")

In consistently pointing to class injustice as the cause of prostitution and the white slave trade, the *Woman Worker* clashed with many reformers like Emily Murphy, who may have bitterly denounced pimps, but often also cast blame on prostitutes themselves for their selfish desire for luxuries, or for getting into problem situations by going to "indecent" public establishments frequented by foreigners, such as "Sicilian ice cream parlours." Working-class mothers too were blamed by Murphy for not instilling in their daughters proper judgement and morals. Other reformers, like Methodist Church speaker Beatrice Brigden, who was more sympathetic to the prostitutes' plight, pointed their finger at the double standard of sexual morality for men and women. Some reformist women's groups, like the National Council of Women, recognized economic insecurity as a factor, but only among the Left was there an insistence that the abolition of prostitution depended on the destruction of capitalism.

References to male "licentiousness" and "bestial sexual appetites" found in the *Woman Worker* ring of moral distaste for prostitution, but they may also suggest an abhorrence of men's sexual domination of women. Moreover, at least one writer made the specific connection between prostitution and bourgeois marriage, where women legally sold their bodies for "an easier time or for title or social position." The feeling that the sex trade involved women's victimization at the hands of men can even be found in the reprinted review by Harold Begbie, in which men are described in stereotypical ways as aggressors often callously intent on sexually using women. In general, though, Communists were more suspicious of the upper class man who was seen to be more likely to seduce or abuse working-class women, with little or no moral conscience.

Although its gender analysis was limited, the *Woman Worker* developed a straight-forward economic analysis of prostitution. This is not to say that it was seen as a form of work like any other, but rather prostitution was portrayed as an evil by-product of capitalist social relations and the pursuit of profit by procurers and white slave consortiums. This view echoed editorials in socialist papers predating the *Woman Worker*. Both the Socialist Party of Canada and the Social Democratic Party, for example, portrayed prostitution as a direct result of women's "wage slavery." Although a few socialist women provided a muted critique of women's sexual oppression by men, most socialist papers before World War I concentrated on the economic causes of prostitution, also offering images of innocent working women seduced by wealthy, uncaring men. Likewise, the *Woman Worker* tended to ignore evidence that all classes of men could be found buying sexual services. When this was admitted, it was often excused by saying these working-class men were left with little alternative outlet for their sexual energies since poverty prevented them from marrying. The *Woman Worker* was quite correct in seeing working-class women as more prone to becoming sex trade workers. Subsequent studies of many Canadian cities have confirmed that those arrested as prostitutes were predominantly poor or working-class women, often in the lowest paid jobs (such as domestic work), and in some cases more likely to be recent immigrants, without friends, relatives and resources to see them through hard times. There is also no doubt, of course, that the sexual lives of working-class women were more intensely surveyed and policed at this time. Indeed, working-class teens could be sentenced to reform institutions simply on the basis of their perceived sexual "promiscuity."

It is possible that beneath the surface of the *Woman Worker's* analysis of prostitution lay other, less easily articulated ideas and unexpressed concerns. It is not surprising that the reader advocating sex education urged women to instruct their daughters, making no mention of educating sons to their responsibilities in sexual matters. A direct critique of the double standard, which allowed men more sexual freedom than women, was almost entirely absent, but the double standard may have nonetheless unsettled some women readers. The WLL analysis also led them to ignore the continuing existence of prostitution in post-revolutionary USSR. In only one article, excerpted from the writing of a male comrade who visited the Soviet Union, is it admitted that prostitution existed in every country, capitalist or not. Many anti-prostitution reformers exaggerated working-class women's victimization, seduction and capture, ignoring women's involvement in "consensual" prostitution, their agency in choosing this trade, though admittedly from a very narrow list of options. The *Woman Worker* clearly adopted a similar approach, and overall, like the reformers, stressed themes of sexual "danger" rather than sexual emancipation for women. There is emerging evidence that a minority of working-class women, especially those living alone and working for wages, may have been pushing on the bounds of sexual propriety at this time. Their rebellion against middle-class notions of sexual purity make them the "vanguard" for the more affluent flappers who then became linked to ideas of sexual experimentation and liberation. But sexual freedom before marriage was not something Communists could or would advocate openly (even if some practised it quietly), for it would only confirm the claims of the mainstream press that Bolsheviks were destroying decency and the family and in the process perhaps alienating the "respectable" working class. Sexual "danger," therefore, remained the dominant theme in the paper, and the editor as well as contributors remained bound to the notion that a class revolution would bury the evil of prostitution once and for all.

Further Reading:

- Deborah Brock, *Making Work, Making Trouble: Prostitution as a Social Problem* (Toronto: University of Toronto Press, 1998).

- Janice Newton, "From Wage Slave to White Slave: The Prostitution Controversy and the Early Canadian Left," in Linda Kealey and Joan Sangster, eds., *Beyond the Vote: Canadian Women and Politics* (Toronto: University of Toronto Press, 1989).

- Carolyn Strange, *Toronto's Girl Problem: The Perils and Pleasures of the City, 1880-1930* (Toronto: University of Toronto Press, 1995).

- Mariana Valverde, *The Age of Light, Soap and Water: Moral Reform in English Canada, 1885-1925* (Toronto: McClelland and Stewart, 1991).

A LONDON GIRL
By Harold Begbie

A Review

August 1926, pp. 10-11.

"A London Girl" is the story of the downfall of a girl of the working class. Mr. Begbie wrote this book with the intention of bringing to public notice the way girls fall from the path of the "recognized standard of morality and virtue" to lives of prostitution, and the hideousness of that life. In portraying this life he contends that the fate of "A London Girl" is the fate of hundreds of others. He does not fail to show that poverty is at the root of the evil, and that human beings crave for joy, for happiness, for gaiety. If these are withheld or denied, then these desires are expressed in other ways.

"Baby," the girl of the story, does not want to "be good"; this is enforced. She wants to "feel good," which is quite natural. She admires the strong and resolute, but she hates the preacher. She responds quickly to kindness, but brutality crushes her spirit. She must have brightness, laughter, joy. This, to her, is life. And this is so, because all she knew in her childhood days was semi-starvation, a broken home, miserable surroundings, exploitation by a shop-keeper, long hours of toil and poor wages. Work became repulsive. She ran away, got work as a barmaid, and through this means became acquainted with the "so-called brightness of a public drinking place."

At the commencement of the story one is inclined to blame the girl for her forwardness and apparent laxity of morals, but as we proceed we lose this in our indignation against those who set themselves to destroy the lives and beautiful bodies of young girls. Baby moves in the circles of the very rich, and descends to the depths of dives, want and misery. Her end is untimely. She is the victim of a vicious condition and the brutality of vicious men.

The only good man to her was her father—whom she left with the care of children deserted by their mother. His picture was always with her. The types of men in the story are common types. One is the vicious, conceited, over-dressed and wordy middle-class youth, who lives by his wits, and spares neither his mother nor the girl he deliberately ruins. Another is the staid scientist, who forever preaches goodness and moralizes to the point of aggravating his victim, so that she makes up her mind to be more daring than ever in her ways of life. Another is the impulsive Frenchman who considers women creatures for the amusement of men. It is he who discovers Baby and is struck by her great beauty and vivacity. He undertakes to train her, to make her cultured. Then there is the rich man who buys her beauty and vivacity. He pays well for this pleasure until he discovers that Baby belongs to the gutter, the ranks of the despised workers.

The brute, a depraved seaman, is another character. It is he who bargains in shillings, and even pence, for the wreck of "The Girl," and finally gives her blows, and kicks her into unconsciousness.

The story gives a little insight into "The Trade." In the elegant salons of the rich, its character is hidden, and rich men compete with each other for the smiles of the courtesan.

In the hotel rotundas and theatre entrances it is respectable even if a little showy. But on the streets it is unmasked and shown in all its sordidness. Here competition is rife between women who are supervised by evil-looking, depraved types of men and even women. Here the man who has a grudge against a girl in the profession can give her into the hands of the law and laugh at his smartness. Here the newcomers in the profession, if they are not licensed, are hounded from pillar to post. They have no place on which to stand. Here drink plays its part in reviving vivacity, which died early because it was abused.

The prostitute of the story knows she is despised. She tried to console herself with the thought that her kind existed even among the highest in the land, the duchesses and fine ladies. But her experiences with human nature of all kinds hardens her against all influences other than those of drink, and that form of sympathetic kindness she sometimes found with in the ranks of "The Trade."

The story is by no means far-fetched. But, beyond showing the root of evil—poverty—and its horridness, the author does not go. This must be left to those who do not fear, and to those who will not fear to destroy a system of exploitation which brings forth such vicious social results.

A MODERN VIRGIN

By A.D.A.

January 1927, pp. 9-12.

"What have you on your books for out-of-town help?" The man seated at the desk looked up at the questioner. After eyeing her up and down, replied slowly, "Nothing, I'm afraid, that'll suit you."

Again, the girl asked, this time with a desperate note in her voice, "But, you have something, haven't you? I'm willing to take anything."

The man at the desk looked at the girl kindly. He knew, only too well, that all the jobs on his books needed strong, sturdy women, women who could keep going for ten and more hours a day and then get up the next morning prepared for the same tasks. He knew only certain types of women were capable of doing the work required in the hotels and roadhouses of suburban and rural Ontario, and at the moment only this kind of work was on his books.

The apparent anxiety of the girl touched the man. His experience as an employment agent brought him in touch with all sorts of types of women and girls. Some were of the sensitive type; these shivered at the sound of a harsh voice and were quite unfitted for the tough kind of jobs that found their way on his books. Others had become quite hardened to the come-day go-day form of existence that prevailed these days and could cheek a fore-man or even a boss without any prick of conscience.

Now here was a girl with grit, but, it was too bad, without the physical strength to do the work he had on his books. So, as kindly as he could speak, he said to the girl, "Isn't there anything you would care to do in the city? Are you really compelled to leave the city? For a minute the girl could not reply, her eyes filled with tears, she tried to swallow the big lump that gathered in her throat. At last, in a broken voice which told the effort she made to speak, she answered with rising passion in her words, "I want to go out of the city. I want to forget this place. I must go away and bury myself."

"Now, now, see here," said the man, "give me your name and address; I'll let you know as soon as anything comes in that will suit you." "My name is Mary Mason. I'm living in a room on _____ Street. But I'm leaving there to-morrow. Indeed I must get something to do at once. Won't you tell me where those jobs are out of town?"

The pitiful way the girl spoke, her white face and tearful eyes, told the man something was troubling the girl. He felt that the girl needed a cheery word and a little sympathy as much as she needed a job, so he said, "Look here, Miss Mason, you're in trouble of some kind, I can see it. I'm only a plain kind of chap, an old bachelor at that, but I know the ways of the world. I know the pitfalls that lie in the path of working girls just as yourself, so if I can help you I will. Treat me as your brother. Now, what's the matter?"

Mary's Trouble

Mary Mason clasped her hands, closed her eyes for a second as if to battle against her nervousness and gain composure. Then she said, bitterly, "I've lost all trust in men, but you do seem a little different from some of those who have crossed my path. I do not know whether you can help me. I do not think so. I shall tell you my story only that you may know why I must get work at once. If I do not get something to do at once I know I shall feel like doing something desperate to myself."

"Now, surely," said the man, kindly and in a soothing tone, "surely things are not as bad as all that. Come round here and sit down and then you can tell me all about your trouble."

Mary walked to the chair the man placed for her. She threw herself wea-rily into it. Clasping and unclasping her hands, with eyes cast down, and in words which came from trembling lips, she told her new friend her sorry story.

She was a domestic servant, alone in Canada. She had worked as a general servant for a family who had lived in one of the best sections of the city. Her mistress was one of those good housewives who make hard taskmasters. She was an exacting kind of woman who made a servant feel she was a servant. Kind words were few, and kind acts were even fewer. She made Mary feel she was only a tool to perform work in that household.

The master, a business man, was one of the average type who was attracted by a pretty face. So from passing the time of day with her, he began to speak in friendly terms. Then he fell to commenting upon her attractive ways. As time went on his manner grew more and more friendly towards her. Sometimes his friendliness was shown by a pat on the cheek; sometimes he bought her a trifling present.

At first his kindness appealed to her. She had no friends; she seldom went out to cultivate acquaintances. So more and more she was thrown back to shelter in the warmth of her master's assumed friendship and sympathy.

Then came that terrible moment when she had been unable to resist his power over her, when he had broken through her power of resistance with his soft words and gentle voice, and she had succumbed to his passion. He promised her his protection. He sealed her lips by making her promise not to tell his wife because Mary had his love. He, her master, protected himself at her expense.

As the months passed on and her baby was about to arrive, and at the time when she needed more sympathy than at any time in her life, she received instead indifference. Her master's kindness turned to brutality. He ceased to speak to her, treated her as a stranger. Her mistress learned of her plight, gave her long lectures on the awfulness of her immoral conduct, and then, when she went into the hospital to have her baby, wiped her hands of her completely.

Out of her small wages she had paid all the expenses connected with her confinement. Her baby had been placed in a home. This was why she must find work, not for herself alone, but for her baby.

As poor Mary told her story, her listener bit his lips and clenched his hands. When she was through, he swore under his breath. Aloud he said, "The dirty cur! The miserable coward! The despicable rogue!" Then, as if a thought has suddenly struck him, he said, "Would you be prepared to repeat this story to a lawyer?"

"Why," said the girl, "what good will it do?" "This," said the man, "that this man who did his best to ruin you shall pay for his pleasure." "Will you do this?" asked the man again. "If you will, I know a lawyer chap who is a decent kind of fellow, we'll let him handle your master; we'll show the devil that he cannot ruin a girl, leave her stranded, and all for nothing."

Taking it for granted that Mary had given her consent, the man put on his coat and hat, and saying "Come" to the girl, they both made for the door. The man locked the door. He took the girl to a building a couple of blocks away. Fortunately his lawyer acquaintance was in.

The girl repeated her story for the benefit of the lawyer, her new friend encouraging her with kindly words when she faltered. "And your master never gave you a cent to help you through the trouble he brought upon you?" asked the lawyer. "No, not a cent," said Mary. "Well, we'll make him pay. I know the type of man; he'll pay rather than be exposed. This type is cowardly. Such as he want to appear good, faithful husbands to their wives, loving fathers to their children, and respectable to everyone, but are ready to victimize any pretty girl who crosses their path. I pity the domestic servants in the homes of such men."

There and then he prepared a statement which Mary signed. He sent the statement and a letter demanding a sum of money which would tide Mary over for a little while.

When Mary and the man left the lawyer's office, Mary turned to her companion, and holding out her hand said, "Friend, thank you. You do not know it, but you have been my saviour to-day. I went to your office this morning with my mind in a state of despair. When you said you had no work I could do my only thought was suicide. Tell me, please, why you have taken such an interest in me; I'm a perfect stranger to you."

"All right, Mary, I'll tell you this as we walk back to the office." They walked slowly along the street. The man, with a touch of bitterness in his words, told her how all his experiences with the life of the workers make him hate the conditions that made life so wretched for them. He hated the class society of to-day. He despised the rich who took advantage of their position to beat the workers down and down. He detested those wealthy skunks that took advantage of the poverty and loneliness of working girls, using them for their passion and pleasure, then casting them on one side as soon as that passion had subsided. He told how he despised the women of the class of the idle rich; he hated their sham, their inhumanity. I have thrown in my lot with the working class. I am fighting the masters who despise the workers, and I helped you because you are a member of the working class. You have been up against it. But you are worth while. You had courage. This is what all the workers want. Not so much the courage of forbearance as the courage to struggle against those who oppress them."

After this little speech Mary knew that this man was different from any other that she had met. He was a real man. Not one of the kind that was to be met with even in her own ranks. He did not do a kindness and expect some sort of personal favor in return. This man did a kind turn for a fellow-being and member of the class of workers because he had a special mission in life; that mission was to help the workers save themselves.

Then Mary had to listen to a little bit of advice from this friend. This man advised Mary not to go back to service. He told her that girls met more temptations in service than they did in the factories. "It is true," said he, "factory conditions of labor are bad enough, but at least numbers give some form of protection to a working girl. Servants are unprotected. The shelter of a good home is so much bunkum. More servant girls are betrayed by their masters or masters' sons than any other class of working girl."

When he held out his hand to her to say "good-bye," Mary could not help saying, "Friend, you are a real man. What a wonderful world this would be if there were more like you."

A New Outlook

A few days later Mary received a letter from the lawyer who had become interested in her case. As she unfolded the letter she saw a cheque between the folds. The letter informed her that her former master had acknowledged his responsibility and had sent a cheque for the amount named by the lawyer.

That day it was a very different Mary who entered the office of the Private Employment Agency. This Mary had come to thank the man who had befriended her and to tell him how much she owed to his interest in her case.

After a little friendly talk, the man said in parting, "Mary, girl, remember, virgins do not give birth to saviours these days to be worshipped by generations to come. These are days when girls must guard their virginhood, must be their own saviours, must be on the watch against the trickery of wealth, or else pay the price. And, remember, Mary, too, why I took an interest in you, you belong to the only useful class and the best people, for as uncouth and unpolished as most of our class are, they are the people who make life possible." With a shake of the hand the man bent his head over his task at the desk, and the girl closed the door and walked out into the street.

"This man is a new kind of saviour, and his advice is new, but I will heed it, because I have learned by experience it is true."

PROSTITUTES

January 1927, p. 13.

Why should I starve while other dine
And breath of man is fire?
Why shouldn't I live on their wealth
As price of their desire?
My body yields—is sold for gold;
My soul is free—is mine,
Is clean and strong and seeks alone
The truth you call divine.
The truth you never learn. I live
An outcast, and your hate
Is sanctioned by the holy Church

And paid for by the State.
Your preachers preach a lie for gain,
Your statesmen war for loot,
But only I in all the world
Am called a prostitute.

—A Reader.

THE GREATER THE EVIL, THE HARDER WE FIGHT

[Editorial]

September 1927, pp. 3-4.

BECAUSE prostitution is vile—people fear to talk about it.

Because it makes people shudder—they close their eyes to it. But because it concerns the working class and the daughters of the working class in particular—we must not only face the evil—but we must fight it.

Some of the horrors of organized prostitution, known as the White Slave Traffic, are mentioned in an article in this issue of The Woman Worker. "The Trade," as it is commonly called, is but the organized side of the evil. The unorganized side, that which we know exists in our midst, at our very doors, is just as hideous.

The reports given at Geneva, before the League of Nations, gives no room for saying that "only a bad girl becomes a prostitute." Rather, it shows that prostitutes are first of all made, after that they become "bad."

Because prostitutes are made we should be concerned with the conditions and the agencies that make them. These we ought to fight with all our might and main.

Not only must a war be waged against "bogus agencies," but every other agency must be fought that prevents working-class girls living moral lives, lives they wish for themselves.

And among these agencies we must include those immigration agents who entice girls to new countries for the sake of commission for themselves and with no thought of the outcome for the immigrant girls. We must include employers who do not pay their working girls a maintenance wage. We must include those who would deny the right of healthful pleasure to working girls. We must include those who would keep the whole of the working class in the gutter. All these are the promoters of prostitution, and all these must be fought.

We dare to be bolder than the League of Nations. We are not afraid to publish the names of the countries guilty of wholesale prostitution in their midst. IT EXISTS IN EVERY CAPITALIST COUNTRY. Canada is not to be excepted. Reports exist showing the conditions which prevailed, up to quite recently, in the Port of Montreal. We have only to read the newspapers, and every day the evil is proclaimed.

War is horrid, beastly—but it has at least a show of glory.

Prostitution is hideous, vile—it is absolutely sordid.

The uglier the evil the greater energy must we put into the fight.

The organized labor movement must take a hand in the struggle.

Working women must wake up to the horrors, not merely shudder, but must buckle on their armour for the fray.

And working girls must organize to get higher wages for a surer maintenance. They must fight this indignity to their sex and to their class.

Words will not avail to fight the evil. Action is necessary.

HOW THE LEAGUE OF NATIONS DEALS WITH THE WHITE SLAVE TRAFFIC

September 1927, pp. 9-10.

"A THRILL OF HORROR runs through the correspondents at Geneva at the revelations in the report of the League of Nations' Commission on the White Slave Traffic, news of which lately began to filter through the press."

So commences an article in The Literary Digest, May 14th, 1927, issue. The report is described by one correspondent, H.J. Greenwall, as "one of the most terrible indictments against humanity ever compiled."

From the article we obtain the following facts:

That this international trade in women for immoral sex purposes is permitted by the governments of some countries.

That four classes of persons profit from the trade, while the victim receives ill treatment, virtual slavery, and in the end a dishonored grave in an alien land.

That the extent of this vicious trade was disclosed when investigators interviewed 5,000 persons interested in the commercial side of the vice.

That the victims are gathered by the white slavers from the cabarets of European countries.

That the movement of tourists is followed. For instance: women are sent into Egypt and Northern Africa during the winter months for the benefit of tourists, and then sent elsewhere for the summer.

The report discloses the misery of the victims. The following are but two examples:

A troupe of fifteen girls, all under age, were taken by a German woman to dance in an Athens cabaret. Seven of them were sent home in a "pitiable condition" to relate how they were forced into vice to save themselves from starvation.

Another troupe of four girls was sent to Buenos Aires, and was there stranded. One committed suicide, another attempted suicide, a third disappeared, and a fourth accepted the situation forced on her.

The methods used to ensnare these unwary victims are said to be bogus matrimonial agencies, and bogus employment agencies. It is shown that white slave procurers, who pose as theatrical agents, have offices in Belgrade, Berlin, Bucharest, Budapest, Marseilles, Paris, Vienne and Zagreb. Portugal is cited as one of the worst countries in respect to the traffic. There the girls given over to commercialized vice range in age from sixteen to twenty.

It is claimed that licensed commercialized vice is the chief cause of the white slave traffic. The supply of the necessary victims is kept up by importation.

Some of the victims know why they are being imported; others do not. Few fully understand the conditions before them. In foreign lands, friendless, ignorant of the laws and of the language, they are practically defenceless.

As to the remedy of the evil, the report asks the governments to exercise more care in permitting girls under a certain age to accept employment abroad. Also the governments are reminded that it is their duty to see that places of entertainment to which foreign entertainers are brought are properly conducted.

A British newspaper, the London Times, being moved by the horrors of the report, goes a little further. It urges the League of Nations to "pursue the destruction of this traffic to the end, and not to conceal the names of those countries which countenance the evil, including those which, although signatories to the international conventions for its suppression, have not acted up to their obligations."

And this is all that is suggested to wipe out this horrible evil. This is all the League of Nations has to offer.

Knowing the League of Nations to be but a League of Masters, and we say this despite the good intentions of some of those who associate with it, we know that to suggest more than it did would be too dangerous for it.

Were the case not so serious we could laugh at such puny remedies. The remedy of the League of Nations is as if it asked a cub lion to kill its mother.

Had the League dared to strike at the root of the evil it would have been compelled to strike at the foundation of the present social system, the capitalist system which stands on the rock of slavery—wage-slavery. The capitalist system exists on the profit it wrings from the labor of workers, and everything that is, is valued in terms of profit; not a thing exists but is a thing of trade. From this condition springs all the social evils of to-day.

The "white slave traffic," with its hideous purpose, prostitution, is the trade in the flesh of women for the satisfaction of bestial sexual appetites. But this trade produces "profit" unearned wealth, for four classes of persons, therefore the trade is moral. And where does the trade begin? We see the profiteers looking at each other and challenging each other to throw "the first stone." Not one among them dares, for fear of the consequences, the loss of profit unto themselves.

So the great "tragedy," the sale of women's flesh, will go on until the day the workers wake up and dare to destroy the whole profit system.

AS MR. CALVERTON SEES NEW RUSSIA'S MORALS

[Editorial]

November 1927, p. 6.

[...]

The Campaign Against Prostitution

"The same attitude has prevailed in regard to every economic and social problem that confronts the Soviet Republic. Let us take a social evil as malignant as prostitution and observe how it is handled. Every one who knows European civilization realizes how serious and grave is the problem of prostitution. It is impossible to evade it. It glares at you on every side. Every country is festered with it, and Soviet Russia is certainly not immune. Those who come back from the U.S.S.R. with the optimistic report that prostitution has been destroyed one must condemn as either blind or sentimental.

Prostitution does remain, but it is no longer official. In fact, prostitution under the Soviets has been rendered illegal. But the decree does not make it cease. It is true, one must remember, that prostitution was once a profession in old Russia. Brothels were licensed, opened with ceremonies by the police, and blessed by the Church. This evil thus had a sanction which it has now entirely lost.

"A constant propaganda is carried on all over the U.S.S.R. against prostitution. Every means of meeting the masses in this matter is utilized, from the printed sheet to the movie. In a photoplay, entitled 'The Prostitute,' for example, the whole career of the courtesan is portrayed, with a direct attempt to show the dangerous consequences of her life for both herself and those who frequent her haunts.

One of the most direct ways that has been employed to combat this evil has been the organization of homes for unemployed house-working girls. ... The problem has been discussed in detail in many papers and in the edition of Working Paper of Jan. 25, 1927, a resolution was submitted to the Moscow Soviet to the effect that single working women should not be laid off and then prostitution will decrease. It has now been decided that single women must be 'laid off' last. In other words, the moment prostitution is suspected from any one or a multitude of causes, an immediate method is applied to destroy it. ... As a result of these methods, prostitution is on the decline, and one of the best statistical proofs of this fact is that the percentage of infection from prostitutes is far below that of the pre-war period.

MOTHERS MUST TEACH THEIR GIRLS

November 1927, p. 16.

The Woman Worker.

Dear Editor,

I am not good at making speeches, but I feel I want to express myself concerning the case of the Picton minister and the orphan girl he betrayed.

It seems to me that we have been too long the victims of mock modesty on questions pertaining to sex and life. I consider it is about time that mothers knew how and what to tell their daughters on this subject. While this knowledge may not wipe out many of the evils that beset the path of girls to-day, yet knowledge will make them more wary when confronted with difficult situations.

It is about time the church woke up, not only to preach against the "white slave traffic" but to clear some of the traffickers out of its own ranks. There is something more to be done than paying such persons to tell us to be good. Presently this man will be able to roam the world where no one will know him, and folks will think he is all right. The girl, on the other hand, will be shunned, and the finger of scorn will be pointed to her all her life.

While I know it will be difficult for many mothers to educate her child, yet I think this education will have to be done at home. I think this because I am afraid much goes on in our schools that some of us in the days gone by would blush about.

I was an orphan and had to fight my way through life alone. I know something of the conditions which face working girls. Education is the means to fight vice. So let every mother consider this and feel it her duty to instruct her children.

Wishing the Woman Worker every success,

Mrs. A. Trenchard.

GENEVA WHITEWASHES WHITE SLAVE TRADING

[Editorial]

December 1927, pp. 2-3.

WHEN the experts' report on the investigation into the White Slave Traffic was completed the name of one expert was missing, Dr. Pauline Luisi, of Uruguay, had refused to sign the report as important evidence had been suppressed.

Dr. Pauline Luisi has rendered a great social service to the world by her courageous act. White slave international rings and threatening governments did not put fear into her. She knew outrageous things took place in her own country and was not afraid to say so. She refused to help whitewash a most despicable and contemptible trade—the trade in the bodies of young women and girls for bestial appetites.

There is no doubt that conditions revealed in the report of expert investigators were such that governments were so thoroughly ashamed that some denied the truth of the reports, while others demanded their suppression.

We are not surprised that governments want to suppress these facts, they are as deep in the mud as the traders are in the mire, they cannot be blind as to what goes on in their respective countries. They know quite well that the poverty-stricken countries of Europe are sending armies of young girls over to wealthy America and to sub-tropical health resorts for no other reason than to satisfy the cravings of the idle rich and their hangers-on.

It has been admitted that Canada is not without sin, but claims the sin is at a minimum. It is claimed that the trade is confined to seasonal visits of women from the U.S. We know, of course, that this is nonsense. The evil is an every-day evil and right in our midst. The seasonal migrations do occur. When are these seasonal migrations? Do these occur when big conventions are held in Canada? Are exhibitions and race seasons the attractions? We have in mind an advertisement that appeared in a Montreal paper some time ago just before a big convention was to be held in that city that "attractive girls were wanted to act as companions"—the number was definitely stated.

We are of the opinion that Canada, too, has been whitewashed.

And this is our wonderful civilization! What price glory for the defence of womanhood!

THE TRUTH WILL OUT

February 1928, p. 8.

A few weeks ago in the city of London, England, a woman was being tried for "soliciting," that is, for being a prostitute. In Canada, by the way, we are not so frank in our language, we call this "vagrancy." After the police had given evidence the magistrate made the following remarkable statement. Addressing the police, he said, "If I were you I don't think I would press the charges against women like the prisoner, because prostitution is inevitable under this system, and if we drive these women off the streets we will only drive this thing into the home, where dreadful results will follow."

How's that for truth? Here we have a man who occupies a public position admitting that women must sell their bodies in order to live under this system.

Then why persecute these women? Why send them to jail when they are the victims of a social system? How are they worse than women who are looked upon as social superiors merely because they went through a ceremony that legalizes the act, when even they sold themselves for an easier time or for title or social position? Who is worse, she who hides what she really is or she who defies convention and shows the world that she is the victim of a vicious social system?

This makes one wonder what is going to become of the crowds of young women who are being brought to this country as immigrants? I know women who have been out of work four months. Women who employ domestic servants are becoming more exacting in their demands and more stingy with the wages.

There is one thing that can be done to help make our demands for a living wage for women and protection when unemployed by paying unemployment insurance, and this is for women to join the Women's Labor League.

Some people are bound to say when we talk unemployment insurance, "Oh, you mean the dole." That, of course, is only a name given unemployment insurance in order to appeal to the empty pride of the people who don't understand that more people of the so-called upper class are getting a dole than they would ever dream of, but with this difference, the upper classes never did anything in their lives which entitled them to "their dole," that is, they never worked to earn it.

Now, women, it rests with you, are we going to get justice for the women of the working class or are we going to let them cry in vain for help when we know how to help remedy the evil? Join the Women's Labor League and speed the day.

Elizabeth.

A VICTIM OF VICE

[Editorial]

April 1928, p. 4.

THERE comes to us the story of a young girl who was violated —and, by a perfectly respectable, law-abiding citizen. The case is even worse than that of the orphan girl of Picton, Ontario, who was the victim of a minister of the gospel.

The man in this case is reputed to be a Justice of the Peace. In his position, as upholder of the law, he should have been aware of the content of the law in connection with his brand of crime.

The girl in the case is a Ukrainian girl living in Western Canada. This girl, because of the poverty of her father, who, by the way, is a dirt farmer, was forced to go into service at the age of fourteen. The master of the house in which she became a servant, without any regard for her age, fourteen years;

without any regard for her ignorance of the facts of life; without any regard for the fact that the girl was away from her protectors (her parent) —violated this girl, and continued this until, at the age of sixteen, the girl had a child. Her employer sent her to an hospital. When her father asked where his daughter was, the employer informed him that his daughter was at the hospital being treated for appendicitis.

It was only after the girl returned to her father's home that the story of the treatment she received at the hands of her employer leaked out.

The residents of the district were up in arms about the case. Their feeling ran so high that they called a meeting to discuss action. They took the case to the court. But, as was expected, the Court exonerated the man. It is claimed by those interested in this case that the Judge was a personal friend of the accused.

And now, the girl, the daughter of a poor farmer, a Ukrainian immigrant, is left to bear the burden of this man's vice.

Surely this is a case for the Labor Defense League, since "protection of the foreign-born" is one of its objectives. And this, because the girl, as a domestic servant, has no union to help her obtain protection and aid.

IMMIGRANT DOMESTICS THE VICTIMS OF THE WHITE SLAVE AGENTS

[Editorial]

December 1928, p. 2.

WE are not surprised at the charges made by Abbe Casgrain, Chaplain attached to the Immigration Service at Quebec. The Abbe just recently made the startling charge that "immigrant girls from Europe frequently failed to report at their destination after their arrival in Canada, disappearing completely in some cases."

The charge has made the government demand a report from Abbe Casgrain, and the Chaplain is preparing one.

At every port white slave agents are to be found at their job. Women and men alike ply their trade among new arrivals, who are nearly always young and pretty girls. By means of promises of assistance and the like these girls are decoyed, only to be used in cabarets, dance halls, and houses of illrepute to satisfy lust.

The white-slaver is to be detested. But not the white-slaver alone. Abbe Casgrain gives his opinion on the matter and condemns the present system of immigration, inasmuch as it is left largely to the railway companies.

But what do railway companies care about the fate of young girls of the working class so long as they get passage money?

We are compelled to ask, "What are all the various religious, charitable, and fraternal organizations doing?" "Is it possible that they are all in the swim, and care more about the Almightly Dollar than the lives and security of young working girls? From reports we receive from time to time we know that every immigrant girl who comes to this country, even under the auspices and protection of an organization such as the Young Women's Christian Association, has to pay her way or she finds herself alone.

Let us watch for Abbe Casgrain's report. We must demand Protection for immigrant girls.

Marriage, the Family, and Domestic Labour   6

If discussions about prostitution tended to stress sex as a potential danger to women, discussions of marriage in the *Woman Worker* at least hinted at the possibility of altering heterosexual and marital relationships to women's benefit. Though the paper tended to stress an economic analysis of the marriage relationship, it also recognized that marriage and family relations were fraught with difficulty and stress under capitalism, and that these familial relations reflected and reproduced women's subordination. If there was hope for more egalitarian and loving relations between husbands and wives, and for happier children and families, it would emerge, it was suggested, after a major social and economic transformation—much like the one in Soviet Russia.

Communists in the 1920s relied heavily on Frederick Engels' classic book, *Origin of the Family, Private Property and the State*, to explain women's subordination in the family. Engels in turn had drawn on the late 19th century findings of anthropologist Lewis Morgan, whose studies included the history of Iroquois peoples. In a series of articles entitled "The Story of Our Family" Custance presented this position, arguing that the advent of private property had transformed familial ties. Monogamous marriage emerged to ensure the ready identification of legitimate heirs to property, and women lost their equality with men and were expected to trade their former independence in more "primitive" societies for a glorified motherhood role. Excerpts from this series are reproduced as an example of the Women's Labor Leagues' theoretical basis for thinking on the marriage question, and also to indicate the extent to which Custance considered an intellectual education in Marxist thought essential to the socialist movement.

Although the WLLs, like the Communist Party, were critical of existing marital relations, most would not have endorsed the view of one male contributor who, in September 1927, rejected outright the modern family as "legalized prostitution," a mere "convenience" for the working class, and a "weapon in the hands of the masters." According to this view, working-class wives and mothers became the unwitting collaborators of capitalists by making the "wage slave" existence of husbands and sons more comfortable and by exerting a conservative political influence on their families. Although the *Woman Worker* sometimes shared the view that women were more conservative than men, WLLers argued that women would be radicalized and new family relationships would develop when women participated fully in wage work and the labour movement.

Certainly, women correspondents were fully aware that all was not well with marriage and family relations. On the one hand, articles like "Cruelty to Women" and "An Interesting Court Decision" indicate their aversion to the assumptions of male superiority and authority in the family, embedded in the legal and social system. They also worried about their children, particularly the way in which class status prevented their full access to education, steered them into early wage labour and cut short the experience of childhood. For young women, this also made the prospect of marriage an economic necessity—as for the women in the story "Something is Wrong Somewhere"—and one that might well become simply joyless drudgery.

The *Woman Worker*, like the Communist Party in the 1920s, displayed some tolerance for alternative marriage patterns. Indeed, in private, Communists sometimes eschewed marriage as a restrictive, bourgeois institution, attempting to establish freer love and sexual partnerships. Finnish WLL locals passed resolutions calling for the institution of civil marriage, indicating their objection to the imposition of Christian marriage on individuals, and one woman wrote to the paper urging the League women to publicly defend the right of Finnish socialists to live common law. (As the Hollinger Mine Disaster revealed all too tragically, however, Finnish common law wives were left with no legal rights as widows.) A fictionalized story, reprinted in the paper, also defended a woman's decision to live common law with her new found "pal" after escaping from an intolerable marriage. Social conventions accepting only legal marriages, argued the author, could be hypocritical and destructive; instead, women and men should seek equal, loving, companionate relationships. Companionate marriages—based on friendship, closeness and sexual fulfilment—were increasingly the ideal promoted in wider society at this time. But as Janet Inman, a Labour Party member from Hamilton wrote in her submission, such ideals might be difficult to attain within a capitalist society. If the editor and contributors were open to considering alternative heterosexual relationships, nowhere in the *Woman Worker* was there any indication of such tolerance for same-sex love relationships. The paper's silence on the lives and rights of these couples revealed the writers' own heterosexual ideals of family life.

The experience of post-revolutionary Russia was continually hailed as confirmation of the potential transformation of the working-class family. While WLLers did not claim that Soviet family life was perfect, they focused their attention on the positive changes taking place, particularly legal and social reforms, leaving the remaining problems unexamined. It is significant that so many articles on the "new" family in the Soviet Union were reprinted, stressing things such as socialized domestic labour and communal kitchens, legal reforms undoing patriarchal authority, challenges to the stigma of illegitimacy, and the new "candor" about sex. This vision of a transformed family life clearly appealed to women readers of the paper.

Communists were aware that these reforms were very radical by the standards of the day. They also knew that the mainstream press was anxious to portray the wholesale destruction of the family in the USSR, and the "nationalization of wives" by the "wicked Bolshies." The *Woman Worker*, though, was arguing quite the opposite about post-revolutionary Russia. In Russia, the Leagues contended, marriage no longer entailed "economic slavery" for women as they were free to marry for love rather than for economic security as was the case in Canada and other capitalist nations. Moreover, the fact that female workers, married or not, were welcomed into the public sphere had far reaching positive implications for the family. Legal reforms protected women and children within the family, ensuring, for instance, that fathers could not escape child support duties.

Women correspondents to the *Woman Worker* clearly hoped that marital relationships, freed from economic stresses, would become loving and equal partnerships, and women the "intelligent companions" rather than the "sweeties" noted in the chapter on women and wage work. Many of the fictional pieces celebrate the devotion and unity of long-term, heterosexual, monogamous relationships. Contributors did acknowledge women's oppression within the family, but saw this primarily as a consequence of the economic relations between classes. Absent from the analysis was a thorough-going critique of the gender conflict and inequality in the family which were rooted both in material and ideological patterns of family life. For instance, the darker side of family life, such as domestic violence, was largely sidestepped by the editor of the paper. But blatant realities sometimes intervened, forcing her to comment. Women's frustration with power inequalities within the working-class family did occasionally surface, especially in some fiction and in letters to the editor. In reply, Custance's editorials warned against blaming the working-class husband for sexual tensions and inequality when its root causes were to be found at capitalism's door.

The WLL also remained committed to the idea that domestic labour and children's needs *were* fundamentally the province of women. Their notion of marriage and gender roles betrayed an assumption that women were responsible for care of the home— cooking, cleaning, managing the family finances, overseeing the emotional life of the family and raising children. As a result, many editorials appealed to women on the basis of their daily domestic duties.

Because the Party put most emphasis on getting women into social production, they never welcomed a thorough-going analysis of domestic labour, both the way in which it sustained capitalism, and the notion that it *was* women's work. This had both positive and negative consequences for women's political activities and status in the Party. On the one hand, the *Woman Worker* provided an invaluable role, giving public significance to women's domestic labour and describing, with sharp realism, the lives of housewives in mining towns, the difficulties in balancing the family budget, the importance of housewives' daily work to family survival. There was also considerable stress put on providing political education for housewives, and the necessity of organizing them into Labor Leagues or union auxiliaries which might promote the union label, lobby to keep food prices down or press school boards to end militaristic education of children (see "Peace and War" chapter). In the daily activities reports in the *Woman Worker* many local WLLs, comprised primarily of housewives, concentrated on this kind of political activity which recognized the need to draw women into socialism based on their daily, lived experiences of work (see the chapter, "The Local Women's Labor Leagues at Work"). This was a theme which persisted not only within the Communist Party, but within the Left generally for decades to come.

In the last resort, though, the unexamined assumption that domestic labour was women's work meant that women remained more isolated from the centres of political decision making, which put more emphasis on organizing wage earners in the 'socially productive' sector of the economy. It also contributed to an ideal image of the family, shared by the mainstream, conservative union movement, that a male breadwinner was the ideal, making women temporary, secondary workers. A more thorough-going critique of women's responsibility for domestic work would await a much later socialist and feminist movement.

Further Readings:

- Friedrich Engels, *Origin of the Family, Private Property and the State* (1884; reprinted New York: 1970).

- Ruth Frager, "Politicized Housewives in the Jewish Communist Movement of Toronto, 1923-33," in Linda Kealey and Joan Sangster, eds., *Beyond the Vote: Canadian Women and Politics* (Toronto: University of Toronto Press, 1989).

- Suzanne Morton, *Ideal Surroundings: Domestic Life in a Working-Class Suburb in the 1920s* (Toronto: University of Toronto Press, 1995).

1. Marriage and The Family

THE STORY OF OUR FAMILY
(By Florence Custance)

Excerpts from July 1926, p. 14; August 1926, pp. 14-15; September 1926, pp. 13-14; December 1926, p. 13.

[...]

THE STAGES OF THE DEVELOPMENT OF MANKIND

We are very fond of calling ourselves "civilized." This is more often than not said to distinguish us from others we desire to belittle. We are apt to think this name places us in the position of being "cultured."

But civilization has a deeper meaning, and is connected with a development upon which culture itself depends.

When tracing the stages of the development and progress of mankind, Lewis Morgan gives three main stages which are again divided into sub-stages, according to the degree of progress along the line of invention and discovery. These three main stages are: Savagery, Barbarism and Civilization.

[...]

THE GENS

The earliest groupings of mankind are known as gentes. The single gens was a group of human beings whose bond was that of blood relationship. This bond was very strong. It held the individuals as a unit—and an injury to one was an injury to all.

No doubt, fear, and the need of protection, also had some bearing on the unity of the gens.

It is to Lewis Morgan, to whom we have already referred, that we owe much for the insight he has given us of the life of our tribal forefathers. Lewis Morgan spent a number of years with the Iroquois Indians. He lived their life, studied their customs, rooted out the origin of those customs, and has shown us that we, too, are playing our tiny part in that long, long process of Social Evolution.

MARRIAGE—THE EARLIEST INSTITUTION

As far as can be ascertained, the first act of restriction placed by human beings upon themselves was that in relation to the sexes. In the very early gens, marriage or sex relationship, was unrestricted; that is, no regard was paid to blood relationship or age. The first restriction placed on sexual intercourse was that in connection with age. This restriction disallowed marriage outside the generation. For example, let us say, the fourth generation great grand children would be entitled to marry among themselves, the third likewise, the second and so on.

This was an important step, as it forbid marriage between mother and son, father and daughter, etc. To-day, we look askance when we see age mated to youth, and the relationship of parents to children is simply that of guardians.

The next restriction was that of prohibition of marriage between brother and sister. To avoid this it was necessary for marriage to extend outside the individual unit called the gens. Therefore, this next marriage custom extended the range of blood relations, because men of one gens were the husbands of the women of another gens.

The forms of marriage just described are called "Group Marriage Forms." The forms known as Polygamy and Polyandry might be called transition stages, the latter means a marriage condition where a woman has more than one husband, and the former a marriage condition which allowed a man to have more than one wife.

The group marriage existed for the most part as a custom among the savage tribes: The barbaric tribes developed to the point of recognizing the "pairing family." This important development was the forerunner of the present marriage form—monogamy.

THE MATRIARCH

The period of the group marriage forms known as the Matriarch. This is called so because the ancestry of children was traced through the mother. This does not prevail to-day. To-day ancestry is traced through the father. [...]

THE PART PLAYED BY DISCOVERIES

We must of necessity again refer to the method of food producing and the discoveries of our primitive forefathers, for it is through these we get our answer.

It has been shown already that the struggle for life was very hard for our early ancestors. Their struggle was the struggle against "Nature." This struggle kept them together in their tribal units. Each member of the tribe was but a part of the whole, all were equal, all shared alike in times of plenty, all suffered alike in times of scarcity. In their wars against tribal foes, all would fight to the bitter death. In some cases whole tribes would be wiped out.

The division of labor was a sex division, the men were hunters, the women were the home builders.

We have seen that the discovery of fire, the domestication of animals, and the cultivation of food plants did away with the fear of insecurity which was forever facing the early hunters. But these discoveries brought in their train new needs. Fire gave courage to the early hunters so that they moved about to seek new hunting grounds. Flocks and herds required food, so the pastoral tribes were kept continually on the move for new pastures. But, later, agriculture compelled a more permanent abode or settled habitation. It was under this latter condition that more rapid progress began to take place.

So, as the tribes became possessed of more wealth (cattle and all that could be obtained through cattle) new methods of living developed.

In this development women played little part. Their duties were confined to the communal home and the needs of the big communal family. There was no way for them to acquire possessions in their own right. Women's occupations were now looked upon as inferior and dependent on what the men obtained. This outlook prevails to-day so far as the work of the women of the homes is concerned.

TRIBAL WEALTH INCREASES

Unlike the primitive hunting tribes who always killed their enemy tribesmen, the pastoral tribes preserved the lives of their foes, but put them to work. They were slaves and became a new form of wealth for their captors. This condition brought its difficulties into tribal life.

It will be readily understood that our primitive forefathers, the hunters, had little beyond the barest necessities of life. A man might possess his own bow and arrow, but at his death this would be buried with him, as it was thought he might need his weapon in the happy hunting ground to which he had gone, but which those left behind could not see.

At a later stage, the personal possessions a man acquired were inherited by the tribe, that is, it passed to the tribe to which he belonged, to that of his brothers and sisters, and not to that he belonged to by marriage. His children did not receive any benefit from his personal wealth, this was because they belonged to their mother's tribe.

PRIVATE PROPERTY MAKES ITSELF FELT

Gradually the desire of a man who had wealth, that this wealth should be the inheritance of his own children, and not the possession of his nephews, gained ground. But in order that this could be possible another requirement was necessary, and this was, that a new marriage condition must be imposed upon women. The liberty of the group marriage tie must be denied her. Her purpose now must be to raise children for a husband to whom she must be bound, in order that these children shall be the heirs to his property.

From that period of time until to-day this has been at the root of the marriage bond between man and woman. All law relating to private property has been based upon this. The monogamous family (mono—single, gamous—marriage), the family of to-day, was founded on male supremacy, and was for the purpose of having children of indisputable paternal lineage.

The monogamous marriage became a bond of slavery to the woman. To compensate her for her loss of individual freedom, her function of mother-hood became glorified. She was urged to have children as numerous as the sands on the sea shore. And if these were sons she was one of the blest. The barren woman was soon cast on one side.

The marriage restriction forced upon the woman by no means applied to the men. The right to group marriage has remained the right of men. In the early days it was practised very openly. There are many biblical examples of this, the story of Abram, Sara and Hagar is but one. To-day it is practised undercover. It is, for the most part, a special luxury of the rich. According to the law, there can be only one marriage, but actually it is only lack of wealth or disclination on the part of a man which prevents its greater prevalence. [...]

SOMETHING MORE ABOUT MARRIAGE

In one of our previous lessons we discussed Group Marriage Forms. It was shown that as an outcome of the different forms there developed the Pairing Family. This form was certainly the highest form. Both man and woman lived together so long as they were happy. This might mean for life, or for a period, according as their dispositions suited. The right to break the marriage tie was an equal privilege.

But when private property intruded itself into tribal life, this relationship altered. Women were gradually pushed into the background; the man, the conqueror, became the head of the household and lord of all.

At this stage, too, women began to have a money value. A man's daughters were so much wealth to him. A man's wife was also his property, she was at his mercy, he could kill her for unfaithfulness. And not only this, but he could have as many wives as he desired. This marriage form was Polyg-amy.

As we have pointed out previously, the Group Marriage form has never died out. In the early days, daughters were given over to the Temples, and were at the disposal of the rich, the warriors, the nobility, and the priests. This use of womanhood was considered to be part of the festivity of the fes-tivals.

But this "free license," this use of womanhood was sanctified, the young maidens had the protection of the gods, they enjoyed lives of ease, luxury and pleasure.

To-day the group form has become commercialized. The respectability of our civilization demands that it shall be under cover as much as possible, and people speak in hushed tones about it, and shudder when the word "prostitution" is mentioned.

Throughout the world to-day nearly all the forms of marriage described in our story are in existence. This shows the unequal degree of development of the peoples of the world.

Nearly everywhere women are struggling against the fetters that chain them to traditions, and are making a stand for their freedom. The forms of struggle depend upon their status in society. [...]

MODERN VALUES STRUGGLE
By A. D. A.

December 1926, pp. 9-13.

Her home was always spick and span—her three children always looked as if they had come out of a "bandbox"—and she, herself, was always a picture of neatness.

She was a marvellous housekeeper, too; she knew how to make a dollar go as far as some women made two. She could turn an old garment into a new one. She could remodel an old hat into one the latest fashion. She could make a delicious meal out of a soup bone. And she was an artist, for [s]he knew just how to set a chair to make it inviting to a visitor, and how to place a few ornaments and pictures so that the effect was beautifully home-like. Yes, indeed, this little woman was economical, practical and artistic, a combination seldom found wrapped up in a single person.

All this is the more wonderful when one learns that she had always been a victim of poverty. Poverty dogged her, no matter what she did or how she strived. Her childhood days were joyless, loveless days. Her mother died when she was a mere baby, and she was thrust into the factory at an early age. And as a poor little victim of Child Labor she labored for a shilling a week in the factories of that dreadful Chain-making, Black Country District of Old England.

Perhaps it was her childhood experiences that developed her hatred of poverty and a form of society that caused that poverty, and created a thirst for beauty, affection and love, as well as made her the practical and methodical wife and mother of later years.

As is usual in cases where a girl has no home love, she married when she was barely twenty. Soon after the birth of her first baby she and her husband decided that they would leave the misery of the Black Country and go to Canada, thinking that her ambitions would be satisfied in a country which was praised by the papers and call the "Land of Promise."

But a stranger in a strange land is lost, and immigrants who are assisted have to take what they can get without a murmur. So she and her husband found themselves on a farm as the general help, she to help the farmer's wife, and her husband to help the farmer in the fields. A new and strange experience, but all experiences teach their lessons.

After the term of farm slavery was over they came into the city to live. Then another baby came along, and then a third. As her family increased, so did her misfortunes. Her husband was often out of work, as his trade was not a flourishing one in Canada. During these times her husband mixed with bad companions and got into difficulties, and her mind was always in a turmoil and full of fear. In addition to this she was compelled to carry the burden of being the bread winner. Early morning she could be seen hurrying to her work, which was to slave in the homes of the wealthy. After her work in these homes she would slave until bedtime in her own home. And this was her life year in and year out until her children reached the age of youth.

There were times when she upbraided her husband for his indifference to his duties and responsibilities. For it seemed to her that as long as she supplied the food, kept the roof above their heads, and stitched her fingers sore making clothes for the family, that he was quite content. His indifference would not have been so bad had he helped her in the house, but even here he took his ease and left things to her.

So battling and fighting her way through all her difficulties this little woman raised her family. And bright, healthy children they were. They were her pride. No one will ever know of all the sacrifices she made to keep them to school, to give them a little pleasure, and to have them looking as well as the children whose fathers brought home good wages to their mothers. She looked upon this as her duty, and besides, she had always vowed that if she ever had children they should never know what suffering was like, that is the suffering she had experienced in her childhood days. How she planned! How she pinched and screwed! But always the thought was with her that her children would repay her when they grew older and she was worn out; they would love her always for her care of them and her sacrifices for them.

But she had reckoned without her host. Her care and sacrifice, her devotion and love, fell on barren soil. This she did not detect all the time her children were under her wing and she was their authority. It was when they started out into the world of work that she discovered this. Demands, always demands, they made upon her. They looked upon her now in the light of a servant, to cook for them, to sew for them, to wait upon them hand and foot. They even begrudged giving her money for their board, and it often happened that she was compelled to go out to work to keep up with their demands.

Is it any wonder that when she saw through the selfishness of her family that she rebelled? But even this rebellion did not come before she found herself worn out, her health broken, and with one foot in the grave.

Then she told her husband that he could not depend upon her labor any more, that he must support himself henceforth. She told her children they must start to depend upon their own efforts and not look to her for everything. This brought the climax. She discovered that all her sacrifice had been in vain. Her husband left home; he got work, but instead of sending her money he wrote her letters which cut her to the heart, letters of revenge, letters of spite. Her children, unwilling to share poverty with her, one after the other found excuses for leaving home. At last she was left alone.

Perplexities

Words cannot describe the anguish this little woman suffered. She cried, yes, cried bitter tears. Anguish gnawed at her very heart, the pain almost suffocated her. For days during this terrible period she was prostrated. But hers was not the spirit to give up without a battle, even with herself. She realized that to live she must exert herself. But what should she do?

There was one or the other of two things she could do. Should it be to send for her husband and her children and tell them that all she had said to them she would take back, she would work hard for them, give them all her energy as she had before? Or, should she leave them to their own resources to fend for themselves, while she would look after herself and be free, unhampered, to live peacefully without the hundreds of burdens, and the constant "I want this" and "I want that" of her children?

She pondered long over this perplexity. She dreaded the uncertainty of the future, and she revolted against the old slavery. At last she determined that even the uncertainty of the future might hold some hope of happiness in store for her, while a return to the old state of affairs would certainly put her in her grave.

Having thus decided she had to start about the business of getting rid of her home, and looking for something to do, for her purse was empty. For several days she scanned the newspapers looking for work. At last she struck an advertisement that caught her fancy.

"A woman wanted to assist on farm. Small family. (Somewhere in the heart of the Prairies.)"

She applied for the position. In doing so she was able to state that she had had some experience on a farm, so her farm experience now stood her in good stead. She got the position. Then she left the city for this new experience, hoping to gain peace of mind, recovery of her health, but happiness was too much to expect.

The New Experience

And what a place was that farm house in the heart of the Prairies! It was rough, poorly built, and everything in it had been neglected. She discovered that the family was made up of a middle-aged farmer, his wife, and son. The farmer was a man who had taken up a government section; he had come from England and was totally unable to cope with the difficulties of Western Canada farming. His wife laid claim to being an invalid, this explained the condition of the home. The son, a man nearly thirty years old, had shouldered the entire burden. Everything was left to him, and everything that went wrong was a crime laid at his door.

Well, things did not look very cheery for our little woman. She found out that it was the son who had advertised for help. The neglected home was more than he could stand. He warned her what to expect from his parents. And she soon found out that he was the only person worth while in the farm household. Always were the father and mother of the man yearning to return to the Homeland; always did their conversation turn to the thing of their desire; never did they consider their son.

And so months passed. The little woman worked wonders on that farm. As she recovered her health, she brought new life into the humdrum existence of the farm household.

And as is to be expected, the two lonely human beings, each the victims of others' selfishness, found pleasure in each other's company. They often exchanged confidences. They talked of their adversities. A deep comradeship developed. And this friendship became sweet to the woman who had never had genuine words of cheer, much less of affection. Life now seemed more bearable.

Just as she was becoming used to this experience, and accustomed to the conditions of farm life, and hoping that she could make good out of the small wages paid her, a great calamity happened. The farmer and his wife decided they would return to England. They also decided that they would get rid of the farm; their son would have the first offer to buy.

Hopes again dashed to the ground. Again a change—why was there no peace for her?

A Way Out

The Pals, as they called themselves, discussed the new situation. Yes, every phase of it was discussed, particularly as it affected themselves and their newly-found comradeship.

So far as the world was concerned they were alone. Those who should have been their nearest and dearest had new interests, and were living in an environment that, seemingly, gave them more pleasure. The bonds that bind parents to children, and children to parents, were flimsy and fragile threads in these mercenary days. They were only wanted so long as they could be used. Truly, they were the victims of this selfish age of individualism. The only thing that counted was appearance. And so-called respectability covered a multitude of sins. Everything to-day was veneered. People were hypocrites. Only rarely were the true and real discovered.

So they argued, why should they sacrifice happiness and their comradeship for the sake of appearances? Why wait for the time when people would place new and better values on human relationship? This paradise would not be in their day. Now mercenary motives were at the root of marriage.

The relationship of child to parent, and parent to child, and human beings to each other were valued in dollars and cents. A hateful condition, but a condition which made every one its victim.

The Pals decided to remain together, to make their own happiness, despite the world and the wag of tongues. They decided that to themselves they would have true values, the values of friendship, comradeship, love, born out of a mutual appreciation of each other. And in this, the god, Money, and all that could be got through the worship of this god, should have no part.

So, somewhere in the Prairies, two persons are working out their own destinies. Shall slaves of convention blame them? Perhaps, who knows, the Pals may be the pioneers of a new conception of Human Values.

CRUELTY TO WOMEN

[Editorial]

January 1927, pp. 2-3.

THE TORONTO GLOBE calls the attention of women to the fact that there is an old law on the statute books of Ontario of 1790 which permits a husband to go to any length in the treatment of his wife. The Globe advises women's organizations to work for repeal of this law.

Most women know already that before they can get a divorce from their husbands for adultery and desertion, that danger to life, limb and health must be proofs of their husbands' cruelty. On the other hand, a man has only to prove adultery on the part of his wife in order to get legal freedom.

The Globe further states that "although the relations of husbands and wives have changed in many respects since 1790, the law relating to cruelty has not changed." While the Globe makes this statement it does not give the reason for the change that has come about in spite of the law. But we can.

The reason for this change of relations between husband and wife is due to the fact that a certain means of independence has come to women. By this is meant they can go out into the world of work and earn their own living; they are not so entirely dependent upon their husbands. This independence has been in itself a protection against physical cruelty as well as a recognition of sex equality.

But this new condition has brought women in contact with a new relationship, that of being employed by an employer, and they have now to face a new form of cruelty, this is the cruelty of those who exploit their labor. This new condition places them on an equal footing with the men of their class. And this condition will make a new relationship develop, that of comradeship in the struggle against the greed of an employing class.

While women will continue to struggle against all sex inequalities, they will not let themselves be blinded. They will not struggle against men because of old traditions only, but will struggle with their husbands and sons against the common enemy of both, their masters, who rob them of the fruits of their toil.

AN INTERESTING COURT DECISION

February 1927, p. 5.

Property or No Property—Woman is Inferior

That a man is the legal and responsible head of the family, despite the fact that his wife is the property owner, is shown in a recent decision made by Judge Tytler, Toronto. The decision was made in the case of school taxes. Religion, as we know, is the means by which responsibility is placed for the maintenance of the public schools and the separate schools. In placing the responsibility the taxpayer or tenant is always asked, "What religion are you?" One must be either a Protestant or a Roman Catholic. If one ventures to mention any other form of thought other than religious, the assessors look at that person as if he or she had dropped from Mars.

However, in this particular case the religions of husband and wife differed. The wife—the property owner—was a Roman Catholic, the husband —only a tenant—was a Protestant.

The judge ruled that the school taxes on property owned by a Roman Catholic wife of a Protestant husband go to the public school.

It was claimed that this decision did not favor one side more than the other so far as religion was concerned, since another case might be the opposite, a Protestant wife of a Roman Catholic husband.

It is clear that this decision was made in the light of the legal understanding of what constitutes a family to-day and upon whom the law fastens responsibility. The father is still the head of the household, the mother merely bearer of children.

SOLVING THE MARRIAGE PROBLEM
A Review

February 1927, pp. 10-11.

When the land of the Soviets has been placed under a cloud over the marriage question, when the women in this land are supposed to be nationalized, it will be a revelation to those who believe these unfounded accusations when they read what actually has taken place in this land of the New Freedom in connection with the human institution known as marriage.

G.G.L. Alexander, of Moscow, an authority on this subject, supplies this information. She writes the splendid article which is the subject of our review. In this article she not only deals with the actual fact of marriage in Soviet Russia, but also compares the Soviet conception of marriage with the conception of marriage of the German intellectuals, which is also the general conception outside Soviet Russia.

Intellect That is Afraid of the Natural and True

The attitude of the writer towards the German intellectuals is one of ridicule. This is because they place marriage outside the sphere of SOCIAL LIFE. These German writers use any expression other than "social." They write of marriage as "An ethical and cosmic problem," "marriage as a work of art," "Marriage as fulfilment and sacrament." They never attempt to place marriage where it naturally belongs, nor do they treat it as question of life and progeny (offspring) and of personal happiness.

To do this would be to bring marriage within the scope of natural life and this would be to show mankind that they are part of the fulfilment of natural law. This, unfortunately, would reduce the EGO, or the great I Am of man, to the sphere of the animal kingdom.

This would, no double, hurt the intellectual feelings of the great intellects, who prefer to talk about marriage as "Modern Man's Affliction"—something that must be put up with—because it is LIFE'S TRAGEDY.

The writer deals with the German intellect, Keyserling, in particular. She claims that he only endeavors to make the risks and misery of "marriage of to-day" palatable by declaring that "tragedy is a part of human life which must be accepted and marriage the ground on which it can be fulfilled."

Keyserling's statement makes Alexander retort: "Marriage in the true sense is first of all community which fulfils its 'tragic' meaning. Neither cabbage nor cow knows anything about tragedy. But on the other hand, everyone knows, even the most primitive being, that it is only at the 'tragic' stage that marriage begins to fulfil its meaning."

Another writer who is criticized is Jacob Wasserman. This writer, speaking through his novels, shows up the abyss of misery and torment, crime and degeneration of marriage. Every case with which he deals is the marriage of the middle class and well-to-do. The marriage of the working class is never considered. In giving advice through his writings, he claims, writes Alexander, that "the individual is no longer important to the whole." To him it is the couple which is important and that for every man there is but one opportunity to find his affinity—thus—search and you will find.

To sum up the whole conception of marriage as intellectuals would have us regard it would be that marriage to them is a "Thing of the Spirit," something "Eternal," something outside the ability of man to rectify or amend. (To be continued).

SOLVING THE MARRIAGE PROBLEM
A Review (Continued)

March 1927, pp. 15-16 and back cover.

The Natural, Therefore, the True

In Soviet Russia, writes Alexander, where everything depends upon unmasking the false and presenting the true, marriage is not treated with levity, as the world at large is led to believe, but instead the marriage question is looked upon as an important social question of the first order, especially by women themselves.

The marriage question is handled in the same logical way, as are all other questions. The first contention in connection with the question is that **the first need of a healthier state of affairs is a change in the social structure of society.** This change has taken place in Soviet Russia, hence the changes that can be made in the relationship of individuals.

It is contended, too, that apart from the social side, the marriage problem in Soviet Russia remains and will remain the individual problem, and this will be so even when the most favorable social conditions will have been created.

But it must not be forgotten, and this is an extremely important fact, fully recognized in word and deed in Soviet Russia, that **Society has to bear the responsibility for the coming generation.**

Alexander states "That it is just the treatment of the new aspects of the marriage question in Soviet Russia which has been discussed with so much zest during the last few months, has shown that the new Soviet laws are not rigid forms. They are constantly regulated by the development of the life of the young state, which brings all the time new result and new tasks to the fore, and are continually altered in accordance with newly arising requirements and necessities. This attitude is explained by the fact that Soviet legislation does not recognize marriage to be an 'eternal problem' but as a question which is capable of being solved by society organized on a new basis."

In this solution of the marriage question one factor plays a great part; this is, that marriage in Soviet Russia no longer provides a means for material advantage to women, and neither are women brought into economic slavery through marriage.

Marriage and motherhood no longer bar a woman from participation in any form of work she desires to do. Far-reaching laws for the protection of mother and child, together with women's equality with men, make wives so independent of their husbands as cannot possibly be the case in any other country. Not the dead letter of the law, but the newly established institutions, speak the new forms of life under which marriage ceases to play the role of women's only refuge.

The development which shows the tendency towards communal responsibility are communal eating in co-operative or municipal dining halls, communal upbringing and education of children in homes, children's settlements, club life, the Pioneer Movement, etc. On the other hand we see in capitalist countries that the marriage question and problems are at the same time family and property questions.

A Protection Before Unknown

The main question raised during the big discussions on marriage in Soviet Russia was that of legal obligation with respect to unregistered marriages, which, according to the new draft laws, are to be considered marriages in fact with respect to the legal position of the wife and children.

It is interesting to note that the question of payment of alimony for the child born out of wedlock has been newly regulated in such a manner as to show that Soviet legislation supports the principle that the weaker or weakest party stands most in need of protection, **a fact which has already made men complain that women have more rights than they.**

Men no Longer Privileged Sex

According to the law of 1918, the father had to pay one-third of his income for the child born out of wedlock. Whoever was claimed by the woman as the father had to pay. If, in order to deny his fatherhood, the man brought forward one or more friends who also declared themselves to be the father of the child, each one of them had to pay. Naturally, this practice soon disappeared of its own accord when it was discovered that no advantage was to be gained by it. For no longer is this Czarist Russia, or a capitalist state, where no one had to pay as soon as fatherhood became doubtful.

And as it was found that harm would accrue to the child if it could be said that it had several fathers, it was decreed in the new law that whoever is designated by the mother as the father must pay. In doubtful cases the party who is in a better economic position is held responsible. If the father is unemployed the first debt he has to settle as soon as he obtains work is the upkeep of the child.

As in cases of divorce, so also here, the court proceedings are short, and every aid is given to the woman and the child as the weaker parties.

In dealing with these questions existing conditions are taken into account. At the All Union Conference of Communal Women Organizers held recently the Conference expressed itself unanimously for the legal protection for unregistered marriages.

Conclusions

The writer concludes her remarkable article with the words "Unhappy wives, unhappy husbands, brutality out of love, unhappy marriages—all are disappearing in the Soviet Union. The martyred figure of the peasant woman who 'for love's sake allows herself to be exploited, ill-treated and oppressed,' is also disappearing, because she has the protection of the Soviet against the brutalities of the husband. Unhappy marriages ordained by the parents into which sons and daughters (especially daughters) are forced because of material consideration, are also disappearing, because the sons and daughters have now the protection of the Soviets against the parents. The selling of daughters and wives in the East is also disappearing, and with it a portion of the middle ages, a source of misery and suffering for thousands of women."

All of these are already hard facts in Soviet Russia which are confirmed a thousand-fold by the new life, by its new forms of community of interests, which have their own source in an utterly different organization of production.

In the Workers' State the solution of the marriage problems is not attempted by paper decrees, by high-brow reflections, which are utterly helpless in the face of decay within the family of capitalist society. It is accomplished by revolutionizing deeds, by practical construction work of the Soviets, which is cultural and educational, by improving the existing reality and existing facts on the basis of practical experience.

It is this that makes the way in which problems are dealt with in the Workers' State so different from the way the marriage problem is treated in the rest of the countries of the world.

F.C.

SOMETHING WRONG SOMEWHERE
By Trevor Maguire

March 1927, pp. 6-8.

When the six o'clock whistle blew the girls in the laundry went to the locker room and changed into street clothes. They were too tired to talk much. Since seven in the morning each hour, except lunch time, had been filled with monotonous toil in a stifling atmosphere.

Lizzie Lindsay and her friend, Anna Banks, left the building together.

"Well, my dear," said Anna, "I'm darn glad that my days in that dump are about ended."

"What do you mean?" asked Lizzie. "Have you got another job?"

"Not exactly another job, Liz, but I'm going to leave. If you promise not to say a word about it to any of the other girls I'll tell you a secret."

"Alright," agreed Lizzie, "I'll promise."

Slipping her hand beneath her friend's arm Anna said softly: "I'm going to be married two weeks from to-night."

"Married!" Lizzie was very much surprised. "Who to? Tell me all about it."

"To a boy that drives one of the company's trucks."

"How long have you been going together, Anna? You have kept it pretty quiet."

"About three months," said Anna. "And he's just crazy about me. He wasn't anxious to marry me at first, but I saw what he wanted and stood him off, and one night he popped the question, and I said yes."

"Do you love him very much, Anna?"

"Oh, yes, I think I do. I tell you what, Liz," Anna added fiercely, "I'm so darn sick of working I'd do anything to get away from it. What kind of a life have you and I got? Working six days a week and resting up on Sundays! Every day, every week, every month, every year, it's just the same, no matter what kind of a job we have. If we want a new dress we have to half starve ourselves for months to save the price. I'm fed up looking through the papers for sales. I'd like to go into a store for once and buy what I needed without waiting to see if there was a sale on some place. And remember, Liz, you and I are not getting any younger, and I for one want to have a little fun before I get too old. I'm going to have one grand bustup anyway. Sometime ago I made up my mind I'd marry the first nice boy I met, and if you take my advice you'll do the same. If you are careful and play a good game you can always land them."

"Well, good-bye, dear, I have to hurry home and get ready. Bill and I are going to look for rooms tonight."

When Lizzie reached the small single room she called home she threw her hat on a table, kicked off her shoes, and dropped on the bed. Closing her eyes she thought of what Anna had said.

Lizzie had few girl friends and no intimate boy friends. She was not what is called "a good mixer." She had a speaking acquaintance with some young men, but none of them interested her, and she had refused so often invitations to go dancing and boating that she was no longer asked. At times in the evenings the loneliness of her little room enveloped her like a cloud, and then, unable to shake off the terrible depression, she walked the city streets for hours, walked herself into a condition of physical exhaustion so that on her return, sleep would come quickly and be sound. On those lonely excursions she unconsciously made mental notes of the young men she noticed, picking out ones she fancied she might like, or even love. The sight of a young couple chattering light-heartedly on their way to some place of amusement was an actual blow to her depressed spirit.

As Lizzie lay now on her bed trying to rest her fatigued body, her mind became unusually restless. Anna was going to be married, had deliberately and cold-bloodedly enticed a young man into marriage so that she might have a little fun, get a kick out of life. He also had to undertake to feed, clothe and shelter Anna for life, and perhaps they would have a family. Was Anna fair in this? Was it fair to burden her lover, whose wages were rather small, and who might be thrown out of employment any time, with such a tremendous responsibility? Lizzie knew some married women working in the laundry who had either to support an unemployed husband or assist him in providing for their children. All those women said they wished they had never got tied up. "If I had only know then what I know now!" they would say. There was something wrong, Lizzie realized; something wrong somewhere, either with people themselves or with their ideas of life and their customs, but the solving of the great problem was beyond her. Marriage might be a relief to a young girl's loneliness, but how often did it bring happiness?

Feeling another fit of the blues coming on, Lizzie sprang up, dressed and went out. She decided to dissipate to the extent of going to a movie; perhaps the comedy film would brighten her up. But the comedy, instead of being funny, was a piece of ridiculous buffoonery, and failed to amuse. The feature film, however, aroused her to hatred and then self-pity. As the photographs flicked by on the screen Lizzie felt a strong hate for the heroine, not because of her rare beauty, but because she had so much of everything; servants of all kinds, beautiful gowns and jewels, an elaborately furnished home, gorgeous motor cars. This fortunate woman did not have to sweat in a laundry all day, and to cap a life of ease and luxury the woman had added happiness in love; the closing scene showed her and her lover in a close embrace, lip to lip, arms about each other. Why, questioned Lizzie, should some people have so much of everything and others so little? There was something wrong somewhere.

More depressed than when she left it Lizzie returned to her room and went to bed. For hours she lay wide awake. One thought went through her mind again and again: Anna is going to be married. She turned and twisted until, towards dawn, she got up and took asperin tablets to induce sleep.

The next morning, being Sunday, Lizzie slept late, and after making a cup of tea over the gas ring in her room, prepared to make her weekly visit to a married sister, Mrs. Watson, who lived in a distant part of the city. Usually the journey was made on foot, but to-day Lizzie was feeling so fagged out she took a street car. Before starting out she had applied a little rouge to her cheeks and powdered the dark circles under her eyes.

Mr. Watson was a factory worker with a fairly steady job, for which he devoutly thanked God. He was very religious, going to church Sunday morning and evening, teaching a class in Sunday school in the afternoon, and attending the men's club of the church Wednesday night, and prayer meeting Friday night. He liked to talk to Lizzie about the state of her soul and where she was going to spend eternity, and during the Sunday dinner would tell what the morning text had been, how the preacher had developed it and the lesson to be learned therefrom. After dinner, when he left for Sunday school, he took the two oldest children with him.

When he had gone Mrs. Watson and Lizzie cleared the table and washed and dried the dishes.

"Did you know Anna Banks was going to be married?" Lizzie asked her sister.

"No," replied Mrs. Watson.

"Well, she is, but don't tell anybody, for I promised her to keep it a secret."

"Just think of that!" exclaimed Mrs. Watson. "What on earth does she want to get married for? You young girls don't know when you are well off."

"What did you get married for, then?" asked Lizzie.

"Because I wanted a man, I suppose, but if I could have seen ahead a dozen years I would have died an old maid, believe me. I tell you, Lizzie, marriage is not worth it. Here I am with five children, that came one after the other as fast as they could. I hardly ever get out of this house, and it nearly drives me mad sometimes thinking that I have GOT to be here and get three meals every day; I have GOT to wash and dress the children every morning and undress and put them to bed every night; I have GOT to make the beds and sweep and sew. I can't see any rest ahead until they are grown up, and by that time I'll be so worn out I won't feel like doing anything else, even if I want to."

"You don't intend to have any more, do you?" Lizzie asked.

"Not much," said Mrs. Watson emphatically, "not me! I was a fool to have so many. But Watson says it is God's will, let them come. I asked him if it was God's will to make a human incubator out of me, why didn't He get Watson a job that paid more money so we could bring them up right and give them a good education. We aren't bringing them up—we're dragging them up! And all Watson could say was: 'We mustn't question God's will.' It's me that has the kids, not Watson; it's me that has to slave sixteen hours a day for them, not him. I might just as well be tied to a stone wall with a ball and chain! I tell you, Lizzie, things are not right for we women; there's something wrong somewhere!"

After tea Lizzie went back to her room and at nine o'clock went to bed, wanting to get a good night' rest, for the next day was work day.

Sleep, however, would not come to her. There was no doubt about it, marriage was not worth while, but what was a young girl to do? Was she to spend her life alone living like a hermit? Over and over her mind insisted that Anna was going to get married soon. It pictured Anna and her husband in intimate scenes, lavishing caresses on each other.

At eleven, in a condition bordering on hysteria, Lizzie rose and dressed carefully, put on her one pair of silk stockings, used lipstick and powder puff recklessly, and then went out.

Walking along the street she met a man who eyed her closely. When she smiled at him he approached, and raising his hat said: "Good-night. Are you walking or going some place?"

"Oh, I am just walking," Lizzie replied.

"That's good! So am I! But where do we go from here?"

"Can you suggest a place?"

"Oh, that's easy, girlie," he said with a smile. Stepping to the curb he hailed a passing taxi, and after assisting Lizzie in, muttered an address to the driver; got in himself and pulled the door shut with a bang.

A WORKING MAN SPEAKS HIS MIND ABOUT WORKING-CLASS MARRIAGES

September 1927, pp. 12-14.

I read the following article in a paper called The Western Tribune. This paper poses as a conservative, liberal, labor, progressive paper, but is actually a humbug. The article is entitled, "Married Men Ahead in Attaining Wealth." Now read it.

"Marriage is the best financial investment a man can make, according to a survey just completed in Chicago, an average being struck from 700,000 returns. The survey was made on the tax situation with a view of reaching conclusions on economy and money-saving.

"The survey shows that at 24 years of age, the average husbands have about five per cent. less property, money in bank and taxable wealth than the average bachelor of the same age.

"But when both reach the age of 28, the married man is three per cent. ahead and continues to distance the bachelor each succeeding year. The cost of marriage sets the husbands back a trifle at the start. But when both reach the age of 38, the married man will average, in proportion to numbers, 17 per cent. more taxable wealth than the bachelor, and at 48 he will be 20 per cent. ahead, despite the expense of larger home, children, heavier wardrobe and living costs.

"The deduction is that the married man works harder and steadier, saves more and is more intensive in developing his business ability."

Taking this from the working-class point of view, we know that the great mass of the workers are not able to save much from the meagre wages they receive. It also shows the role women of the working class are forced to play under capitalism. She is, in many cases, used as a lure to make a better slave of the male slave, or that is what is expected of her.

During the great massacre of 1914-18 she was used to get him to go to war, to slaughter and to be slaughtered.

I have been in the position of seeing hundreds of girls working in departmental stores and factories, girls of fifteen to twenty, getting tired of slaving for such small pay and long hours, and hanging on to the job hoping some guy will come along and marry them. I have even seen a girl of sixteen ask a boy of nineteen, at a place where I was one time working, if he would marry her, as her home life was a misery to her.

But the great number of these girls do not seem to think of the greater slavery and misery of marriage, under a wage slave system, turns out to be in 85 per cent. of cases—the getting up in the early hours of the morning to get what is generally termed "the bread-winners' breakfast," getting the kids off to school, and then, in a great many cases going to work daily themselves, having to come home and do another day's work there, cleaning, mending, washing, etc.

Marriage, as constituted under this capitalist system, is just a convenience for most of the working class, and the last war to end war proves my statement, as any one who takes the trouble will find by looking up the statistics of the quick marriages performed in those days. I could write some very interesting things, and also some very disgusting matter on that subject, especially of England, France and Belgium.

In Canada we have seen workers interested in the Labor Movement who have become holders of property, that is, possessed of a wife (for that is what most of them look upon the woman as) who have dropped right out of the movement, as they did not want to interest their wives in the Labor Movement, for they feared they might lose a little of the interest in them.

Unless both sexes understand their class position beforehand, I consider marriage, as constituted under this wage slave system, a useful weapon in the hands of the masters, as they are the ones who profit by it. First there is the cannon fodder, and slaves, created by the children of such marriage; second, the male slaves are better and more easily satisfied; and third, the male slave can be more easily used to scab in times of lockout and strikes.

Marriage, to-day, for the working class, and for that matter for the other class, is based upon what "gain" we can get out of it. It is not for "comradeship." It seems to me to be just what Madam Kolanti definitely named it, "legalized prostitution."

I recognize that there are some few exceptions to the general rule in spite of the system of capitalism. I am one of those who want a change.

A. Padgham

"AS MR. CALVERTON SEES NEW RUSSIA'S MORALS"
[Excerpt]

[Editorial]

November 1927, pp. 6-7.

[...]

Marriage and Divorce Laws

"Under the Czar marriage had fallen entirely into the hands of the clergy.... Marriage now is entirely a civil function. All the old impediments to marriage—religions, prohibitions and the like, are destroyed. The empty noise about the 'nationalization of women' is nothing more than myth. Instead of the nationalization of women, what is to be found is the emancipation of women. The marital laws of the U.S.S.R. give no right to the man which is not granted to the woman.

"The inequality of sexes which is prevalent throughout the rest of the Western World, the double code of morality, have no existence in Russia of To-day. The laws of nineteenth century England, which reduced woman to a chattel, without the semblance, economic or legal rights, seem the attributes of a barbarous civilization compared with the rights and freedom of the new woman in Soviet Russia.

"The new sex attitude in Soviet Russia is based upon the principle that the matter of sex relationship in itself does not constitute a social problem unless children are involved. Marital relationships between the sexes are regulated by registration, the same as in any other country. It is in divorce that the U.S.S.R. deviates from the Western standard. The first consideration in the case of divorce is that of the children. This is the social side of the problem. If there are no children divorce is singularly simple. If two people find their marital life marred by incompatibility of temperament and reaction, they can get a divorce on that ground.

HOW THE WICKED BOLSHIES NATIONALIZE THEIR WOMEN

January 1928, pp. 10-11.

Gee, how I shuddered when I used to read that women were nationalized in the Land where the Bolshies live!

I must admit I was not altogether sure what was meant by this. But the newspapers gave me the impression that when women walked along the street that men, vicious and ugly looking, simply grabbed them and took them off somewhere and used them as they liked. Honestly, I thought that nationalization of women meant a terrible, terrible sort of prostitution.

As you may suppose, my fear caused me to read everything I could lay my hands on about the Bolsheviks and the Soviets. And so little by little I found out the truth, for truth will out, you know.

I found out that it was all bunkum about the women being nationalized in a harem sort of way. From what I have read from books and articles written by reliable persons who have been to Soviet Russia, I really should not mind the kind of nationalization they have there.

Only the other day I read an article that was in one of our local papers (it astonished me to find it in a master-class paper) and this article told that Soviet Russia was the only country that has a woman ambassador and women as heads of important state departments, to say nothing of the numbers of women who were members of the local Soviets.

Sure, women are nationalized, but so is everything else. That's the beauty of the whole thing. Nothing is left out. Everyone and everything is taken care of. The railways are nationalized, they belong to the people. The factories, mills and mines are nationalized; they too, belong to the people. In fact, everything of social value is nationalized, all belong to the people, and mark you, the people are the workers and peasants, or farmers, as we say in Canada.

Now it is easy to see that this nationalization of things means that the people must fit themselves into this nationalization process, and so they, too, have the appearance of being nationalized, and this means not only the women, but the men and children, too, bless you.

And it seems that all this nationalization is done through the workers' and peasants' state, that is, the institution of the workers' and peasants' government. And as this government is elected by the workers and peasants themselves you will quite understand why those who work receive the benefits.

In other countries the opposite is the case. Were it not a serious matter it would make one laugh, but in other countries, and Canada is one, the workers send their masters or their masters' representatives, the lawyers, to parliament and put them into power. And what do the masters do when they get there? Why they look after themselves. And the poor, silly workers, have to cry on the outside, "Please give us old age pensions." "Please give us unemployment insurance." "Please do not let the soldiers shoot at us when we are on strike." And "Please say we can strike."

It is clear to me now that the governments of the masters only wanted to frighten us so that the women would not want to have a government like the one they have in Soviet Russia. Well, one day, I am sure, they will wake up and find they have been fooled. Speed the Day.

A.I.

THE HOLLINGER MINE DISASTER.
The Federation's Letter to the Timmins League.

March 1928, pp. 6-7.

February 15th, 1928.

TO THE TIMMINS WOMEN'S LABOR LEAGUE

Dear Sisters and Comrades:

On behalf of the Executive Committee of the Canadian Federation of Women's Labor Leagues, we extend through you our deepest sympathies to the wives and children of those who were the victims of the Timmins mining disaster. We are filled with sorrow, because of the suffering this terrible disaster has brought to the mining community of Timmins and especially to the Finnish section of that community.

But, dear comrades, mere sympathy is not enough—it is but a feeling that overwhelms for the moment and then passes away. We must recognize the fact that the early days of sorrow which our bereaved sisters and their children will endure will be followed by the stern realities of life—the Struggle to Live.

It is in this connection we desire to bring to your attention the fact that we note already a question has been raised concerning Compensation and the right of our Finnish women comrades to this Compensation because their marriage form is not recognized by Canadian law. We ask your League to take this matter up immediately with the Union representatives in Timmins and ask them to see to it that our Finnish women comrades are not put on one side because of this. They have a right to the full Compensation and must dispute any decision that is made by the authorities which would rob them of that right.

And the future, comrades, is before you, too. All of us have been too in-different to the chief safety device the workers have, which is UNIONISM. We have not encouraged our husbands to join the Union, or to attend to the business of the Union if they are already members. And yet it is through the Union that working conditions as well as wage rights are demanded. There-fore, it is up to you, at this time, to use all the influence you have to help along Unionism in your district, for as you can see clearly now, it is Union-ism and safety for your husbands, or golden profits for Hollinger investors.

We ask you not to hesitate to call upon us for any assistance you may need to help along your work.

We remain, your Sisters and Comrades,

The Executive Committee of the C. F. of W. L. L.
President, Ellen Machin,
Secretary, Florence Custance.

COMPANIONATE MARRIAGE

April 1928, pp. 12-13.

Ben B. Lindsay, Judge of the Juvenile Court of Denver, originator of the term "Companionate Marriage," has been much criticized for his ideas and conclusion of companionate marriage, and legalized birth control, as a rem-edy for the "failures" of youth that have passed before him during his many years in the Juvenile Court.

One of the criticisms has appeared in a recent number of the Outlook—written by Dr. Joseph Collins, of New York, a medical practitioner and author. While we could not agree to all that Dr. Collins has to say, yet it is not without interest. He says in part "his opposition to birth control is be-cause it makes youth selfish, and that in the event of children being born to the "companionate" married that their parents assume the responsibility of caring and providing for them. This could only be done by those that could afford it, and not by the working class."

This shows us that the remedy of companionate marriage, like all other social service remedies, does not meet the need of the working class.

This is why we need a working-class movement, working-class literature and The Woman Worker, as an educator for working women. But we be-lieve Judge Lindsay had this in mind when he asked for legalized birth control with it.

Dr. Collins, after debating the inconstancy of human nature and how it might be helped, says: "There is one instrument to shape the human race,

enlightenment; it might be called education were not that word used syn-
onymously with learning—when the fundamental principles of biology,
physiology, psychology and sociology are taught in the schools at the expense of algebra, history and rhetoric. Then race improvement and
individual happiness will gain momentum." This we agree to, beginning
with sociology; in fact it takes in all the others.

Dr. Hardie, of the Social Hygiene Organization of Toronto, is a great advocate of early marriages as a stabilizer of youth.

But when Dr. Hardie lectured before a Hamilton audience—on social
hygiene—he did not touch upon the economic side of it. We ask: How can
young men earning $17 dollars per week provide for a future home to
bring his bride to? How could a girl earning but the Ontario minimum
wage of $12.50 per week—without unemployment—without mornings
off in the dull season—provide a full "Hope Chest" no matter how full of
hope her own chest might be? We know it is not sufficient to pay board and
appear as a business girl is expected to, and which is an economic necessity these days.

Judge Lindsay says he is in favor of Al Smith for the Presidency of the
United States, provided the Governor does not let his religion dictate his attitude towards marriage and birth control.

Meanwhile, let us march forward to economic liberty—the only way to
solve the working-class youth problem, but also the problems connected
with childhood, middle life and old age.

Janet Inman.

LETTERS WE HAVE RECEIVED
Too Dear at Twenty a Month — So Married

April 1928, p. 16.

Some time ago I met a friend of mine whose wife had died and left him
with three small children and he had to hire a housekeeper to look after
them, paying her $20 a month. I happened to run into him again the other
day and, after the usual greeting, he said, "You know, I'm married again." I
said I had not heard about it. So he said, "You know I had a housekeeper and
was paying her $20 a month, but I couldn't afford to keep it up, so we got
married." Is not this interesting?

A.P.

2. Domestic Labour

TRADE MARKS AND LABELS
By a Supporter

November 1926, pp. 6-7.

Mistress Housewife—when you go to shop to buy food and clothing for your family, and tools for your own work, and furnishings for your home, etc., do you give any thought to your purchases beyond their price and their use? Well, if you do not, you should.

We know, as a rule, the average housewife, like the good housewife she is buys the most of the best for the least amount of money. This is good buying.

But how does our good housewife know she is getting value for her money? Well, she has become accustomed to rely on certain goods and these goods are known to her by their trade marks or their labels. These trade marks and labels are manufacturers' signs. These signs are registered with the Government, and by this means they obtain protection for their products. Also, these signs aid the manufacturers in advertising their wares. We all know that attractive advertising takes the product more than half-way to the consumer. This is why so much money is spent on advertising.

But there are labels and labels, as the saying goes. There is another kind of label—for the moment, we admit, a rather uncommon label, but a label that should have a more significant meaning to working women than the trade marks and labels of the manufacturers. This label is THE UNION LABEL. Look on the front cover of THE WOMAN WORKER and you will see a label with the number 35 beside it. This label speaks volumes. It tells us that the place where THE WOMAN WORKER is printed is a FAIR SHOP. This means that the men are paid the UNION RATE OF WAGES and that ALL OTHER CONDITIONS OF LABOR ARE FAVORABLE TO THE UNION.

In the great majority of cases when we buy goods without a union label it will be almost safe to say that these goods were made under sweatshop conditions, that is, by workers working for low wages and, in many cases, in unsanitary surroundings.

Some times manufacturers put on campaigns for HOME INDUSTRY. BUY IN CANADA is their slogan. This is all very well. But when we buy we want to know that the workers are receiving more than work only. We want to know that for that work they are receiving wages that will allow them to live decent lives.

Particularly does this apply to the clothes we wear. When we women buy our hosiery and our underclothing we certainly look for the labels of the manufacturers, but that is all. Unfortunately not any of these carry the union label. They cannot, because the workers in the textile factories in Canada are not organized. How do we know that the hundreds of girls working in these factories are getting decent wages and working under conditions which will not injure their health? WE DO NOT KNOW, but we can guess THAT ALL IS NOT AS IT SHOULD BE.

So, Mistress Housewife, when you buy husband's clothing, your children's clothing, and your own, as well as the other things you need, do not worry so much about the manufacturer's label—if the UNION LABEL is there the goods are bound to be all right. You will know that the clothing was made in a sanitary shop, by workers working under fair conditions, and at the union rate of wages.

Labels may be small things, but they may have big meanings. THIS IS SO WITH THE UNION LABEL. Demand THE UNION LABEL.

DEMAND WAGES FOR WIVES

February 1927, p. 6.

The Provincial Council of Women (Ontario) visited Premier Ferguson. They presented to him a number of demands. One of the most interesting was that husbands should be compelled to give a portion of their salary or income to their wives as wages for managing the home. They presented a clear case as to the necessity for this.

This demand cannot be applied in the case of working-class housewives. It would be safe to say that the majority of workingmen after receiving their pay envelopes from their bosses, place them in the hands of their wives.

The domestic problem of the workingman and his wife is to eke out the wage in food, clothing and shelter. Their struggle is the struggle for bread.

SCHOOL DEMANDS OF THE LABOR PARTY

April 1927, pp. 8-10.

"The Supremacy of Science in the Teaching of Children—The Elimination of All Religious and Semi-Religious Forms and Ceremonies."

This demand has proven itself to be the most contentious of all the educational demands. As a matter of fact it is merely a demand for the fulfilment of the present Ontario School Act. No special provision is embodied in the Act for the receiving or giving of religious education.

Yet Bible reading, and without question Bible explanations by the teacher, as well as religious ceremonies, form a part of the education of the children of the workers.

The popular opinion on this question is that this is the source of moral training for the children. Without Bible reading our children will grow up rogues, vagabonds, and thieves.

Labor demonstrates its contrary opinion on this point by making the above quoted demand. Labor's stand on the question of morals is that these are born out of the social conditions which prevail. If these conditions are bad, then morals reflect these conditions. We cannot expect figs from thistles.

By merely arguing the point we cannot truly convince. The best way to convince is to give proof, or examples.

A few weeks ago Miss NeTannis Semmens, Field Secretary of the School of Religious Education for Children's Workers, when speaking at a large meeting of mothers in Old St. Andrew's, Toronto, made some interesting statements concerning THE RIGHTS OF CHILDHOOD. The most outstanding, and the most remarkable, because it was made by a Christian worker, was the following: "That, as a result of a national survey, it was found that THE STATUS OF THE CHILDREN IN RUSSIA IS HIGHER THAN THAT OF THE CHILDREN IN GREAT BRITAIN, WHICH, OF COURSE, INCLUDES CANADA."

Now, here we have a woman, a Christian, whose word will not be disputed because of her standing in the Christian world, declare that the standing of the children in Russia is higher than that of the children in Canada. This, to be said of a country where, as is so well known, RELIGIOUS TEACHING AND CEREMONIES are not allowed in the schools.

The speaker may not have realized to what extent she made admission to the contentions of Labor—Not religious teaching, not Bible reading, but knowledge, knowledge of LIFE ITSELF, and the conditions in which that life is placed, form the basis of the teaching in the schools in Soviet Russia.

In our schools much is taught that could very well be left alone, and much that should be learned is carefully kept from the children. No attention is paid to the life of the children, that is, their existence, and why they should safe-guard it. The social outlook on life is foreign to the children. Some may say, "Why do we not allow the children to become members of the Junior Red Cross, sell tags for Hospitals, teach them to be kind to animals?" "Are not all these social in outlook?"

These are merely apologies. They do not touch the fringe of the outlook we have in mind.

The outstanding and appalling of all the ignorances of our children is that in relation to their understanding of Life.

Our whole concern is to teach the child to be a good, docile wage-earner, or, to use the disagreeable but more popular term, wage slave. This is because our society is a society of classes, ordered and governed by the class who exploit the needs of life as well as the worker for the sake of profits.

Such a society thinks only of its own appetite. It cares little about the children of the present, and nothing about the generations of the future.

In place of Bible reading, which Labor claims can very well be left to the churches and other religious institutions, of which there are an abundance, it is required that scientific knowledge shall be imparted to the children. What more important knowledge can be imparted than the knowledge of their own bodies, how and why they function, and the process of life propagation. It is high time we ceased to deceive our children by telling them that they came from a "cabbage bed" or "the stork brought them" or "they came in the doctor's bag." Such "moral lies" show we are ashamed of ourselves, ashamed of our actions, ashamed of natural human processes, ashamed of the truth of Life Itself.

It is not without good reason that people who investigate the educational systems of Soviet Russia are astounded that children are looked upon as young human beings, having their own outlook, with their own rights. In no other country are children treated so. Rather the opposite is the case—they are looked upon as nuisances, little creatures to be tolerated because they are here.

The writer of this article spent five months in Soviet Russia in the year 1922. This stay provided a good opportunity to study the social life of the people of that country under the developing New Social Order. The most interesting study of all, that is to one interested in children and teaching, was the treatment of Child Life and its standing in the new order of things.

A visit to one of the educational institutions will never be forgotten. This particular school was the School of Natural Science. The school house was formerly the summer residence of a very rich man. It was set in spacious grounds. These grounds the children were using for their practical work. The school house itself was under the entire management of the children, the teachers were advisers. The school curriculum was one that should form a part of the education of every child. As a result of this training, all things pertaining to life and necessary for life were known to the children. Their practical work consisted of gardening and looking after pet animals. Life and its propagation was no mystery to these children. They knew its course in plant life, they knew its course in animal life, and they knew it in human life. Quite naturally and frankly one boy, a lad of fourteen, told us about their pet rabbits and their young. In fact, their knowledge of the Mendel theory would put university students to shame.

The education of the children in Soviet Russia is scientific. It is also beautiful because it is so real. Such a scheme of things would be impossible in our public schools, because it vibrates with freedom and is freed from every form of superstition.

The demand of the Labor Party is not born out of mischievous wickedness, as many of our opponents infer, but is, instead, an attempt to make the best use of the limited years of education granted our children, so that when our children leave school we shall be assured they know something of their life's tasks and duties other than those connected with obtaining Food, Clothing and Shelter.

F.C.

MONTREAL
League Organizes a Camp for Workers' Children

June 1927, p. 14.

The Women's League in Montreal will have a camp for children this year in one of the most beautiful spots around here, in the Laurentian Mountains.

Of course there are many kinds of camps. Especially are there lots of Charity Camps, and it is painful to see how the children sent to these camps are exploited for patriotic purposes. I happened to be in one of these camps. I spoke to some of the children and they told me they will never go to such a camp again.

But our camp will be altogether different. It will be run differently and the children will learn something of the co-operative side of life, the life that they will sooner or later have to build for themselves. We want them to see something of the communal system and how it differs from the present system of society.

Therefore it should be in the interest of every class conscious worker to send his or her children to the Camp to help the work.

It is also important for every working class woman to join the Labor League Movement, because women will have to learn to struggle with the men to abolish slavery and to fight for a better system in which the working class can enjoy a fuller, better, and more enjoyable life.

B. Shachter, Secretary.

LIFE IN A MINING CAMP IN ALBERTA

November 1927, pp. 10-11.

News of the general disorder in the world comes to the apathetic miners and their wives through the press of the master class. Even this place was a little moved by the horrible murder of the two working-class victims, Sacco and Vanzetti, although many who came to the protest meetings heard of the case for the first time. There are some people here who never read the newspapers, so when they heard us talking of Sacco and Vanzetti they wondered why justice could not be shown these men. And what a funny idea they have of justice! They really believe that there is justice for everyone, rich and poor alike.

There is one day when our little town is full of life. This day is pay day. The people hurry and bustle about as if eager to get rid of the few pennies they earn. Much of their earnings is taken to the liquor store. It might be said that the owners of these stores ride around in big cars and they certainly think they are far superior to the miners.

I have often walked the full length of the Main Street, which, despite its shortness, has plenty of business establishments which are totally dependent on the miners. Besides the many business establishments, we have many lodges and societies which try their best to get every penny from the miners. These organizations have many dances, teas, whist drives and the like, in order to drive from the workers' minds all thoughts of their own welfare.

The union men give scarcely any regard to their wives and children. True, last year there was a picnic at which the wives and children of the miners were given ice cream and candy. Our group of women suggested to the union that it should form a woman's auxiliary, although the suggestion was greatly approved, no action has been taken as yet.

But the wives of the miners have changed considerably. They no longer stay at home contentedly to darn, wash and mend while their husbands go out for amusement. They often go to the movies, where they see the finery of the upper class women, which is such a big contrast to their own. So from the movies the women get their pleasure, while the men amuse themselves in the gambling dens and drink shops. It is a sorry thing to tell, but even the class conscious workers do not shun these places; it seems as if they are pleased to be acquainted with drink shop managers.

Here and there on the streets you may see women whose husbands are in the drink shops enjoying the company of drinkers who make a loud noise to show their enjoyment. When the husband seeks other company to that of his wife, the wife does the same thing, and thus we find many homes wrecked.

Not content with robbing the miners of their wages in drink, other forms of pleasure are organized. Just now carnivals are the rage. These are set in an open space, there is a dancing platform and all kinds of games. The men are willing to part with their money for a few hours' pleasure, no matter whether or not the wife will find it difficult to manage with his too small wage. Here we find the workers spending their money for a little but senseless pleasure, while many of the militant workers are in prison suffering confinement because they struggled against wretched conditions. Every spare penny should be spent to help them.

It does seem as if the workers could never arise from their stupor. But our hope is—the youth—the glorious youth. But you may say, how can the youth be glorious in such a life? But we who have some hope for the future should help our youth to understand their task and how they can carry on the work we know must be done for the workers' freedom.

I know this education will not be easy. We shall not receive encouragement from outside forces. It is easy to see the difference given to our teaching and that given, say, for the sake of an example, the Salvation Army. The Army is allowed to stand on the streets every night to preach, but we are not. The government is willing to have every kind of religion supported, but it must suppress every rebellious idea that enters the workers' heads.

It is true we try to agitate in the unions. I have been successful in getting locals of the union to subscribe to some workers' papers, but the members seldom if ever take the papers home to read.

The women, although not as advanced as the men, will not take much educating to have their eyes open. At the present time they are laboring under the old ideas planted through capitalist class education in the schools. But once they are started they will advance in such a manner as to force the men to take action in getting the necessary changes in this little mining camp.

A Miner's Wife.

EDUCATED HOUSEWIVES

December 1927, pp. 5-6.

So the "housewife" is about to be educated. Good! That we are in black need of much knowledge along the many lines is a sad and serious fact.

To be sure we are not entirely ignorant: most of us have taught the three R's, and we've been trained to be respectable and religious, to be patient and patriotic, and above all, to be sober and THRIFTY.

Millions of us have learned these lessons well and faithfully, but somehow the knowledge has little or no cash value. With all our thrift, our patriotism, etc., etc., very few of us are able to secure comfort and safety for our families or even moderate independence for our old age.

Our children have to work in mill or factory, often before they are fully grown, and always before they are fairly educated, and the difficulty of paying the winter's coal bill is hardly settled before the next winter is upon us.

Thus it has been—and so it continues to be.

So if there is any system of education that will explain to us why we should not be discontented with such a state of things, we are willing to listen.

But we can't help feeling that we have the right to be discriminating in our choice of teachers. Unless our education is actually related to our lives as workers we have no time to waste on it. And so, if Mrs. Flora Drummond, who was on this continent recently, or anyone else, wishes for pupils, we must demand certain qualifications—we would ask, for instance, that they first answer a few questions which occur to us at random, but which relate to our more immediate problems.

First: Why, in a rich and almost empty country like Canada, with more than a million people able and eager to work, should there be such a thing as "Hard Times," with unemployment and so much poverty?

Second: Is it even decent that we should parade this poverty by advertising its great increase in the press through FRESH AIR FUNDS in summer, and SANTA CLAUS stuff in winter?

Third: Why should the hardest and most necessary work be always poorly paid—such as the section men on the railroads?

Fourth: Why is it thought quite natural to explain to visitors when taking them through the shabby part of the town, that this is where the "working people" live?

Fifth: Why are workers frequently put in jail or even shot down, as in Colorado to-day, merely because they are insisting on the right to live decently? Does government only exist for the protection of the employer?

And we have hosts of other questions—all of them having to do with our daily lives—so you see we must claim the right to "pick" our teachers. In the meantime, however, quite a few of us are learning a little, directly, through experience, and sometimes, indirectly, after we get through reading the "bargain list" in the paper. Sometimes the description of the bargains calls to our attention the huge quantities of things that are now produced by the marvellous new machinery—the modern miracles.

And who is going to keep us from being discontented—that is, if we are not feeble-minded, when we remember who makes the machines, and who operates them, and when we wonder why life is still so hard for us.

I hate to shock Mrs. Flora Drummond, but I fear I shall when I tell her there are a few housewives, even now, who actually believe that no slaves ever produced so much and got so little as the workers of to-day. And as this belief is apt to turn into not only intelligent but an active discontent, at any moment, we doubt if we need to bother with an outside "teacher" after all. Mrs. Drummond has a tall order on hand to explain the discontent now in England and in trying to cure it.

H. D. P.

WHEN WINTER COMES — BUDGETS ARE NOT FAR AWAY

December 1927, p. 15.

Dear Editor,

Very soon the newspapers will be flooded with "Budgets" compiled by women who never kept house in their lives. Soon they will be telling us what "nourishing soup" can be made from bones. They will also tell us how to gather up cinders and wash the ashes from them and then put them back on the fire again. They will tell us how to repair our old boots and clothes.

Now really, my dear women, if this were not sarcasm it would be laughable, because the working class have been doing these things all their lives.

Last winter, in Toronto, we had a dear sweet lady who tells Bible stories in a Mission House telling us how a man, wife and five children could live on $26 per week. After rent, gas, electric light and clothes had been budgeted, she had to admit there was nothing for candy. Also she forgot sickness, reading matter, fruit, dental treatment, and the rest of those things which are necessary these days. All she thought the working class required was a shelter and the cheapest food.

What about the "rainy day" we hear so much about, and what will happen when some employers tell the breadwinner, "Sorry, but you are too old."

These budgets are an insult to working women, and we should not heed them. Working women are always compelled to eke out their housekeeping allowance and stretch a dollar to breaking point. Instead of bothering about budgets we should spend more time thinking about organizing. We should organize to demand MEAT in place of BONES!, wages that will enable us to enjoy life as it ought to be enjoyed, and not crawl through the world thankful for the advice of those who have everything worth while. Join the Women's Labor League—and speed the day.

E. W.

THE STRAP IN TORONTO SCHOOLS

February 1928, pp. 6-7.

During the past few weeks there has been quite a lot of discussion on the merits and the evils of corporal punishment in the schools.

Dr. James L. Hughes, for many years inspector-in-chief of the schools in Toronto, is opposed to corporal punishment. He states as his reason for this that corporal punishment implants fear, and fear has an evil influence on a child's life; it represses and blights.

Dr. Hughes claims, too, that the home life of a child is reflected by the child's conduct at school. Often this is marked by neglect, that is, it is negative, as expressed in terms of Don't—Quit—Stop. To counteract the use of "the strap" by teachers, he urges that higher salaries should be paid to teachers who get results through kindness.

Much of what Dr. Hughes states is quite true. Often we find that home training or lack of home training and school discipline are at variance. If we inquired into this we should find that parents have too little time to spend with their children. The mother with her household cares finds she cannot spare the time to reason with her children, hence she commands and she threatens in order to obtain obedience. Those few who take the time irrespective of household duties are few and far between. Then, again, it must not be overlooked that many married women go out to work; if these women have children it can be easily seen that these children are a law unto themselves. So we see that behind the home conditions there is the larger thing—the economic condition of the home.

As much as it may be disputed, even by teachers themselves, it can be seen that a certain economic condition has a great bearing on the teacher. The teacher knows that he or she must get results. In this process the child is only an instrument, the results mean "livelihood" to the teacher. The method of obtaining results largely depends on the teacher. Some may be blessed with a forbearing nature, others may not have this, and yet this enters very largely into teaching methods.

Many of the existing difficulties could be overcome if other conditions existed, and among these can be mentioned—smaller classes, better training for the teachers, results based on the general tone of the school instead of so much per teacher, and, above all, perhaps, at this moment, higher salaries all round for teachers, for it must be remembered that the mind and temper of a teacher is affected by the stress of making ends meet.

Working-class mothers must pay more attention to this whole question. It is a much bigger thing than appears on the surface. We have a right to demand the best education for our children, and we want good teachers too. This point we want to press home, because the public schools are the places where our children spend one-half of their waking hours, and the other half bears the stamp of the influence of school training.

It is in the interests of our children that we should support the teachers when they make demands for higher wages and fairer conditions under which to get results. Teachers have many things to contend with of which the average parent has no knowledge. A case in point is that of a Toronto teacher who, on receipt of his pay cheque, found he had been stopped half a day's pay for absence from school when this absence was not his fault, but happened because he had been summoned to a court session as a witness.

The Toronto teachers are not getting a square deal all the way round from the Board of Education. The above-mentioned case is a piece of abominable treatment. It will not be far wrong to state that such an arbitrary act would not have occurred in any other place or country.

There is much to be rectified in the schools—methods of teaching, the kind of subjects taught, etc. Some of this can be done by helping the teachers to understand Labor's point of view on many things. The Women's Labor Leagues can do much to help towards this end.

F.C.

Birth Control and Abortion   7

By the 1920s the practice of birth control—by various means including abstinence, the "rhythm method," withdrawal, abortion, and
even for some women in desperate circumstances infanticide—had
a lengthy history in Canada. Most Canadians, however, were reluc-
tant to acknowledge or discuss this reality openly. Privately, women
had always shared with daughters and friends their knowledge and
methods of controlling family size through, for example, the use of
herbs, home-spun recipes (some rather frightful), and vaginal
sponges. Public discussion, however, was limited by lingering Victo-
rian morality and, more importantly, by the fact that the advertising,
sale, and distribution of contraceptive products, devices, and information, had been made illegal in 1892. So too was abortion.
Although it was common knowledge that women determined to
avoid childbirth often risked their lives through self-induced or
"back street" abortions, women seeking abortions and practitioners
offering them were both penalized harshly under the Criminal Code
of Canada. Under these conditions, it is not surprising that a
broadly based birth control movement—with representation from
radicals, reformers, and capitalists—did not fully emerge in Canada
until the 1930s. The appalling and pervasive economic misery of the
Great Depression, and the social and political unrest which accompanied it, eased moral scruples about "artificial" contraception in
favour of more practical, even instrumental, thinking.

It was not middle-class reformers and industrialists, however, who initiated the first round of public debates on the issue
in Canada. Rather, a handful of male and female sex radicals, anarchists, and socialists in the political left had been the first public
promoters of birth control as early as the late 19th century. Among
them were the English socialist couple in British Columbia, Dora

Forster Kerr and R.B. Kerr, who linked the demand for fertility control to a new vision of sexual and social relations between men and women which challenged monogamy and insisted on the importance of women's sexual pleasure and economic independence.

Generally Finnish socialist groups were more frank than their English counterparts, even advertising contraceptive devices and methods in their press. Reluctance in Canadian socialist parties about taking a public stand in favour of fertility control was linked partly to an old fear that such "women's issues" were irrelevant to the working class and diverted precious attention away from the class struggle. Suspicion was also deepened by the lingering association of birth control with the socially conservative views of 19th century English economist Thomas Malthus who saw family limitation as a cure for working-class poverty and unrest.

The positive attention given to birth control in the pages of the *Woman Worker* in the 1920s therefore represented an extension of an earlier but distinctly minority tradition within socialist circles. Through the paper, the practice of limiting family size and its implications for working class freedom were confronted more directly and thoroughly than ever before, and at a time when reformers were still uncomfortable with the whole idea, despite their increasing familiarity with the activities of well-known birth controllers and reformers Margaret Sanger in the United States and Marie Stopes in Britain. Even the highly controversial question of abortion, previously taboo in the left, received limited, though surprisingly frank, attention. Granted birth control, along with most other "women's issues," was still no burning priority for the male Communist Party leadership. But women in the Communist-linked WLLs insisted on championing the causes of birth control and, more generally, sex education, by calling for the de-criminalization of birth control (and occasionally abortion) and the establishment of what they called "Mothers' Clinics." These were to be public institutions where information about fertility control and pre-natal care itself would be readily available to all women, not just to the wealthy who had always had privileged access to information and health care services. If the Communist Party did not applaud the actions and opinions of the WLLs and its Federation, nor did it try to censor them.

The selection of articles reprinted here testify to the personal and political importance of fertility control to many working-class women connected to the Communist Party. Florence Custance had always maintained that birth control was an immediate and pressing need among working-class women. She noted, for example, how membership in the Toronto WLL increased significantly during

1927-28 when the birth control issue was made a priority in the paper and the Federation, and then just as suddenly dropped from sight when this discussion ceased. Her observation of the centrality of reproductive issues for women of the working class was based largely on her experience with the Toronto League, which seems to have been the most vocal and persistent advocate of contraception. It is likely that the high visibility of the issue reflected in part the extent to which the paper was influenced by the Toronto League with which Custance worked. Still, of the many contributors to the debate in the paper, only one, Margaret Crowder writing from Los Angeles, outrightly rejected "scientific" (or "artificial") birth control. All other commentators were supportive, even insistent, that sex education, birth control access, and quality maternity care were all crucial for the liberation of working-class women.

In taking up this platform in the 1920s, the Women's Labor Leagues and other left-wing contributors to the *Woman Worker* separated themselves even farther from the community of white middle-class reformers and feminists who, apart from a few lone individuals, were still opposed to contraception. There is no doubt that the birth control issue was considered too politically contentious at this time for mainstream reformers to consider seriously. Some women reformers had moral and religious concerns about the practice. Some, alarmed by the sharp post-World War I drop in birth rates and by recent waves of immigration from eastern and southern Europe, spouted racist concerns that the British population was already in decline in Canada and needed boosting, not limiting. Some feminists could not reconcile advocacy of birth control with their idealization of motherhood as women's primary role and source of power in the family and the nation. Others worried that artificial contraception, rather than giving women more freedom, would actually decrease their sexual autonomy. After all, without the fear of unwanted pregnancies, what grounds would women have to exercise choice and refuse men's sexual advances when they were not welcome?

The Labor League women and other contributors to the *Woman Worker* also differed in their thinking from the majority of birth control advocates in the United States and Great Britain who, since the nineteenth century, had been heavily influenced by Thomas Malthus' socially and economically conservative argument that the root cause of poverty was overpopulation. Most WLLers distanced themselves from any birth controllers who by neo-Malthusian logic would blame working-class poverty solely on family size, thereby ignoring the most obvious cause—capitalism. In an article reprinted here

("Birth Control and Working Women"), a member of the Toronto WLL attacked the old Malthusian doctrines and re-directed readers' attention to the inadequate size of working-class wages. Large families certainly strained the limited resources of working-class families, and therefore contributed to family impoverishment, but the majority of writers in the *Woman Worker* were too class conscious to accept the notion that birth control alone would ever end working-class poverty. A 1928 editorial ("Immigration—Now Birth Control") warned readers of the wealthy "lords and ladies" in Great Britain who were supporting birth control as a solution to the pressure of unemployment. Turning Malthusian arguments on their head, the editor reminded women that "Capitalism is overpopulated by the parasitic class," and unemployment is caused by capitalism. Mrs. Lillie Broadhurst was unusual in her acceptance of distinctly neo-Malthusian judgements, but Custance, while disagreeing with her, allowed her space to voice her perspective. In a column spanning three monthly issues, Broadhurst pushed family limitation specifically on poor and working-class families, and insisted that it was a "calamity" and a "crime" for workers to have more than two children.

Broadhurst and also Z.L. Burt, who appears to have been a member of the Toronto League, were among the few writers to draw specifically on eugenic arguments linking family planning to "race" improvement. In the context of the Great Depression of the next decade, both neo-Malthusian and eugenicist thinking would take centre stage as white middle-class reformers and industrialists turned increasingly to birth control advocacy, and for some, sterilization, as means to limit the fertility of the poor and the *so-called* "unfit." The sterilization of the mentally ill, legalized in Alberta in 1928 and in British Columbia in 1933, was endorsed by many medical professionals, as well as interwar reformers and feminists of various political stripes, like Agnes MacPhail and Nellie McClung. Following the tradition of earlier socialist women, most contributors to the *Woman Worker*, while not attacking the racism and ableism inherent in eugenicism, generally avoided linking contraception to racial purity. Instead, they focused their discussions on class. Pointing to recent alarming reports documenting the extent of maternal mortality in Canada, they argued most strongly for birth control as a means of securing the health and peace of mind of working-class mothers and their children. Without safe and accessible means of controlling fertility, working-class wives were consumed with worry and burdened with ill health as each pregnancy brought with it little chance of quality pre-natal care, greater pressure on the family budget, and concern for the future of her children. Was it any wonder that it was women of the working class, not the wealthy, who died most often in childbirth? In an article not re-printed here ("Working-Class Mothers—Save Yourselves!" May 1928), Custance relayed the story of one woman from the Peace River District who died in her sixth month of pregnancy, 135 miles from hospital or medical services. "The hen house had to be torn down to provide boards for her coffin," and the family crumbled: the children turned "wild" and her husband became a "wastrel." Moth-ers' Clinics would reduce maternal mortality and improve the health and happiness of working-class family life. This was an argument centering on both collective and individual, though class-based, rights: the collective right of working-class families to reproduce was defended alongside the right of individual working-class women to survival and health through practising family limitation.

Writers in the *Woman Worker* also were motivated to advocate birth control out of concern for the numbers of women who suffered death or injury through abortions either self-induced or obtained at the hands of back-street abortionists. Working-class women fran-tically determined to end a pregnancy were not only subjected to life-threatening procedures, contributors argued, they were also victimized by the high prices charged by practitioners of abortion. Socialists had long pointed to abortion (and also infanticide) as damning evidence of the brutality and immorality of capitalism, and they assumed that in a socialist economic system there would be no reason for women to resort to such desperate measures. The WLLs continued this line of thought, taking a defensive economic ap-proach rather than entertaining any abstract notion of a woman's individual right to end a pregnancy out of personal preference. Only occasionally could contributors be found calling for the legalization not only of birth control information and devices but also abortion. Two examples of this unusually progressive stand are found in the article by the Toronto WLLer entitled "Birth Control and Working Women," and the excerpt from a column applauding the situation of women in post-revolutionary Russia. But most often the argument went that birth control, especially in a socialist context, would do away with the need for abortions and the dangers they entailed for women. The specifically feminist argument for abortion based on women's right to control their own bodies would not gain popularity until a much later period.

The advocacy of birth control and the tentative explorations of the necessity for abortion, especially under capitalism, put those as-sociated with the *Woman Worker* in the vanguard of a movement that would only gain broader popularity in the depressed conditions of the 1930s. By then, however, most advocates were anxious to use birth control as a social and political stabilizer. Family planning was aimed most pointedly at the working classes, especially non-Anglo Canadians and people with physical or mental disabilities who were judged "unfit" to reproduce. Although this mainstream coalition served to increase the general respectability of contraception, and birth control clinics were established in several centres in the 1930s, the popularity of eugenic ideas and social conservatism meant the movement as a whole took a turn to the right. The emerging socialist feminist analysis was overshadowed for the moment, but came to the fore in the 1960s to 1980s, blending insights from the distinctive but overlapping historical traditions of socialism and feminism in Canada.

Further Reading:

- Catherine Annau, "Eager Eugenicists: A Reappraisal of the Birth Control Society of Hamilton," *Histoire Sociale/Social History,* XXVII, 53 (May 1994), 111-134.

- Diane Dodd, "Women's Involvement in the Canadian Birth Control Movement of the 1930s: The Hamilton Birth Control Clinic," in Katherine Arnup, Andrée Lévesque, and Ruth Pierson, eds., *Delivering Motherhood* (London: Routledge, 1990).

- Angus McLaren and Arlene Tigar McLaren, *The Bedroom and the State: The Changing Practices and Politics of Contraception and Abortion in Canada, 1880-1997* (Toronto: Oxford University Press, 1997).

- Angus McLaren, *Our Own Master Race: Eugenics in Canada, 1885-1945* (Toronto: McClelland and Stewart, 1990).

MRS. ANNE KENNEDY SPEAKS ON "BIRTH CONTROL"

February 1927, pp. 8-9.

When asked why the United States Government was afraid to publish statistics of women's deaths as a result of childbirth, Mrs. Kennedy, the field secretary of the American Birth Control League, replied, "That it was not so much fear as it was shame." Mrs. Kennedy claimed that two or three millions of women died each year as a result of child-bearing. She also gave the appalling figure of the practice of self abortion by women as from 5 to 40. This latter was a discovery made through the medium of the Birth Control Clinics, a few of which have been established in some of the States.

Birth control must not be confused with abortion. Birth control could be defined as the prevention of conception. It did away with the dangerous practice of abortion.

In dealing with the attitude of various countries towards birth control, Mrs. Kennedy said that Holland had practised it for fifty years. France had prohibited it as its policy is "cradle competition." Recently Japan had tolerated it. There were four clinics in Tokio. Russia's attitude had been that it had allowed the practice of abortion. Germany had permitted birth control methods.

One of the greatest objectors to birth control in India is Gandhi, who preaches "self-control." The greatest force of opposition in England is the attitude of the Church, but England has some clinics. Despite the opposition of the Roman Catholic Church, individual women of that faith practised birth control. In fact, 30 per cent. of the women who attend the clinics in the U.S. are Roman Catholics.

Uncle Sam's reply to Mussolini, who requested that the United States Government open its doors to permit Italian immigration, because of Italy's state of over-population, is very significant. This reply was, "Your people must stop spawning."

Suppression Brought Forth Its Fruit

Birth control teaching had thrived and advanced as a result of suppression. Mrs. Sanger, who could be called the founder of the present movement in the U.S., had been prosecuted and persecuted, but the movement had grown. Mrs. Sanger, who was a nurse by profession, felt herself morally compelled to take up this teaching because of the great waste of motherhood and womanhood through childbirth in conditions of great poverty. Mrs. Sanger believed in prevention.

The law in the U.S. is still very rigid. Only birth control information is allowed in the case of women who are diseased. The weakly woman with impaired heart, kidneys, or lungs, to whom child bearing would be a decided burden and injury, is not allowed to receive birth control information at the clinics. This prohibition forms the subject of a special Bill which the American Birth Control League has before the Senate.

It was a noticeable thing at the clinics that of all the many women who came for information and assistance, all were married women, with the exception of two cases. This goes to prove how wrong those people are who think that birth control knowledge will result in laxity of morals, and that unmarried women will have recourse to methods.

Birth control was intended to be a measure to cope with the tremendous increase of the world's population, which during the past 100 years had increased out of all proportion to that of the previous years. And birth control knowledge, too, could play some part in making some of the things that were wrong, right.

WORKING CLASS MOTHERS PAY WITH THEIR LIVES FOR CHILDREN
Mothers' Clinics Must Be Established.

March 1927, p. 11.

The press of the Province of Quebec is up in arms because the Sun Life Assurance Company has a special rate against French-Canadian married women. It is claimed the company is unfair. The company answers this charge by giving a few facts.

The company claims that from the period of 1901-1923 the mortality has been 175 per cent of the French-Canadian married women insured in a large number of companies in Canada and the United States.

While "childbirth" claims 7.8 per cent. of these women, other diseases, such as tuberculosis, pneumonia, pleurisy, peritonitis, take heavy tolls.

The company claims that recently it has been able to make some alterations in its rates. These alterations apply to French-Canadian women married to professional and business men.

The statement made by the president of the company speaks volumes and should be heeded by working women. He says: "Too often the wife of a farmer or artisan does not take sufficient rest after the birth of a child, but is up and about in a very few days, attending to the household and other duties at a time when she is physically unfit for tasks that are frequently burdensome and exhausting. One cannot but admire her pluck and sympathize with her difficulties, but the result may be disastrous."

He goes on to state that it is this neglect of health that leads to the other diseases.

This is the fate to which working-class motherhood is condemned. Can this be justified by Church or State? If we want further proof of the conditions that prevail in Canada, let us read what Dr. Helen MacMurchy states in "Child Welfare Work in Canada" (1922). On page 10 it is stated:

"On the list of seventeen civilized nations arranged in order as regards maternal mortality, Canada and the United States stand at the foot of the list. We are **seventeenth in a class of seventeen**. It is a disgrace to us. We must make a better record. Surely the first step in child and maternal welfare is to save the mother and child alive."

Is not this statement damning enough? Is anything more necessary to prove that something must be done to save the lives of mothers? But who will save them? **It is up to working-class mothers themselves**.

Despite condemnation we must make a bold stand for the establishment of MOTHERS' CLINICS. BIRTH CONTROL KNOWLEDGE must be considered a necessity and an immediate means of dealing with a condition of poverty. We must rally to our side all those who will help to SAVE working-class motherhood. But even this is not enough. We must demand higher wages, and support our husbands in their demand for higher wages, in order to keep up a higher standard of health. It is poverty, tortuous poverty, that lies at the root of the terrible death toll of working-class motherhood.

F.C.

A VIEWPOINT OF BIRTH CONTROL

September 1927, p. 12.

There is so much involved in the question of Birth Control that one is at a loss which phase of it is most important. Sometimes the population problem of every country seems to be of the first magnitude. We cannot help wondering how long the human race will go one breeding numerically without a thought to the intelligence or quality of the offspring, and whether or not they will be able to give them opportunity in life.

It is very encouraging to know that the most progressive portions of society are giving their time and holding meetings for the discussion of Birth Control. It is no longer a fad but a necessity.

It is said that religionists offer the strongest resistance to the subject of Birth Control. However, the challenge has gone forth and they must give answer to some of the most pressing questions of the present day.

If organized Christianity is sincere it must tell us why, after the third child, poor people, under our present social system, no longer maintain their self-respect, and all kinds of diseases, especially undernourishment and poverty, set in. Statistics have proved this to be so.

Again, the church does not believe or preach fatalism, why not children by choice instead of chance? Or, as Dr. Louis L. Mann, Rabbi of Sinia Congregation, and member of the faculty of the University of Chicago, would have us say, "voluntary parenthood."

Dr. Mann says: "Without Birth Control woman becomes a mere breeding machine, as she was in ancient Greece, void of a soul, but necessary to produce slaves and soldiers for industry and war."

From a brief review of the attitude of religionists towards contracepted unions, and their assertion that Birth Control is destructive of love, we reply in the words of Professor Thomas D. Elliot, of the Sociology Department of Northwestern University. Prof. Elliot maintains that "Birth Control among refined people need not impair love; procreation by sensual people does not necessarily spiritualize the union."

If religion is concerned with the well-being of the mass, should not religionists encourage those physically and morally capable to have children, and give some time and effort to segregate and discourage the propagation of the unfit and degenerate?

Many of us have glimpses of a time when this subject will be put on the plane of ethics. Instead of tradition we shall have science. Instead of bondage we shall have an intelligent motherhood responsible for each human being.

Z.L. Burt.

THE CASE FOR BIRTH CONTROL

Another viewpoint by Mrs. Lillie Broadhurst.

October 1927, pp. 10-11.

I know of no single question that is of more far-reaching vital importance to the human race than is the question of Birth Control. Directly, or indirectly, it touches every man, woman and child, nay more, it touches the child not yet born.

But before we can discuss any question intelligently we must know just what the subject is. Briefly it is this:

We believe that under any conditions and particularly under our present economic conditions, human beings should be able to control the number of their offspring and to accomplish this result we demand the knowledge of preventing undesirable conception, and that it should not be considered criminal knowledge.

There is no element of force in our teachings, that is, we would not force any family to limit the number of their children against their will, though we would endeavor to create a public opinion which would consider it a disgrace for anyone to have more children than they can bring up and educate properly. We should consider it an anti-social act to bring children into the world who would be sent out to earn a living at a tender age in mills, shops and streets. A working man should not have more than two children. Every child after the second and particularly after the third is a calamity. The mother's health is exhausted. It is nothing less than a crime against the mother—a crime against the father and the other children, also a crime against society.

Every doctor knows that too frequent childbirth, nursing and loss of sleep exhausts the vitality of mothers and makes them prematurely old, or they turn into chronic invalids. The knowledge of prevention would do away with this evil. We believe that a woman is, can be and should be, a human being besides being a mother, and if she is to take a place in social life she must not be forced to bear children when she does not wish to.

The first right of the child is to be wanted, that is the slogan of the Voluntary Parenthood League. But how many children, think you, are wanted?

In Holland, a country in which prevention is legally sanctioned, the children are wanted, planned for and surrounded with love and care from their advent, and the people are very happy. Look around you in this city and count the worn, weary faces of some of the mothers you see and think of their many agonies. If men had to go through what women do, if men were the bearers of children, the laws against prevention of conception on our statue books would never have been written. Look at the women who were high-spirited and talented! After a few years of marriage and childbearing, what are they? Spiritless drudges without any ambition but to wash and feed their little ones. How can a woman who has four or five children in the first ten years of married life follow up her studies and live up to her ideals and aspirations?

Children are a blessing when properly spaced and wanted. Conscious and limited procreation is dictated by love and intelligence. It improves the race. Unconscious, irresponsible procreation produces domestic misery and half-starved mothers and children.

What we want is quality, not quantity.

The babe is so important a thing that it demands it shall be created in love, and only as a gift to parents whose hands are held out in loving welcome. Our love is a noble one which forces us occasionally to deprive ourselves for the pleasure of children for the children's own sake.

There is no danger of the parental instinct dying out. Dr. Robinson, of New York, says: "When I see the risk and expense woman will go to, endangering her life, I am speaking of numerous Caesarean operations, and prospective mothers will undergo in order to have a living child, I have no fear that the use of preventatives will result in the dying out of the human race—it is the height of folly to argue that because people object to six or a dozen children they would object to two or three. I believe in the scientific principle of birth control because it works. It is no new idea, it has long been tried and has not been found wanting."

In Holland there are fifty headquarters where women may be given this information as a health measure. The death rate among the children has dropped from 180 to 90 a thousand in a period of thirty years, which is a record for Europe. These Clinics also help the mothers who are in distress because they find themselves unable to bear more children, and after instruction and treatment they will joyfully come to thank those who have helped them and tell the joyful tiding that they are now expecting a little one. There are very many women in this condition. The last war is responsible for many sterile mothers and fathers, the mothers becoming so from their work in munition factories, and the fathers from dreadful wounds in vital portions of their bodies.

(To be continued.)

THE CASE FOR BIRTH CONTROL

(Continued from October issue.)

November 1927, p. 13.

You must remember we are not speaking for the mothers who have maids, nurses and doctors to wait on them at the birth of their children, good food, warmth and every comfort during the weary nine months that precede the advent of the child, but of the poor, half-starved mother who had to depend on the kindly ministration of her neighbour and perhaps the attention of a physician at the birth of her child. In these cases very often the nourishment that the mother should receive is impossible to obtain in the husband's limited wages. I have personally received my education along these lines.

I once stood in a small flat in London, England, and took a child from the doctor's hands and in the next room, the bailiff was counting the spoons, knives and forks (three of each, I think) and wanted to know if he could have his dinner. There was no food in the house. The husband had been out of work for some time. One other child, aged two, was in the house. This is only one of many thousands of cases. Do you think this child was wanted, and would you think it right for that woman to give birth to any more under like circumstances?

What inducement is there for the intelligent, sober, class-conscious worker holding a twenty-dollar a week job to bring more wage slaves into the world. As the family increases, do the wages. No! Very often, knowing full well that he has a large family they will give him less money, for the master class know that when a man has a large family he will do anything rather than lose his job. So you see the large family is like a club at his head.

Think again of the many young folks, who would like to marry, but because of the small amount they earn they fear to do so. It is the thought that they will bring little ones into the world who would need food and clothing out of the same small amount that deters them. Once more I would remind you that it is not the mothers who have lovely homes, kind, wealthy husbands, who can afford to give them every care, that we speak of. To these we say reproduce and raise the standard of manhood and womanhood if you are so willing, and may your efforts be crowned with success. When I see a lovely woman without children, I think of that quotation of Shakespeare's— "Lady, you are the cruelest she alive if you lead these graces to the grave and leave the world no copy." I believe I am talking to a group of women who are above the average in intelligence and I ask you to give this your earnest attention and support the Birth Control Movement, also the Voluntary Parenthood League and at all times help and instruct all young people in these matters. Always read and advise the reading of Dr. Marie Stopes' books, also Dr. Robinson's. There are none better and none as good. Should we not, as a progressive body of women, try to get a speaker from the Control direct; it is not so much for ourselves, but for the good of the generation to follow and the many poor souls asking for help.

"What shall be done to quiet the heart cry of the world?

How answer the dumb appeal for help we so often divine below eyes that laugh."

No, I do not think that Scientific Birth Control would cause more immorality. I think it would help to do away with it. If young folks could have Scientific Birth Control instruction, they would lead normal, happy lives, and when they felt they desired.

(To be Continued)

BIRTH CONTROL (Concluded)

By Lillian Broadhurst
December 1927, pp. 10-12.

A little one theirs would be the joy of voluntary parenthood. The cause of immorality, as it is called, is the effect of a cause. That cause is the fear to marry and bring into the world babes unwanted.

Our civilization, instead of advancing, is retrogressing to barbarism. The forcing of young girls into marriage will bring forth idiots and morally insane. This also leads the race into degeneracy and, eventually, race suicide. Unless the child can be born well and brought up well it is better it would not be born at all. A mother is physically strong only when she bears her first child in mature age. When she becomes a mother she has to rest a long time to recuperate and bring up well her first child before she is in condition to have another one. Frequent children cannot be healthy ones, physically or mentally, and economic conditions will keep them in deficiency and misery. After a few generations, the nation, instead of having strong and brave people, will have weak and cowardly ones, and gradually will fall into degeneracy. For the sake of the country and the nation it is necessary to resort to contraceptives.

Abortion is a crime, celibacy is immoral, prostitution is an abomination. The only honest, decent and moral remedy is prevention of contraception.

From the moral and philosophical view, every unwelcomed child is a burden to itself and to society. Unhappy lives of millions are caused by their being forced into existence.

Physicians from their profession, priests from the confessional, know of thousands and thousands of women seeking destruction of their unborn children because they want no more babies.

Why should they be forced into compulsive motherhood or why should men be compelled to unnatural celibacy?

This compulsory celibacy is a frequent cause of men's immorality. A man confesses that he assailed or seduced a girl because his wife is sick and afraid to have children. If there were a way to prevent conception he would be moral and good. But he has now seventeen children and the doctor said that the next pregnancy will kill her. Recently there was an action for separation in Pennsylvania because the woman wants no more children.

We know that priest-ridden Poles, Slavs and Italians have weak and sickly children because there are too many and they are underfed.

In these children that are born year after year, there is always an inborn immorality.

Polish men are often immoral because they have been born of too young mothers or preceded by many born before.

There was a case in Nebraska of a girl of 12 who became pregnant. Priest and parents compelled the man to marry her. Now she is a mother of sixteen children; she is only 29 years old and just a skeleton.

Dr. John Doe in Lincoln, Nebraska, was arrested for procuring an abortion. Four hundred names were found on his register—women that want no more children.

And we want no more abortions. We want and we will eventually gain Scientific Birth Control. Yes, there are women who are too lazy and self-indulgent to bring into the world children, although they are surrounded with every comfort. But would you come to them? No, I think not. You like to see these women mothers—would you envy the babes that would see, these wealthy women can obtain Scientific Birth Control—why should not the poor workers do so? May I ask why they should not enjoy life if they wish?

Yes, I know that some think that it is only for procreation that you should have unions, but you all need a great amount of study along these lines. Do you know anything about the laws of your country? You are only your husband's chattel and the law is on his side. You cannot refuse by law to cohabit and if you do; because you do not wish to conceive, he can and will divorce you, or neglect you and seek other comforts elsewhere and you, his chattel, can be very thankful if he does not illtreat you as one type of man does, and the law will not give you a divorce, unless you can prove cruelty and adultery, the world will blame you for not conforming to your wifely duty forsooth.

The higher intelligence of the breeder restrains a beautiful mare; she is not allowed to foal every year, only at special times, when her condition is good and circumstances favorable. It is the same with high-grade cows. Surely the higher intelligence of man should not think animals more important than children.

We know there are many methods in use that are detrimental—that is why we want Scientific Birth Control. Then we should not have so many nervous wrecks to look upon.

Note: —The writer of this article wishes to state that very little of it is original. She is indebted to the works of Dr. W. Robinson, of New York, whose books should be ready by all intelligent people. She is also similarly indebted to Dr. Marie Stopes, of the Birth Control Clinics, London, England, whose valuable works should be read by all mothers, more especially her book entitled, "A Letter to Working Mothers."

Lillie Broadhurst.

Editorial note: Mrs. Broadhurst has informed us that she is indebted to Dr. W.J. Robinson, of New York, for a number of quotations she uses, and whose permission she obtained to use them. Her article was first of all prepared for a debate for a Women's Group. She also expresses the opinion that it would be good if other opinions were expressed besides her own.

In the next issue of The Woman Worker another article will appear which will deal with Birth Control from another point of view.

AS MR. CALVERTON SEES NEW RUSSIA'S MORALS
[Excerpts]

November 1927, pp. 7-8.

[...]

Candor About Sex and Life

"In many other ways the moral life of the U.S.S.R. is constructed upon a different plane, with entirely different shibboleths, from that of the rest of the Christian world.

"Sex is considered a sane topic that is discussed everywhere with clarity and candor.

"Birth control is written about in a manner that would at once astonish and terrify a modern American. Pamphlets on the topics are numerous. Indeed, they can be bought at any book-store or even railroad stations. One pamphlet entitled "Prevention of Child Birth," by Dr. U.Z. Shpak, discussing all possible means of contraception, has already gone through many editions. Abortion, to cite another instance of this different attitude, is not condemned but legalized. The Commissariat of Public Health in 1920 issued the following mandate in reference to abortions:

1. Operative interruptions of pregnancy without charge are permitted in the hospitals of the Soviet Government.

2. The performance of such an operation by any other than a physician is most strictly prohibited.

3. The midwife or nurse who shall perform such an operation shall be deprived of the right to practice her calling and shall be turned over to the courts for trial.

4. The physician who performs such an operation in his private practice for motives of gain shall be handed over to the trial court.

"In conclusion, one can certainly say ... that the moral life of the New Russia is built about the pivot of social co-operation."

Thus does Mr. Calverton, who is now in the Soviet Union, write of the social life and morals of the people.

Who would be a party to the destruction of such progress? Certainly not members of the working class. The workers of the Soviet Union have dared where other workers have feared as yet to tread.

Mr. Calverton is an educationalist of the highest order, contributing articles to the very best periodicals of America and Great Britain, and his interpretation of the social life of Russia of To-day is one that should receive the widest publicity. His contribution to Current History for November will do more to break down prejudices towards Soviet Russia than anything that has come to hand of recent date.

He shows that the Ten Years of Struggle of the New against the Old have been worth-while.

BIRTH CONTROL AND WORKING WOMEN

January 1928, pp. 7-9.

About a century ago there lived in England a man named Thomas Malthus. He was a professor of History and Economics. He lived in a period very like the one in which we are living, a period of revolution and war, of changing orders and new ways.

We all know that a century ago saw the beginning of a new industrial age, the age of machine production. This started first in England. To-day sees machine production as a world method of production, and we live in a period of that age that can be called gigantic machine production.

Just as new machinery to-day displaces old types of machinery and tends more and more to displace labor causing unemployment and misery—so, over a century ago, the introduction of the machine into industry displaced the handicraft worker, and a terrible condition of unemployment obtained. The workers in those days hated the new invention, the machine, and at times smashed and destroyed the factories where they were.

Now, you will ask, "What has all this to do with Birth Control?" Well, let us see.

Thomas Malthus, whose name has been mentioned above, knew of this misery of the workers, their unemployment and starvation. He saw, too, the evil after-effects of the wars of that time, the Napoleonic War. And he, like a very wise man, tried to fathom the cause of it all so that he could suggest a cure.

He wrote an essay on the subject entitled, "Population." In this essay he said that the cause of the social misery of that day was due to the fact that there were too many people in the world—there was "Over-population." He predicted that if over-population continued the world would be faced with utter starvation, because not enough food, etc., could be produced.

A hundred years and more have passed since he wrote his essay, and I think it can be agreed that production has always been ahead of the growth of population. To-day some professors tell us that the cause of trade troubles and unemployment is "Over-production." However, the conditions called poverty and starvation are still with us. So Thomas Malthus' theory has been proven all wrong by history itself.

With our own eyes we can see that social misery—(poverty)—is the lot only of one class—that of the workers and poor farmers. And these are slowly but surely learning that the reason for this condition lies not in the size of the population of a country, but because of the fact that a country and all its wealth are in the hands of a few persons, and these determine how the rest shall live.

Yes, indeed, Malthus was wrong in his calculations. But, in spite of this Malthus' theory is taught in the universities and colleges as a correct theory, and this, because professors and teacher dare not tell the truth concerning the cause of poverty and social misery.

This theory, too, is accepted by social service and uplift organizations. One of the most outstanding uplift organizations, the Birth Control Movement, has adopted Malthus' theory to justify its existence and to gain a standing as a social organization.

And this is why we have found it necessary to give to our readers the foregoing introduction to our statements on Birth Control. We must draw a line between the theories of the Birth Control Movement and the actual practice of Birth Control and the scientific knowledge this entails.

The only advice received from official quarters was to the effect that if we had knowledge ourselves, to pass it along quietly.

Now this is just what the Women's Labor League Movement will not do.

The demand for Mothers' Clinics is a legitimate demand. This demand carries with it the end of "illegal operations" and the danger to life these entail—it carries with it the end of robbery of working women by doctors whose practices are on the decline—it places the propagation of life on a more scientific basis and spells death to mock-modesty and ignorance.

Working Women Have Few Illusions

The average working woman knows already that the size of her family does not alter the root of the maintenance of the life of herself and family. The wages system still remains. The thing pans out for her something like this, quoting the words of one woman: "The only difference it makes is one largely affecting the children. A small family makes larger cultural demands on parents; you feel you must send your children to high school or business college; you must have them taught music and let them have a good time at athletics, and these things bring their financial worries—whereas a woman with a large family is forced through necessity to let her brood take potluck."

Malthus was wrong in his theory as to the cause of poverty, unemployment and social ills. The Birth Control Movement is wrong, too, when it supports and advocates this theory. But when conditions prevail, as we have them in Canada, then Birth Control is not merely a matter of individual relief but carries with it a struggle against narrow-mindedness on the subject of Birth and the evil practices that obtain as a result of this narrow-mindedness.

Member of the Toronto League.

POVERTY KILLS WORKING-CLASS MOTHERS

[Editorial]

April 1928, pp. 1-2.

CANADA loses more than four mothers every day. So states the government report on Maternal Mortality, publication No. 37.

We have become so used to hearing it said that Mrs. So and So died in childbirth that we take such happenings for granted, and after merely expressing words of sympathy for those left behind, we have simply let the incident pass from our minds. Such is our indifference!

To appreciate what this death rate of motherhood means, the figures given in the report should be studied. From the period July 1st, 1925-July 1st, 1926 there were 237,199 births in Canada—1,532 mothers died—giving an average maternal death rate of 6.4 to every thousand living births.

Imagine, in a single year 1,532 mothers died! And the average age of these mothers was thirty-one years! Just young women!

We are appalled when we read of mining disasters and the loss of life in the mines. And yet we have up to the present given very little heed to the frightful loss of life of our working-class motherhood. Now that fairly accurate figures are given by the government concerning this loss, we may shake off some of our apathy and get down to action.

To a certain extent apathy on the matter is the result of the fact that working-class mothers die in isolation—in their poverty-stricken homes out in the bush, or on the farm, or in the crowded city where everyone minds her own business in times of sickness. There is nothing dramatic about such a death, and nobody is held responsible. Hence the indifference!

Yet the women who die are the working women of farm and city. That this is so can be proven from the words of Dr. Helen MacMurchy, who prepared the government report. Speaking in Toronto on March 21st of this year, Dr. MacMurchy stated that "Canada had a total of 1,532 maternal deaths, most of which might have been prevented. The children thus left motherless numbered 5,073, including 768 new-born babies. Investigation has proved that half these mothers now deceased were in poor health for a long period of time. Some suffered from heart disease, some from tuberculosis. Many were exhausted through constant care of home and children, and a few were the victims of extreme poverty. More than 300 were in poor condition on account of toxaemia (blood poisoning), and 100 came to their death through hard labor. Over 1,300 had received no pre-natal care." (The Globe, 21/3/28.)

When we boil down the words of the report the cold, hard fact which stares us in the face is that these mothers need not have died. The reason they died was because they had not the wherewithal to pay for medical attention nor to obtain help and relief from their household duties. They died—the Victims of Poverty—the Victims of the small pay envelope—the Victims of the wages system which cares naught for the life of the man who earns the wage, nor for that of his wife who has to eke out, week after week, that miserable wage-pittance.

The Solution! Medical experts advise "education," and that interested organizations should be asked to co-operate in educating mothers to demand pre-natal care.

To us this advice is late. One of the objects of our organization is THE CARE OF MOTHERHOOD, and we have consistently asked for the establishment of MOTHERS' CLINICS at which our working- class mother can get the care and attention needed.

But Mothers' Clinics will not cure all the cares and worries of burdened working-class motherhood. That pay envelope has to be bigger; it has to contain more dollars with which to buy necessities and to obtain help. This means that working-class mothers will have to support their husbands' demands for higher wages. The demands of working-class mothers must be "More Wages to Live On" and "Mothers' Clinics for Medical Attention."

BIRTH CONTROL—ANOTHER VIEWPOINT

April 1928, pp. 11-12.

I see a great deal in The Woman Worker about scientific birth control, but from what I can gather it seems that what you want is artificial birth control, or sated lusts, with consequences aborted.

If you will search such history as is left to us of the civilizations that are now being dug up from under the sands of time, you may be surprised to find that even the workers of every one of them was fairly well acquainted with such variety of preventive.

The fact is that the only scientific birth control is self control, and until the human animal uses it he is a slave to his baser passions.

Creative force is the same throughout the universe. What we sometimes call a difference is not a difference in force but a difference in the application of the force.

The same force that turned downwards created a child or goes to waste—if turned upward through the spinal nerves creates intellect, and it is a provable fact that all past civilizations have died because the great masses of the people, in other words the workers, lacked intellect to continue on the path of progressive evolution, and either gradually or speedily devolved according as the waste of creative force was violent or less violent.

The very ancient Caldeans taught self control, but it was hard to get the masses of the people to practice it, and eventually a cunning priestcraft got in power that encouraged satiation of lust which gradually devolved the mass intellect to where the masses of the Caldean people were no more. The last empire of Babylonia, and especially the City of Babylon, dedicated itself, from the start, to the enjoyment of lust in the most violent way, and her death was as violent and speedy as her waste of creative force was.

The same can be said of all nations, and also of individuals.

Horace Greely was considered a powerful intellectual in his younger days, but he was one of the worse sex perverts in American history, and was in the insane asylum before he had reached middle age.

As for the rich having access to scientific birth control, they may have control, but the enormous number of congenital idiots they are pouring into the world by ones and twos to the family would soon swamp civilization if workers poured such intellects into the world as fast, in proportion to their numbers.

If you doubt me, examine any Sunday magazine of the big dailies. You would not find as many, absolutely imbecile, intellects in all the peasantry of France as is displayed along the Riviera in silks and satins. The same is true of all other large cities in varying degrees. But people have worshipped at this shrine of Mammon for so long that even the workers are wont to substitute the dollar for intellect.

Of course we have been told, by priestcraft, that such abuse of the genative function was natural for so many ages that we are inclined to believe it, from sheer force of habit, but as a matter of fact there are about three other animals in nature that indulge as man does—the ape, the jack-ass, and the goat. Is it any credit to man's will or to his pride, either, that he wilfully classes himself with such?

"Man, only, breaks his chains when self control he gains."—Heindel.

The worker cannot afford to imitate the rich in their debauchery.

Priestcraft encourages such in order to keep the intellect so impoverished that it is a garden spot for superstition, and, through fear—the deformed off-spring of superstition—they enrich themselves.

MARGARET CROWDER,*
Los Angeles, California.

MARGARET CROWDEN ANSWERED*

June 1928, pp. 14-15.

Margaret Crowden, in the April number of The Woman Worker, disapproves of scientific birth control and suggests that the only way to limit the number of children is by self-control. We would all agree with her that self-control is most important in matters of sex, but I doubt if this would have the desired effect. Most modern psychologists agree that absolute continence is harmful to the average person and often results in serious nervous disturbances. Moderation in all things is the ideal to be attained.

In the early development of man, in order that he should survive, it was necessary that a great many children should be born, and a few of them might have a chance to escape the many dangers which beset them. Now that we are able to protect the lives of children better it is not necessary that so many should be born. People, however, have not changed physiologically nor psychologically to the point where it is natural for them to have only one, two or three children, so it is necessary to use birth control.

At any rate, if we depend on the self-control method we will find the few superior individuals having small families and the many continuing to have large families.

The ills of society will never be overcome by lessening the size of families. We can see in Holland, where scientific information regarding birth control has been given out for many years, they still have the evils of present-day society. The only cure for our present ills is a co-operative commonwealth. Yet the limiting of the number of children is a great benefit to the whole family. It preserves the health and strength of the mother and gives her more time to develop mentally. It relieves the father from the terrible strain of providing for an ever-increasing family. It gives the few children more advantages than the many would have.

The advocates of birth control do not encourage unbridled license. They only believe that in this as in all other matters man should use his knowledge to govern nature in such a way that he may attain a more perfect life.

I.E.H.

*[Editor's Note: Crowden was spelt inconsistently in the original.]

A FEW WORDS ON BIRTH CONTROL

October 1928, pp.15-16.

Birth control means much to the working-class mother. It gives her a little freedom, it enables her to have time to think of other things than just her children and her work for them, it gives her the chance to bring a healthy child into the world when she wants it and to bring it up according to her ideals. All these things are impossible if she bears a child too often. We know many workers' homes are wrecked, because the burdens of child raising have been too much for the parents. Sometimes the mother has deserted her family, but more often the father goes away and leaves the burdens to the mother.

How I delight in seeing a worker's family with parents fully class conscious, and these with a limited number of healthy children to whom they
teach the germs of the great struggle ahead of them! Such parents, to my
mind, are giving their children a square deal in giving them strong bodies
and healthy minds to fit them for the trying conditions they will have to face
later on it life.

But, of course, this question of Birth Control has another side, too—a
dark side. I know homes that have become worse than can be imagined just
because the wife held the reins in Birth Control. She wouldn't spoil her
looks just to please her husband. She wouldn't be bound to her home by a
child, or children, perhaps. No! She'd live and be happy even though she
was married. Gradually the society she mingled with dragged her so low
that she wasn't even good enough to mingle with it any longer. Or, again,
perhaps there is a child already. The mother hops after the latest mode in
dress, habit, slang of modern times: she does everything to be smart and
girlish, and she neglects her child entirely. This child wants to know so
much, so very much, and the mother hasn't time for the little fellow. He
goes hungry, ragged, dirty, while his mother mends her facial beauty or her
silken hosiery. And the father, if he isn't like his wife, goes to work steadily
and has no chance to console his child. In cases like this I often wonder if
bearing a few children wouldn't shake silly, butterfly ideas out of the heads
of such mothers and force them to contemplate life a little more seriously
from the real working-class point of view and thought.

But, of course, I wholly agree that the knowledge of Birth Control should
be spread among the working class.

Sofie.

IMMIGRATION—NOW BIRTH CONTROL

[Editorial]

November 1928, p. 5.

WE are informed by press dispatches that an appeal signed by Lady Bal-
fom, Lord Buckmaster, Lord Dawson, and so many other Lords and Ladies
of the Realm, for subscriptions for the establishment of birth control clinics
in mining districts, has been issued in Great Britain.

"The clinic in Rodeham," a dispatch says, "has been visited by many
miners wives under the pressure of acute economic necessity."

The appeal states that birth prevention is "a scientific and humane way of
helping to solve problems of depressed and over-populated industry."

And so the cat is out of the bag. A quack scheme for the solution of the unemployed scheme. First emigration, now birth control. Not birth control

from the point of view of having a woman determine if she wants a child or not, but birth control because of economic pressure, due to an over-populated industry.

Over-populated industry forsooth. If the Burleighs, the Buckmasters and the Dawsons were off the backs of the workers, the economic pressure would disappear.

It is here that the danger has in the birth control agitation. "The Woman Worker" has supported the demand for the abolition of Birth Control literature and information. We must be exceeding careful, however, not to fall into the trap of being drawn into quack schemes for the so-called easing of the "burden of the poor" by appeals from our Lords and Ladies for a reduction of the birth rate, to solve the problem of "over-populated" industries.

Capitalism is over-populated by the parasitical capitalist class. A steadily growing unemployed army is a product of capitalism. Beware of the nostrums of our masters, with the bleeding hearts for the bleeding workers.

Solidarity: National and International   8

Since the 19th century workers across Europe and North America organized to support each others' efforts to build trade unions and socialist parties. Organizations like the Second Socialist International had connected socialists and social democrats before it was divided by World War I, while unions too organized internationally. A commitment to solidarity, encompassing notions of common struggle, political and moral support, as well as economic aid, was an existing cornerstone of both trade union and socialist traditions by the time the Communist Party was founded.

Most trade unions operating in Canada had also become "international" by 1920. Within North America, international unions (though often dominated by the larger American membership), were constructed in the hopes of providing more effective means to protect workers' rights across borders, and to deal with capital which itself was international in organization and power. Within national boundaries too, trade unionists realized that workers had to create links that would facilitate the exchange of information and organizing assistance, and which would act as a unified voice for workers rights and needs when confronting both employers and the state. Since the 1880s successive efforts to build links between workers had been attempted, first with the broadly based Knights of Labour, later with the narrower (craft-dominated) Trades and Labour Congress, founded in 1883. In the immediate post-World War I period, a new wave of militancy momentarily posed hopes of a broadly based movement again: the 1919 Winnipeg General Strike and the unsuccessful attempts to build a One Big Union after World War I were but two examples of militant efforts to create an inclusive workers' accord designed to secure concessions from the state and employers. After 1919 and the decline of the One Big Union, the vision of unity and solidarity did not entirely disappear. It did take on new forms, including the commitment of small groups of workers across Canada to the newly formed Communist Party.

The emphasis on building links between trade unions within Canada, as well as with workers around the world became a central goal of the Communist Party, and is clearly evident within the *Woman Worker*. Indeed, the emphasis on making international links was especially crucial in the 1920s, in part because the Party was a member of the newly established Communist International, but also because in the 1920s, the Communist International, as well as its dominating leaders from the Soviet Union, still placed important stock in the idea that revolution could not easily succeed in one country: it must be fermented and supported in other countries as well.

Drawing on existing traditions as well as new political loyalties, therefore, the *Woman Worker* tried to build solidarity in a number of crucial ways. International news in the paper provided basic information, absent in the mainstream press, to women interested in labour and socialism: material ranged from descriptions of socialist leaders like Clara Zetkin to accounts of working-class organizing in Canada and around the world (see "Chicago Women to Organize Federation"). Accounts of organizing were especially utilized as educational lessons to drive home the destructiveness of capitalism and the links between capitalism and imperialism. While international news had always been a feature in some pre-World War I socialist papers, the *Woman Worker* offered more coverage of women's struggles and also more attention to colonized areas of the world such as China, in an effort to draw class links across racial and geographic boundaries. By publishing articles on child and female labour in Japan and China, by pointing to the need to "free girl slaves" elsewhere, the paper was trying to persuade Canadian working-class women to identify with the exploitation of Asian women, and also to see that all working-class struggles were intertwined in combat against the same oppressive masters.

Many articles on workers and women in Asian countries showed some sympathy for the nationalist, bourgeois revolutions occurring at this time (see "China Awakened"). In the *Woman Worker* at least, Communists expressed some support for the project of female emancipation that such liberal, nationalist rebellions called for. Certainly, there is also an element of Anglo-Saxon superiority in these accounts of Asian populations and gender roles. There is little respect for existing Asian cultures which are portrayed rather one-dimensionally as "backward" and oppressive to women, in much the same way Protestant missionaries at the time portrayed them. Nonetheless, the attempt to develop empathy for Asian workers and political solidarity across cultural and racial lines was noteworthy in the 1920s.

Solidarity could also be constructed with countries which had even stronger ties through immigration to Canada. One of the major struggles in Britain in the 1920s was the 1926 General Strike, sparked first by the coal miners and later spreading to workers across the nation. The *Woman Worker* gave the strike significant coverage and urged women in Canada to support the miners' cause with financial contributions and moral declarations of solidarity. The message was clear and direct: these workers and their families faced the same obstacles to organizing and to securing a decent living that Canadian workers confronted. Their struggles are both connected and parallel to ours.

International cooperation might be fostered in other ways as well. In the "Open Letter to the Labor Movement of Great Britain," Canadian Communist women tried to initiate discussion with British women about immigration across borders, indicating how British domestic workers might be misled into emigrating to Canada in search of "plentiful" jobs which did not really exist. In some cases, the paper would make comparisons between occupations in various countries, arguing, for instance, that an attack on the working conditions of female teachers in Canada bore a frightening similarity to attacks on women teachers in places like fascist Italy.

Contrasts were used to highlight the differences between capitalist celebrations and socialist ones, or to expose the hypocrisy of capitalist mainstream traditions such as Christmas, which called for expressions of joy but also exposed the suffering and poverty of many workers. Contrasting 1 July, Dominion Day, and 2 July, marking the International Cooperative Movement, for example, the paper argued that it was difficult to "celebrate" a country in which poverty was still rampant, and more rewarding to mark a day of international solidarity based on cooperative principles.

In promoting the cooperative movement or in condemning the political execution of the famous American anarchists Sacco and Vanzetti, the paper was expressing a solidarity that went beyond the confines of the Communist movement. Communist thinking at this time, as we have seen in previous chapters, endorsed political solidarity with a broad spectrum of left-wing causes: this was both educationally and politically advantageous to the Party's overall aims. The paper's editor undoubtedly realized that the readership of the *Woman Worker*, which included a wide spectrum of socialist and labour women, supported these causes and could be drawn into the

Communist movement through active, though sometimes critical, support for other progressive causes.

Similarly, the *Woman Worker* did not just print articles about unions which had ties to the Communist Party, although there was a tendency to secure support for unions where the Party had some base. In the latter case, for example, there were repeated calls for aid, both material and moral, for the United Mine Workers' unions involved in bitter strikes in Nova Scotia and Alberta. The unions and their wives' auxiliaries included a few dedicated Communist organizers who could pass on crucial information about these struggles to the *Woman Worker*. Such calls for strike aid complemented those articles describing daily life in the mining camps of Alberta and Nova Scotia, often written by miners' wives and asking housewives in other areas of the country to identify with their struggles to house, clothe and feed their families.

As one of the most important symbols for international and national solidarity, International Women's Day was promoted energetically by the *Woman Worker*. International Women's Day, first suggested by German social democrat Clara Zetkin before the war, became an important ritual for Communists around the world in the 1920s. In Canada, the day was used to mark past victories and current battles of women wage-earners, and to encourage connections between women struggling for socialism in many campaigns and organizations—from anti-war work to unions to housewives' organizations.

There was probably no country that held out more symbolic importance for international solidarity work than the Soviet Union. As an example of a successful workers' revolution, the Soviet Union provided hope and illustrations of women's and workers' emancipation. The Soviet Union also provided international leadership to other Communists through the Communist International. Articles on the Soviet Union, therefore, are not only found in this section, but are also reprinted in the chapters on peace and war, and marriage and the family.

Further Reading:

- Ian Angus, *Canadian Bolsheviks: The Early Years of the Communist Party of Canada* (Montréal: Vanguard, 1981).

- Jane Degras, ed. *The Communist International, 1919-1943; documents* (London: Oxford University Press, 1965-71).

- William Rodney, *Soldiers of the International: A History of the Communist Party of Canada, 1919-1929* (Toronto: University of Toronto Press, 1968).

WORKING WOMEN OF CANADA RALLY TO AID THE BRITISH MINERS!

[Editorial]

September 1926, pp. 4-5.

THE Coal Miners' Strike is still in progress in Great Britain. All have watched the various stages of the miners' struggle. Those who know the conditions under which the miners and their families existed are in full sympathy with them.

Every effort has been made by the mineowners and the Baldwin Government to break the strike and discredit the chosen leaders of the miners. But these leaders, while hated by the owners and their sympathizers, have gained for themselves the highest respect and confidence of the intelligent workers throughout the world.

One of the features of the strike is the attitude of the miners' wives towards the strike. A spirit, hitherto very rare in the labor movement, has developed. The wives of the strikers are to the forefront in demonstrations against both mineowners and those who would break the strike.

The courage and fortitude of the miners' wives have rallied the whole of the forces of women in the working class movement to their support. Women's Co-operative Guilds, Women's Sections of the Labor Party, Women's Trade Unions, in fact, women in every section of the movement are working in unity and harmony for the benefit of the miners' wives and children.

During the next few weeks representatives of the British Miners' Relief Committee will be travelling through the country. Their mission is to collect material help for the miners, as well as to tell the truth about the strike. It will be the duty of the women of the working class to render every bit of aid to these to make their mission a success.

Working women know full well what it means to pinch and screw in ordinary times to make ends meet. Let us try to imagine what it must mean to the miners' wives at this time. Let us remember they are fighting against slavish conditions. Dig deep into your pockets and give till it hurts.

THE CO-OPERATIVE MOVEMENT

October 1926, pp. 2-3.

THERE is growing up in Canada a movement which working women should known something about. This is the Co-operative Movement. In the big cities of Canada little is known of this movement, but in many small towns and farming districts the co-operatives are flourishing institutions.

In Great Britain the Co-operative Movement is very strong, and Old Country women are well acquainted with the Co-operative Stores and the Women's Guilds which work in conjunction with the Stores. Every article sold in the Stores is discussed by the women, and they know why the prices are fixed, and they "share in the dividends or profits" made through careful buying. Co-operative buying proves a benefit to the workers in Great Britain.

In Canada there are some Consumers' Co-operatives, but the strongest side of the movement in Canada is "co-operative selling." The farmers of Canada have learned that it doesn't pay to compete with one another, to undersell one another, to try to put the weak farmer out of his farm. They have learned that by putting their products together they can demand a higher price for these products, and all share in the benefits. This is the meaning of the Farmers' Wheat Pool, which the newspapers discuss, but do not very well explain for the benefit of the workers.

Some farmers have also undertaken co-operative production. The object is to do away with the trader—the middle man—as he is called. For example, the farmers do not sell the wool from their sheep to the wool merchant, who again sells it to the manufacturer, who makes it into goods, who then sells it to the merchant, and so on until it reaches the consumer. The farmers of Ontario have erected their own factory. The wool from their sheep is sent to this factory, and the farmers' wives get their blankets, etc., at cost price. They no longer wait for bargain day at the big departmental stores, as the wives of wage workers do.

The Co-operative Movement is a world-wide movement. Those connected with it have established July 1st as their day of International Celebration. On this day this year a big conference was held by Canadian Co-operators in Edmonton, Alberta.

It is very evident that the farmers of Canada are more alive to their needs than are the workers in industry. The farmers are learning quickly the benefits of unionism and co-operation, the workers of Canada have yet to learn these things.

ARE THE BRITISH MINERS BEATEN?

[Editorial]

October 1926, pp. 3-4.

THE newspapers that are controlled and owned by the masters take great pleasure in announcing that the British Miners are going back to work, because they are tired of the strike.

Those who have followed the struggle between the mine owners and the mine-workers know now that the courageous British Miners have been left to shoulder their struggles alone, they have been left to the mercy of a group of masters determined to make the men work longer hours for less pay.

The chances of the miners of success in keeping their hours of labor and wage rates intact are remote.

Complete success depended upon the solidarity of all organized workers with the miners. The general strike expressed this solidarity, but the leaders became afraid, and called off the general strike. Not only was solidarity necessary in Great Britain, but it was necessary in Europe and America. Coal was shipped to Great Britain, so that manufacturers had no need to bring pressure to bear on the government. The mine owners have received assistance from every source—the government—their class brothers—the workers in Great Britain who feared to struggle with the miners—and the miners and transport workers of other countries, who helped to send coal to Great Britain.

The British miners do not ask for impossible things. They merely ask that their wages shall not be lowered, and their hours of toil, in the darkness and dangers of the mines, shall not be increased.

The Miners' struggle shows that even yet the great masses of the workers are not conscious of their power. And it shows the need of solidarity of the workers. The miners are the victims of the cowardice of others. This, and not starvation, will have been the main cause of their defeat.

THE GREATEST SOCIAL CONSTRUCTOR OF OUR TIMES

[Editorial]

February 1927, pp. 3-4.

THREE years have passed since Lenin, the greatest social constructor of our times, died. Throughout the world workers of all shades of working class thought paid tribute to his memory. And this tribute is seemly. It can be said quite truly that no other working class leader of modern times placed so much faith in the workers as did Lenin. Never did he rebuke them, shun them, despise them, although they were the people who had the dirty hands and wore the shoddy clothes. Never did he belittle them, although they did not possess high culture and speak correct language. Instead, he was always patient with them. He made every allowance for them.

And why was he so patient with the masses. It was because he contended that the workers would be called upon by necessity to take the road to Power, to take the power out of the hands of the rich rulers, and to order their own lives. He claimed they would have to bear the burdens, first of revolution, before they could get freedom from their oppressors. Therefore he made it his duty to guide them so that the burdens should not fall too heavily upon them.

As a result of his guidance we see in Soviet Russia to-day the greatest force for social reconstruction raising its head above all else. This is the great co-operative movement. Lenin maintained that the basis of the new social order which the workers and peasants of Russia must build would be the big co-operatives of production and distribution, and that it was possible for Soviet Russia to lead the way.

If the great co-operator of one hundred years ago, Robert Owen, could see what Soviet Russia is achieving to-day he would say, "At last I see my ideal." Robert Owen tried to help the workers out of their poverty in the early years of factory exploitation by means of co-operative plans of all kinds. But he failed. The hearts of the rich who robbed the poor were not touched when Robert Owen pleaded with them, and told them of his plans. This was because the profit system brought benefits to the rich.

Lenin claimed that successful co-operation could not be achieved in a country side by side with the profit system, that the Co-operative Commonwealth must be ushered in by a workers' and peasants' government.

Two great forces exist to-day in the world. One, competition for profits benefiting the few, and the other, Co-operation, for the good of all. One will have to give way. This will have to be Competition for Profits. The Co-operative Commonwealth has found a strong foothold in Soviet Russia, one-sixth of the earth's surface. Lenin guided the workers' movement to make this possible. In the history of mankind Lenin will live forever.

WOMEN TEACHERS SUBJECTED TO ATTACK

February 1927, pp. 5-6.

In Canada we find that the Winnipeg School Board has revised the scale of salaries for women teachers. After January 1st, 1927, the teachers taken on by the Board will have to work for $100 less per year. Thus the new wage scale for women teachers registers a great reduction. Last year it was the Toronto teachers who were thus humiliated. Surely, here is work for the Teachers' Associations to handle. And the community too should have something to say about it—Poor Pay can only result in Poor Teaching.

In Italy we find that women teachers have been prohibited from teaching boys in high schools and universities. The reason given is that they feminize the boys and youths.

This is another of the Mussolini concepts that would like to keep women confined to the home and be the abject slaves of men.

What if Mussolini should wake up one day to find that the women of Italy had decided to copy the example of their sisters of ancient Sparta? A Birth Strike would show such as Mussolini, who, after all, could play the bigger part in wars and against oppression. The spirit of the womanhood of Sparta is only sleeping!

THE MINE EXPLOSION IN COLEMAN, ALBERTA
By Our Labor League Correspondent

February 1927, pp. 13-14.

This winter seems to be a winter for mine explosions. It seems as if people have become so used to them that they soon forget. But those who lose loved ones cannot forget.

Workers are doing lots when they go down into the darkness of the earth to dig riches for those who live in luxury, while they themselves receive hardly enough to live on.

This mine in Coleman has killed so many from the ranks of the workers that one would suppose that these would not be forgotten, that is, in the sense of thinking about what to do and what to demand, instead of only mourning.

In this disaster many children have been left to mourn their fathers. The wife of a certain fire boss became sick when she heard the news that her husband was dead. The compensation paid to the family is not at all large.

Among the dead, which number ten, are a few young men just at their best age. There are six men still in the mine. Because of the fire which was raging within the mine, water was pumped in. Now with the aid of pumps they are trying to drain the water, but it is a slow job.

I was conversing with one of the men of the rescue party and asked him when he expected to be able to get the bodies out of the mine? He said he expected "in about three months."

The men employed by the company who runs the mine are all at work in other parts of the mine, while the rescue party is at work in the explosion area. Do you not think it horrible to go and work when they know that there has been a fire and that water is carrying around the bodies of their comrades?

Those alive should learn from such things as this explosion to better their conditions. The death of each worker should urge them more and more to work to such an end that human lives would not be so cheap. Workers should join unions. They should demand better wages, or they will be shoved lower and lower down in life.

It is said "That it is the poor who help the poor." This is true with people in this district. The Union Local here collected $5,000 to aid the widows and the children and to bury the dead. The Blairmore Local Union gave $100.

MARY NORTH.

CHINA AWAKENED

[Editorial]

April 1927, pp. 2-3.

THE events of world importance at this time are events in China.

Each day the newspapers tell the happenings. But their tales are so varied and so conflicting that their readers can only know that something is wrong in China. From the workers' press alone can the truth about China be learned.

The Chinese people, oppressed and plundered for years by the "money kings" of the world, at last arose against their oppressors. At this moment the Chinese people are near complete freedom.

They have overcome their own native opponents who were in the pay of the governments of the "money kings," chiefly Great Britain. They have captured important "treaty ports" which were also "slave pens." In the cotton and silk mills of these ports, Chinese women and children were compelled to work for twelve hours and longer a day, seven days a week, for the great wage of a few cents per day.

These were the horrible conditions in the factories of Shanghai which caused the workers, supported by the students, to go out on strike in May, 1925. The world knows how those workers and students were treated. How they encountered British guns.

From that time the Chinese people have been determined to end the oppression of the foreigners within their borders.

Shanghai, this stronghold of Great Britain's power in China, is now in the hands of the Chinese people. But this, not before hundreds of Chinese workers suffered the penalty of death for wanting "freedom."

During the recent "one week of strike" in Shanghai over 4,000 workers were arrested. Even some of the newspapers of the master class have admitted that 2,000 workers were murdered and executed.

And now the City of Nanking is the scene of fray. The guns of both British and American boats have been used on the Chinese people. War is on; it cannot be disguised any longer. Foreigners are warring on a nation in its own territory.

Right is on the side of the Chinese people. It is our duty to join the protest against the conduct of the tools of the money bags, the imperialist forces in China.

WOMEN ADVANCE WITH CHINA'S AWAKENING

April 1927, p. 5.

Women's advance into active political life has ever been obstructed. China is not proving an exception. It is reported that Chinese husbands in Hankow held a demonstration of protest against the changed attitude of their wives since the new government has taken over Chinese affairs.

But Mrs. Sun Yat Sen, the wife of the late Dr. Sun Yat Sen, the founder of the great freedom movement which is sweeping China, pays little heed to these protest. She is organizing a special school where women will receive instruction and be trained for political and social work.

In the new order of things whither we are quickly speeding, women must be co-equals with men, and women are learning this.

FREEING GIRL SLAVES

July/August 1927, p. 7.

The Kuomintang, the Southern Nationalist Government, has ordered a thorough investigation of the girl slave evil. A group of feminists under the leadership of a woman lawyer, Su Han-Sang, has pledged itself to drive slavery out of Canton. While the Municipality of Fatshan, a town twenty-five miles from Canton, has already passed a set of laws forbidding the buying and selling of women. Not even the name "slave girl" is to be permitted within the town limits. From now on there are to be only "adopted daughters."

All the girls now owned must be registered. Names, birthplaces, and two photographs must be filed with the courts.

For many of the "adopted daughters" these regulations will involve little change. Generally the girls have been decently treated and have shared the food and home of the family. But there have been cases where the girl has been made to work 12 or 13 hours a day, she has been flogged, half-starved, denied education and forbidden to marry.

To such girls the new law will be a liberation. Food, clothing, a decent place to sleep, spending money of her own and education in a workers' or vocational school, the right to marry, these things have been given slave girls by the new law of Fatshan.

Even this, however, does not mean that these girls will be as free as European or Anglo-Saxon women or as their Chinese sisters. They will still be bound to give reasonable service to their masters. They cannot leave the master's house without permission nor buy their freedom except by his consent. Together with most of the other Chinese women the slave girl must resign herself to restrictions concerning marriage. She will not have the right to choose her own husband except by the special leniency of the head of the house.

But in one way she will be better off than the real daughter of the family. The law states that she is not to be the victim of "blind marriage." She is to be allowed to veto the men who are offered to her. Also she cannot be sold as a concubine. Fatshan figures by these new regulations that the town will be entirely free of slave girls within 15 years.—Canton Gazette, China.

AN OPEN LETTER TO THE LABOR MOVEMENT OF GREAT BRITAIN—TRADE UNIONS AND WORKERS' POLITICAL PARTIES—FROM THE CANADIAN FEDERATION OF WOMEN'S LABOR LEAGUES

[Editorial]
September 1927, pp. 1-3.

Comrades:—

FROM time to time we are informed through the medium of the press of visits to Canada by women who claim to be connected with the British Labor Movement.

Some of these women are known to us to be associated with the British Labor Movement, others are not. But all come to this country either for the express purpose of "seeing for themselves what possibilities there are in Canada for women workers from the Old Land" or for "investigation purposes to discover whether or not adverse reports of the treatment of immigrant girls are true."

It is with regret we have to state that with a few exceptions these persons do not come near the organized labor movement of Canada. Most of them prefer to go to organizations that are distinctly "anti-labor."

Recently, a Mrs. Cohen from Leeds visited Canada. Mrs. Cohen's qualifications were given as—Chairman of the Leeds Trades Council, Chairman of the Women's Employment Council for Leeds under the Ministry of Labor, and district organizer of the National Union of General and Municipal Workers. These qualifications would indicate that Mrs. Cohen was a responsible person in the Labor Movement.

However, the Labor Movement of Canada, and the Labor women of Canada, did not have the pleasure of meeting Mrs. Cohen, although Mrs. Cohen claimed, when interviewed by the press, that "she came to find out what possibilities existed in Canada for English working women." And we infer from other of her remarks that the visit was to find out if unemployed girls who had worked in the Textile Industry in Yorkshire could be placed in the textile mills of Canada. If this is so, then it would be well for the British Labor Movement to know that the textile workers here are without a union, and that working conditions are not those that the labor movement would desire.

The short time Mrs. Cohen was in Toronto she could not have found out much along this line. Also, since she stayed at the Canadian Women's Hostel (this institution is known to us as being a strictly business institution), she would not get any information other than favorable as to conditions of work and care of immigrant women workers.

Her impression is quoted by the press, "She had nothing but praise for Canada's care of the incoming people." "If your newcomers but have grit and adaptability, I see a fine future for them in so wonderful a country with such marvellous resources," are Mrs. Cohen's words.

We women of the Canadian Labor Movement want it understood we are not opposed to immigration. We know only too well that workers are forced to move about the world to get their living. We are well aware there is room in Canada for many, many millions of people—but room is not the only thing—the main thing is whether the possibilities to live exist in a country, and we know that these possibilities are limited through economic necessity.

You, in Great Britain, are led to believe that there is a continual dearth of domestic servants in Canada. Even granting this to be so, then why the continual scarcity? This condition prevails because the great majority of girls who come to Canada on the "domestic servants assisted passages schemes" leave their places of employment immediately they have met their financial obligations—and it must not be overlooked that these girls are watched over lest they become defaulters.

After leaving domestic service, these girls drift into factories and stores, there to work for what an employer cares to pay. Not knowing of the existence of a minimum wage, they supplant the older and established workers. Not troubling to find out whether or not there is a Union they can join, they act as strike breakers and bring down the wage standard of the organized workers. This condition of affairs is the outstanding menace of the needle trades unions here.

It is because we are engaged in work connected all the time with the "wages" struggle, that we know of what we write. As stated before, we have no desire to deter working girls from coming to Canada, but we strongly resent them being brought here in absolute ignorance of wage and working conditions. We consider it a gross injustice to unwary and unsuspecting girls that they should be at the mercy of certain types of advance agents of immigration agencies, who profit personally as a result of the trust these immigrant girls repose in them.

We hope that by calling these things to your attention, you will use your influence through your press and organizations to inform working girls how matters stand in the country to which they immigrate—things which concern their life, security, and moral well-being, and not let them come to a country ignorant of conditions and fearful for their very existence.

With sisterly greetings,
Canadian Federation of Women's Labor Leagues,
Ellen Machin, President
Florence Custance, Secretary.

CLARA ZETKIN

[Editorial]

September 1927, pp. 4-5.

FEW, who are active spirits in the working class movement live to be old. But Clara Zetkin is an exception to thus rule. Recently our veteran comrade celebrated her 70th birthday.

Her years in the struggle for the cause of the workers are full of interest, and this because they were full of struggle. She was active in the Socialist Movement at a time when it was neither safe nor respectable to be a Socialist. She became a leader in the Social Democratic Party of Germany, and in 1892 she became editor of the women's newspaper, The Woman Worker.

In her speeches and writings for the freedom of working women, she never separated this struggle from the greater struggle of the working class for freedom from wage slavery. Even when the great struggle for The Vote for Women was on in Germany, she kept this position very clear.

During War, 1914-18, she and Rosa Luxemburg worked against those who stood for the defense of the "fatherland," and spoke against war. After the War, she joined the militant wing of the workers' movement, this later became the Communist Party of Germany.

Clara Zetkin has been through many struggles. May she live long enough to see the workers of the world freed from the tyranny of the world of masters.

YULETIDE AND THE WORKERS

[Editorial]

December 1927, pp. 1-2.

WHAT a season is Yuletide! What a feast time it has become for manufacturers and shopkeepers! Who would have supposed that this old pagan holiday of our pagan forefathers would be turned to such account! But there it is. Commerce and gain have put the religious side of the festive season completely in the background; the name Christmas is all that remains of this side, the pagan feast time triumphs.

For a month before Christmas Day the busy working-class housewife answers the ring at the doorbell "scores" of times during the day and wishes the agents and pedlars of good cheer many miles away. She can light her furnace with the circulars and private letters of suggestion for Christmas gifts she receives through the mail. The children, too, are kept in a state of mental turmoil with Santa Claus parades and Santa Claus stunts in the big stores.

The poverty stories of unfortunate workers are told the public through the newspapers. Appeals are made for the poor. Collections are taken up at factories and workshops. The firms get the credit, but the workers give the cash.

"It pays to advertise" is the business slogan of the bosses. We must not think that the Santa Claus stunts are to give the children amusement; we must not think that the firms who send private letters through the mails do so to make things easier for us. No, indeed, these are only means by which advertisement for goods is made. "It pays to advertise."

But what of the goods that are advertised. Who makes them? Look at the trade-marks and labels. Made in Great Britain, France, Germany, Japan, China, and so on. Trade is international. It matters not to those who want profits where these goods are made, or who makes them, so long as they can get 100% profit on their deals. But they do care that the workers who make the goods shall be divided, shall hate one another, shall despise one another, so that they shall be ready to tear at one another's throats when the masters and governments squabble among themselves over trade and profits.

We have no kick against "goodwill," but it is the kind of "goodwill" we question. Christmas "goodwill" is a commercial "goodwill." The kind we advocate is "international goodwill" among the workers of the world, the producers of the needs of life, the only useful class of people upon whose shoulders rest the maintenance of life itself.

International goodwill is not a one-day feeling arising out of a feeling of a satisfied stomach. International goodwill of the workers of the world is determination to break down all and every barrier that keep the workers of the world divided. This division must not be. We all have a common condition—we wage-workers—wage slaves. We should all have a common goal—to free ourselves from this condition. Our goodwill and solidarity must be with the workers of all climes, and not with the masters who exploit us, even though some of these live in our midst and are advertised as public benefactors.

Let us, then, be among the heralds who proclaim to the workers, International Goodwill among the workers! International Unity of the workers! For then Geneva Peace Conferences will not be required. The Unity of the workers will bring Peace to this War-Stricken World.

CHICAGO WOMEN TO ORGANIZE FEDERATION

February 1928, pp. 10-11.

Seven working women's organizations met December 18, 1927, in Chicago, in a preliminary conference to work out plans for calling a city-wide conference of all labor organizations of women. The seven organizations who took the first steps were the United Council of Working Class Women, Swedish Women's Club, Lithuanian Working Women's Alliance of America, 3rd District, Finnish Working Women's Club, Mothers' League of N.W. Side, Ukrainian Women's Progressive Association, Russian Women's Progressive Mutual Aid Society. Total of 2,000 members represented.

A Committee of Action for organizing a Chicago Federation of Working Women's Organizations was elected of nine members. The chairman is Miss Edith Rudquist, of the Swedish Women's Club, and Nellie Katilus, of the Lithuanian Women's Organizations, is secretary. The city-wide conference will be called February 26, 1928, at the Ashland Auditorium. All organizations of working women will be invited to co-ordinate the work of the existing organizations, or working women in their fight for shorter hours in industry, against child labor, to combat high cost of living, for more and better schools, against the dangers of war, to support workers persecuted for participation in strikes, for general social reforms.

The first task of the Committee of Action is to arrange a mass meeting to be held on the International Working Women's Day, March 8th. An invitation to speak will be extended to prominent speakers.

The Committee of Action is of the opinion that this will be the biggest organization of women of any in the city of Chicago. The beginning of the work is very encouraging.

(Printed by request.)

INTERNATIONAL WOMEN'S DAY CELEBRATIONS OF TO-DAY

[Editorial]

March 1928, pp. 1-2.

FOR twenty years, March 8th, International Women's Day, has been celebrated by women the world over, and this for the purpose of demonstrating international unity and giving voice to those things which would help along that social process known as the emancipation of womanhood. For the first few years only small groups of women met in their annual celebrations. Now these celebrations are mass demonstrations in many countries.

International Women's Day owes its origin to a conference of Socialist and Labor Women which was held in Switzerland in 1907. While its founders could not possibly foretell the outcome of their decision, yet at that time its purpose was to provide a means of educating women to look at the world as a whole, to break through narrow national boundaries, and in this way to fight the War Danger as well as to strengthen their forces for the struggle of sex equality.

The event which brought this day to the fore and made it one of history was the action of the women of Petrograd (Leningrad) who, during the height of the war fever in 1914-1918, demonstrated against the war and the miseries it brought to the people of Russia.

It was on March 8th, 1917, that they joined forces with the workers of mill and factory and demanded PEACE and BREAD. This action started the revolt movement in Russia, a movement which did not cease until the workers and peasants of Russia came to the top, thus paving the way for the ending of class oppression and the beginning of a new order of things.

Since this year one class of womanhood in particular has claimed March 8th as their "special" day; these are the women of the working class. The lesson that has been learned by them is that freedom cannot come to women so long as one thing in particular remains, and this is a system which permits oppression and exploitation of man by man, and which allows the few to rule the many because these few possess the wealth. And, also, as this condition was that which began with the dawn of civilization and which caused the enslavement of women in the first place, this condition must go before women can be truly free. The system which is at the root of all the misery in the world to-day is capitalism, or, as it is called in terms of its latest development, imperialism.

At our celebrations we shall find ourselves compelled to denounce imperialism as the breeder of greater hatreds than existed in the past; as the cause of the strife and slaughter in China; as the cause of the filled prisons in Europe; as the cause of the oppression which the workers of all lands are enduring.

But words are not enough. We must prepare ourselves so that we can take active part in the struggle against imperialism. This means more organization, more enlightenment. Let this be our resolve on March 8th, 1928.

MAY DAY—1928

[Editorial]

May 1928, pp. 6-7.

MAY DAY is one of the popular days of the year, but not everyone likes its popularity. The employing class and the governments of capitalist countries fear this day because they are uncertain as to what it holds in store for them. For the workers it has one great meaning—International Solidarity.

The first of May, or May Day, as it is called, is a Workers' Festival. It was instituted by workers and for the benefit of workers. It is the one day of the year when militant workers throw down their tools and declare "We are our own masters for to-day."

May Day was declared an international day by an international gathering of delegates from workers' organizations in the year 1889. This gathering was called the Second International. The reason for the decree at that time was that the forces of the workers everywhere could be united in order that the Eight-Hour-Day could be established for the workers of all countries.

Thirty-seven years have passed. It is now 1928. The workers are still struggling for the Eight-Hour-Day. This is so even in Canada.

But although this small privilege is denied the workers of many countries by the privileged few of these countries, this has not prevented the workers from growing more conscious of the cause of their enslavement. In fact, it has helped along this process.

So now the workers who celebrate May Day make their celebrations political demonstrations. They demand not only the Eight-Hour-Day, Higher Wages, Old Age Pensions, Compensations, and the like, but they challenge the power of the privileged few. And this year they will say in more decisive tones than ever before: "IT IS YOUR POWER AGAINST OUR POWER."

Already in one country, the Soviet Union, the workers have taken power out of the hands of the privileged few. In this country the workers, with the peasants, are managing their own affairs and ordering their own lives.

This is why the privileged few the world over hate the Soviet Union. They fear this country will be an object lesson to the workers of their respective countries.

This is why they say and do everything that is harmful to the Workers' and Peasants' Republic.

This is why they are seeking always for some excuse to make war on the Soviet Union.

But we, as workers, will not heed the knavish tricks of the privileged few. Instead we will declare our international solidarity with the workers and the peasants of the Soviet Union.

And, too, we will pledge our international solidarity with those other workers, who, like ourselves, are enslaved. We will hold out a brother's hand to the struggling working men and women of China, to those of India, and to those lying in the dungeons of Europe.

Also, we will pledge ourselves anew to the cause of the Workers' Freedom. For this cause is the only cause worth while. The struggle of the workers for freedom from capitalist class control has also a wider freedom, that of the freedom of all humanity from class wars, trade wars, exploitation of man by man, and the miseries suffered by the young, the weak and the helpless.

Then, let us hail May Day as the herald of the international might of the workers of the world. Let us go forward with more courage to accomplish our task. We have nothing to lose but our chains, and a world to gain.

THE POSITION OF THE WORKERS' CHILDREN IN CHINA AND JAPAN

May 1928, pp. 9-10.

Capitalist Industry and the Proletarian Child in the Far East.

The forms of capitalist industry differ in China and Japan. In China modern economics depend on international financial capital, whereas in Japan a curious fusion between imperialism and survivorships of the absolutist state has taken place.

A common characteristic of the capitalist economic system of China and Japan is the frightful exploitation of child labor. In all Far East countries embued with capitalism a continued absorption of juvenile labor forces from the country in industrial centres goes on.

It can truthfully be said that in these countries the basis of capitalism is constituted by the exploitation of the labor of little boys and girls. At the commencement of capitalist industry the total number of juvenile workers reached 50 per cent. of the total number of workers.

Another characteristic is the absence of all legislation for the protection of the child, or at any rate the radical insufficiency of such legislation. In the whole of China there is no trace of any legal limitation to the exploitation of child labor. The natural consequence being the extraordinary long working days, and the extraordinarily low salaries. In factories, and particularly in mills, one sees young children working night and day from 12 to 14 hours. Very frequently these children are under 9 years of age.

There is without doubt a law in Japan for the protection of children. It is forbidden to employ children under 13 in factories, but this law is not heeded thanks to a second law allowing children of 11 to work in factories provided they have finished their elementary schooling, or they attend the factory schools.

In the same way the working day for minors under 15 years of age must not exceed 13 hours. But night work will be forbidden from the year 1930 for children under 15.

Japan: Prohibition of All Proletarian Schools; Official Military Preparation

Japanese workers and peasants knowing that all official education could be nothing more than a thing of constraint destined to teach the ideology of the governing class, tried educating the children in schools of their own, but the government took in hand all education, any form of proletarian school was prohibited. During strike periods, prohibition of demonstrations, dissolution of mass meetings and arbitrary arrests of leaders, the strikers refused to send their children to the State schools, and endeavoured to teach them in schools of their own, the government prohibited this school strike and empowered the provincial governor to imprison whoever provoked school strikes for a period of anything up to 30 days.

The military preparation instituted in July, 1926, is destined to turn the Proletarian youth aged between 16 and 25 into a faithful soldier of the state.

—Dr. T. Oki, from the Teachers' International.

WHAT I SAW IN THE LAND OF THE SOVIETS
(A special article for The Woman Worker.)

July/August 1928, pp. 12-13.

Soviet Russia! Backward, Barbarous, Bolshevik, Russia!! The land where the workers and peasants are enslaved under Communist rule! The land, where the workers are ground down under a terrible oppression and are awaiting a chance to demonstrate to the world that they have had enough of despotic rule and are eager and willing to adopt Capitalism once more!

Such is the picture presented to the workers of the world by their class enemies—the Capitalists. And they present such a picture because they realize that the very existence of a Soviet power is a menace to their system, consequently they do not scruple to misrepresent and slander most vilely the achievements of the Soviet Government.

To visit Russia after over ten years of Soviet rule is to realize how it is that the capitalist class the world over try by every possible means to create prejudice against the ruling class in Russia, for in Russia to-day is being built up a new social order, a new economy which results in real material and cultural benefits, not for a small privileged class, but for the great mass of workers and peasants. It is therefore useless to expect that the capitalist press will ever give us the truth as to conditions in Russia. It would be folly for them to emphasize the achievements in the realm of Labour Protection, Social Insurance, etc. So the various organs of capitalist expression remain discreetly silent about these matters, but on the other hand in the midst of preparations for an offensive against the workers and peasants of Russia, they raise all kinds of bogeys to undermine the class sympathy which un-doubtedly exists between the workers of the world and their class brothers and sisters in the Soviet Union.

Conditions Formerly

It is a fact that under the Czar's rule the workers and peasants were terri-bly exploited, long hours of labour, miserably low wages, and horrible housing conditions were the lot of the masses. Under such conditions it will be readily understood that the social and economic status of the women of Russia was very low indeed.

Conditions To-day

Tremendous changes have taken place under Soviet rule. The Soviet Code of Laws relative to hours of labor, conditions of employment, etc., stand out as a contrast to the old conditions.

The seven-hour day is being put rapidly into operation. Those engaged in heavy manual labor, such as miners, etc., work six hours a day, and in some industries as low as four hours per day are worked. Holidays with pay, vary-ing according to the industry from two weeks to one month, are granted every year to each worker. There is no distinction between men and women in the matter of wages. The principle of EQUAL PAY FOR EQUAL WORK is adopted. Women are not looked upon as competitors with men, but rather as companions in industry.

Women as Reconstructors

Women are playing a very important part in the social and economic re-construction of Russia. The trade unions organize the women wage-earners and draw them into active trade union life and work. There are over 2,569,000 women in the unions, they take part in the routine work, attend the meetings, participate in discussions, etc. And the number of women who are elected to responsible positions in the leading trade union organizations is over 1,000. This is apart from the number of women holding minor positions.

The women are not only active in the trade unions, but they are also active in the co-operatives, etc. In one district which I visited the percentage of women active in the co-operatives was 25% of the membership. I do not mean by this that they were merely members of the co-operatives, but that they functioned definitely in responsible positions.

In various other phases of social life the women are very active. For instance, in addition to being members of Trade Unions and Co-operatives, the women at an enterprise, office, or plant will form a group, they will become the patrons of a village away in the backwoods, they will discuss ways and means of assisting the development of educational and cultural activity there. What they are able to do in this connection can be best described in a word picture given me by a woman comrade who was a member of such a group.

"We formed our group and selected a village where the cultural level of the peasants was exceedingly low. We sent down a woman comrade to give the community some practical help. This comrade found the peasant's home life very primitive, from a hygienic and sanitary point of view things were terrible.

"So our group of comrades in the city were faced with a big task. Material assistance had to be given. Slowly simple laws of hygiene and sanitation were adopted. Conditions generally began to improve. Then the comrades thought the time was ripe to introduce a creche into the village. This had been found necessary because it had been noted that the women would go to work in the fields, leaving their children in the hovel called home, absolutely unattended. Sometimes the children died from lack of attention.

"After a suitable building had been erected as a creche there were other difficulties. So backward were the peasant women that it was difficult to get anyone to leave a baby in the care of the nurse who had been put in charge. At last two of the women consented to leave their children. But so fearful were they that something terrible was going to take place that they came peeping through the windows to make sure their children were not being murdered. However, in less than a year all of the children of the working mothers were being cared for in the 'creche in the backwoods.' And the group of women in the city had become very proud of 'their' village and were planning further educational and cultural work." [...]

F.C.

LENIN, KARL LIEBNECHT, ROSA LUXEMBURG

[Editorial]

January 1929, pp. 4-5.

WITH the coming of the month of January, we are reminded of the deaths of three great leaders of the working class: Lenin, Karl Liebnecht and Rosa Luxemburg.

The tragic circumstances connected with their deaths are well-known to all class-conscious workers, and will never be forgotten by them.

At this time, when again war clouds are hanging heavily over the world, we cannot help but recall that it was the last world war that brought to the front the leadership of Lenin, Karl Liebnecht and Rosa Luxemburg.

When war broke out in 1914, Karl Liebnecht, then a member of the German Reichstag (Parliament), stood alone when he refused to vote for war credits to help the German armies.

Rosa Luxemburg, too, among the women of Germany, practically stood alone when she supported the stand of Karl Liebnecht. She gave the most open expression of denunciations of the war, exposing, too, the organized interests behind the war. For this she was sent to prison.

When war broke out, Lenin was in exile, having been banished from Russia because of his activities in the working class movement. He returned to Russia during the turmoil of revolution in 1917. Under his leadership, the social revolt of the classes, brought the working class of Russia to the top in November, 1917. By means of this leadership, the workers' and peasants' power (Dictatorship) has been maintained, for although Lenin died in 1924 his leadership remains.

Throughout the world memorial meetings will be held. But these meetings will not be for the purpose of mourning the deaths of these great leaders; they will have a much greater purpose than this. Instead of mourning, those who participate in such gatherings will rejoice that such leaders arose to teach their lessons to the working class.

Such leaders as Lenin, Karl Liebnecht and Rosa Luxemburg never die; their lives are so much a part of history that they live forever.

The lessons taught by these leaders were of great importance during the last world war. Today, they are of even greater importance to the working class, for the workers have gone through the fires of experience and should be the wiser for this.

Without a doubt, the actions of the workers, both today and in the future, under the stress of war conditions, will reveal the power of the lessons taught by these three great leaders and teachers: —Lenin, Karl Liebnecht and Rosa Luxemburg.

LETTER FROM A JAPANESE WORKING WOMAN

January 1929, pp. 15-16.

Women comrades! You must hear how we live!

We work the whole day amidst tears and at night our troubled dreams give us no peace. What we have to suffer is more than human strength can bear.

At half past four the overseer wakes us up roughly, and at five o'clock we are in the dining room of the factory.

Bad, cheap rice, such as we never ate at home, constitutes breakfast. The soup has neither strength nor juice, it is merely salt water. Then we get two or three pieces of salted turnip, and that is all.

We cannot eat this stuff, for it makes us sick. But one must either eat or starve, and we must pay very much for this food. If we come in too late for breakfast, we are beaten by the overseer.

The day's work begins.

We work the whole day in the sweat of our brows. But we get only 70 to 75 sen. The unskilled girls, when first taken on, get 55 sen.

If we are working in the textile section on bad machines, we produce bad material which tears, and for this we get blows and deductions from our pay. Sometimes, as a punishment, a girl is put on unskilled work at a wage of 50 sen.

If, in spite of this, we succeed in earning something, at the end of the month we hardly have a few yen over, for, in addition to the fines, the company makes various other deductions from our wages for insurance, etc. And none of us has the courage to protest.

We work from six in the morning, without interruption and without anything to eat, until noon. At midday we are at liberty to eat, but, as the machines are still running and work is not interrupted, one girl must attend to two machines, while the other girl gulps down a little food. We have learnt to eat at the run.

They do not leave us time even to drink a cup of hot water during working hours. The canteen is so far away that those working on the night shift eat at the dirty machines.

In the afternoon we work on until six in the evening and even longer, without a minute's interval. The result is a working day averaging thirteen to fourteen hours.

That, however, is not the worst! The overseers in our mill, impudent rascals, can do just what they like. Woe to the girl who does not submit to them! She is put on to a bad machine and endless fines are inflicted upon her. For us this is such a menace that we are very unhappy. The company never takes any notice of our complaints.

Listen again, comrades! For the work in the mill we must buy an overall at 5 yen 50 sen; a hat, a cape and a rubber apron at 155 sen. For all these things we pay double prices at the shop belonging to the company, so that these expenses swallow up our miserable pay. We can leave the mill on Sundays only, but it often happens that even on Sundays we are prevented on one pretext or another from going out, and we have to spend the day in doors.

If a girl becomes ill, she is not permitted to remain in the hostel; she has to go to work like the others; indeed, she must work still harder than the healthy ones, for the company is afraid through her death to lose the advances made to her and is therefore anxious to recover as much as possible while the chance remains. If a girl is so ill that she cannot get out of bed, the overseer goes up and drags her out. Numerous girls die in the mill at the machines.

There are only two ways out of the factory: to the hospital or to the graveyard. The hospital is so terrible that we call it the sepulchre. Nobody who enters there ever returns. They give one cup of rice per day there. When the attendants bring the food, they hit the patients on the head as a sign to sit up and eat. We have no faith in the medicines that are given there, for they have never done anybody any good.

Our sleeping quarters are dusty and dirty, and a ray of sunshine never finds its way in there. They are like a terrible prison. The girls from the North all fall ill here; this year no more of them have entered the mill.

But the worst off of all are the peasant girls, who are used to the fresh air of the fields.

I will tell you, comrades, the story of a woman who worked along with us. Her name was Hissa. She came from the North-East of Japan.

When she first came to the mill, she was a strong, healthy young woman. But after two months of work in the mill she became ill and suffered with her lungs, as we all do here. The company forced her to continue at work, as they were anxious about the advances made to her.

It was terrible work. The drops of hot water from the steam of the machines fell on her face and head, while her feet almost froze to the wet, cold floor. The rubber aprons make the legs and body cold, and they are also very heavy.

One day, when she was already very ill, Hissa was working without her apron. When the overseer began to shout at her, she said that she was not able to stand the weight of the heavy apron, as she was very ill and could hardly stand on her feet. The overseer flew at her and began to beat her.

From that day on Hissa could not get up; she spat blood until she died.

There are thousands of such cases.

I cannot describe our unhappy lot; I should have to talk day and night.

The will and the ideas of an individual being will not suffice to release us from this life, or, rather, to save us from this death. We must unite.

Last month we entered the trade union and two days ago we began to strike for an improvement of our position and an increase of wages.

We are in a difficult situation, but we shall fight bitterly to bring the strike to a successful issue and to vindicate our right to live.

INTERNATIONAL WOMEN'S DAY IN TORONTO

April 1929, pp. 7-9.

The 8th of March, 1929, will long be remembered by the women of the Toronto Leagues. The fight to get a hall should be of interest to all our Leagues.

Our first attempt was blocked by the "edict" issued by Chief of Police Draper. We found that through this the English language only could be spoken. But as it was our custom to have speakers using languages other than English, we were advised to go to the police for a permission to abide by our custom for our celebration for this year. So armed with a membership card, a copy of our constitution, and a copy of the programme for our meeting on the 8th, two delegates proceeded to have an interview with the chief.

This, to the delegates was a very interesting event. But, of course, the Chief, himself, was too busy with big things to attend to us, so we were referred to the deputy, he was good enough for us. The deputy looked over our constitution, with satisfaction—he didn't see the word revolution there—so that was all right. But when he read our programme and discovered that we were to have "foreigners" speak in their own language—why—that was a different story.

Well, we had to do some tall talking and explaining. We had to tell Mr. Deputy that this was an International celebration and WE HAD TO HAVE GREETINGS FROM OUR WOMEN IN THE LANGUAGE OF THEIR COUNTRIES, and this was why we had listed Finnish, Ukrainian, and Jewish speakers.

But the poor fellow was not quite so sure that we would not violate the constitution of the country and have sedition served up to us in a foreign tongue. He wanted to know what they would say, and why they could not say it in English. (We felt like saying it with bricks). But, of course we had to be very polite and patient and only say what he was capable of understanding.

Another thing he found it hard to understand was that we had Communists in our League. He wanted to know if we thought it was possible ever to change their views. Our comrade, Mrs. Burt, said "that we wouldn't want to change their views," and proceeded to tell him what brave people the Communists were. He got very impatient about this information and said "he had read all about the horrors of Red Russia, in fact he had read all this in the newspapers." So according to his own confession he must be very well informed.

After being interrogated for nearly an hour, he consented to us having the meeting, but—the two delegates who had interviewed him must be responsible for everything that was said there.

When our executive committee heard this proposal they very promptly turned it down and asked the women to return to the police and demand an unconditional permit. This time the deputy insisted that we could have our meeting and stated that "free speech" was not being attacked by them, and that he would instruct the hall owners to that effect.

Now comes another side of the story. On going to rent the hall, however, we were met with a statement that a written guarantee had to be given that there would be no Communism, Bolshevism, or mention of Russia in our meeting. So once again we were without a hall, because we would not consent to this.

The next move had to be drastic. After some consideration we decided to arouse the interest of some outside people. We went to interview the Rev. Mr. Cameron, who had written an article on "Free Speech," which was published in the Toronto Star Weekly. In this article he had stated that if the police would not grant free speech and free assembly in public halls, then the churches would have to open their doors to the labor people. We told him that it was a hall we needed in which to hold our celebration meeting.

We found Mr. Cameron a real sympathizer. We had a message from him the next day that permission had been given us to hold our meeting in the church hall. In addition to this he himself got on the job. He told the police that their action was illegal and that we were having the church hall to say what we pleased.

As a result of all this we were informed that we could have the hall we went after in the first place. As this was more central and better for our purpose, we took it. So when Friday, March 8th, came around we had a splendid meeting in Hygeia Hall. And our programme went the way we had it arranged.

Greetings were extended by our Finnish, Ukrainian, and Jewish women comrades in their respective languages. Chairman Mrs. Burt in her opening address told of the terrible struggle to get a meeting place, but she failed to tell the meeting that it was mostly through her efforts that the meeting had been made possible, for it was herself who did the interviewing throughout the struggle.

Comrade Florence Custance was the speaker in English and she gave a splendid address. Some of the things touched upon were—the birth of International Women's Day, the War Danger, and the heroic part played by the women of the Soviet Union. Comrade Custance called for support of the only workers' country in the world, and stressed the necessity of the workers spilling their blood if need be in the interests of their own class and not for the interests of the capitalists.

Music was provided by the orchestra of the West Toronto Ukrainian Labor Farmer Temple Association, under the leadership of Comrade Duffy. This children's orchestra is worthy of our special praise, and Comrade Duffy should be complimented on the wonderful music produced by workers' children under his teaching. Two recitations given by Comrade Lily were well received. The meeting was brought to a close by an appeal for funds by our President, Mrs. B. MacDonald, and another for The Woman Worker, by Mrs. A. Campbell. The latter, too, contributed to the musical programme; she sang the stirring workers' song—Toilers Arise!

A. C.

The Local Women's Labor   **9**
Leagues at Work

The Federation of Women's Labor Leagues was formed to create a working-class women's movement dedicated to the long-term process of socialist revolution under the leadership of the Communist Party. The Leagues were linked to a political party with a great deal of centralized power. The Federation itself, and its locals, were expected to respond to Soviet and Canadian Communist directives on the nature, methods, and priorities of their work with women. In practice, however, the Leagues were able to assert some measure of independence, bending the party line on many issues to include discussions on issues like birth control, male-female marital relations, sex education, and childrearing. The WLLs also asserted themselves, as we have seen in earlier chapters, by not immediately or completely cutting their ties to bourgeois feminists and pacifists as they were directed after the Stalinist turn of the Party in 1928. Both the Federation and the WLL locals in fact operated with a surprising amount of autonomy and decentralization up until the 1930s when they were absorbed and restructured under the male dominated Workers Unity League.

As secretary of the Federation and editor of the *Woman Worker*, Florence Custance herself may have had more control over the WLLs than the Communist Party leadership was able to assert. Certainly it is Custance's ideas and perhaps those of other members in the Toronto WLL to which she belonged that dominate in the pages of the *Woman Worker*. Custance used the paper to pass on the Party's, the Federation's, and her own directives and advice for educational and agitational work, imposing on the Leagues in this way some ideological consistency and common directions. But each League shaped this advice according to its own resources, beliefs, and local or regional particularities. The ethnic composition of locals also influenced their priorities. As a result, activities varied between communities and provinces. The Toronto League, for example, was much more focused on birth control and wage-earning women than were the WLLs in the coal districts of Glace Bay, Nova Scotia and Coleman and Blairmore, Alberta where the women were preoccupied by the struggles of their husbands in the mines. The Finnish Leagues had a special interest in the unionization of Finnish domestic workers and in certain family reforms such as the recognition of civil marriages. The Montreal League was the only one to report interest in setting up a "Children's Home," (day care) for mothers wanting to work outside the home.

Local Leagues sometimes met in regional conferences to pass resolutions and share strategies, but one of the most important avenues for the sharing of information was through the *Woman Worker*, especially the short reports that locals were urged to submit monthly. For much of the paper's duration these were printed in a section called "Our Labor Leagues at Work." In the absence of a national convention—a dream that never materialized—these reports provided a crucial way for the Federation executive to stay abreast of local happenings across the country. For WLL members themselves, the reports helped counter the political and geographic isolation that occurred when locals were scattered across the country in communities often hostile to their purpose. A sense of national political sisterhood could be kindled as members from east to west had the chance to read about what their comrades in small and large communities were doing. Individual League reports were considered a crucial part of the paper and an important way of stirring women to action. Not only do these columns suggest how the ethnic orientation of the Leagues and the nature of their local communities shaped their work, they also permit insights into Communist women's diverse concerns and methods of organizing in the 1920s. We can see, for example, how traditional female political experience in support work through auxiliaries and fundraising were utilized to draw women into the socialist movement. Many of the Leagues' activities were related in some way to the domestic work performed by the housewives who dominated the membership. Organizing Communist summer camps for children, for instance—a particularly strong focus in Montreal—was an extension of women's childrearing duties. Similarly, taking advantage of housewives' role as household managers, several Leagues emphasized consumer actions. The Toronto League, for example, attempted a boycott of non-unionized bake shops in the fall of 1926. The political mobilization of women's domestic interests and skills proved indispensable in drawing women out of the home and into the streets, although their organization around women's domestic skills was not used as a springboard to unseat the traditional assignment of gender roles.

By economic necessity, fundraising work received high priority within Leagues. Much of this work was done through social events which were useful not only to raise money but also to keep members connected and draw in new people. Almost every local report contained references to events like tea parties, whist drives and euchre nights, plays, dances, and picnics. Sewing circles were also popular, providing members with more items for the bazaars they also hosted. There was no shortage of activities and causes inspiring their fundraising efforts. Leagues had a host of costs connected to local initiatives for speakers, public meetings, summer camps, and special celebrations like International Women's Day. Locals also contributed to the campaigns of municipal Labour candidates and sometimes paid for local delegates to attend regional conferences. Some, responding to the pleas of the Federation, raised money for the *Woman Worker*. Not surprisingly, Custance's own local in Toronto was most vigorous in its fundraising for the paper. In demonstrations of national and international solidarity, Leagues supported the Canadian Labor Defence League in its work with imprisoned radicals and trade unionists, often sending contributions to relieve the plight of Canadian, American, and British workers and their families hurt by strike actions or industrial accidents in Canada.

Most League members were also keen to educate themselves about socialism, something the Party certainly encouraged. Study groups were popular forums for the discussion of current issues and theories of socialism, and some classic texts, like August Bebel's *Woman Under Socialism*, were read in some Leagues. Lectures, by Communist and non-Communist speakers, both male and female, raised awareness too, and Custance herself addressed Leagues whenever she could. In northern Ontario a travelling library was started, aimed especially at young people in isolated areas.

While the League reports tell us a lot about the nature of the various locals and what they were up to in these years, it should be remembered that members tended to stress the positive side of their operations, giving few glimpses into the problems they encountered. Individual Leagues sometimes admitted periods of declining activity (see the Edmonton report in October 1926), but there is no direct acknowledgement of the difficulties they faced among themselves as they tried, for example, to bridge the linguistic and cultural barriers that divided women into separate Finnish, Ukrainian, English, Jewish, and sometimes Russian branches. Reports of various events organized to bring women together across their differences make no mention of the tensions that inevitably surfaced when, for example, members who did not speak English were invited to attend an evening featuring an English-language lecturer. Because the paper only printed English-language contributions, a great many voices went unheard and perspectives unreported.

Despite these tensions, the local WLL reports printed most months in the paper convey the high hopes women had for the work of their individual Leagues, the strength of their commitment to revolutionary politics and practice, and the excitement women felt at being part of a national network of like-minded souls working with a common vision of class and gender liberation. The female-centred nature of activities, and the combining of the social with the political—all of which are apparent from the local reports—clearly strengthened the Leagues and the women themselves. Sophia Mackie, from Nakina, Ontario, likely spoke for many others when she observed in her May 1928 report the growing confidence of women in her League: "We are no longer asking our men how we should think or how we should have to say aloud our thoughts."

Further Reading:

- Ruth Frager, "Politicized Housewives in the Jewish Communist Movement of Toronto, 1923-1933," in Linda Kealey and Joan Sangster, eds., *Beyond the Vote: Canadian Women and Politics* (Toronto: University of Toronto Press, 1989), 258-275.

- Steven Penfold, "'Have You No Manhood in You?': Gender and Class in the Cape Breton Coal Towns, 1920-26," *Acadiensis,* 23, 2 (Spring 1994), 21-44.

- Varpu Lindstrom-Best, *Defiant Sisters: A Social History of Finnish Immigrant Women in Canada* (Toronto: Multicultural History Society of Ontario, 1988), ch. 7.

CALGARY

October 1926, p. 14.

Calgary League reports through its secretary, Mrs. M.L. Parkyn, that the League got three new members, and that each of these at once became subscribers to "The Woman Worker." There was a women's conference held in Regina and the League was able to raise enough money to send a delegate. The League was satisfied that the money spent was worth while. Now and then when a comrade has been in great need, a Whist Drive was run in order to give some assistance.

A study class has been organized, and the members meet in each other's houses. The women are planning to attend a special meeting being arranged for women to be addressed by Professor Scott Nearing. The members of the Calgary League are determined to go forward and make their organization a success.

EDMONTON

October 1926, p. 14.

The secretary, Mrs. Pallot, reports that things have not gone well with the League in Edmonton. Active members have left the city and consequently the work has gone down.

We ask our Edmonton secretary not to despair, and certainly not to give up. We feel sure the League can be built up again. New blood will come into it. Edmonton is too important a place to be without a Women's Labor League.

CALEDONIA AND NEW ABERDEEN LEAGUES

November 1926, pp. 11-12.

The secretaries of these leagues report that they joined forces and organized a Tag Day for the British Miners. They sent committees to the office of the collieries and collected $85.00. This they sent on to England.

The leagues also worked together in organizing a picnic. They raised about $40.00. The Caledonia League gave its quota over to the Labor party to help the Labor candidate in the Federal election. All the leagues worked hard for the Labor candidate, D.W. Morrison. But he was defeated.

Both leagues sell their bundles of The Woman Worker regularly, and the money is sent to the office just as regularly.

Mary Campbell, secretary of the Caledonia League, writes about The Woman Worker: "The Woman Worker is becoming more interesting each issue, it is easy to read and understand."

We take this opportunity to thank Mrs. Dobson, the secretary of the New Aberdeen League, and Mary Campbell, secretary of the Caledonia League, for their regular reports, and also the membership of the leagues for their loyal support of THE WOMAN WORKER.

We want also to congratulate the leagues for the splendid work done on behalf of the British miners. They will be pleased to see that the secretary of the Miners' Federation of Great Britain, J.A. Cook, acknowledged the resolution sent by the executive of the Federation to the miners' wives.

TORONTO LEAGUE

November 1926, p. 12.

The Toronto League reports that it is going to do its part in helping the Toronto Trades and Labor Council organize the bakers. After hearing their delegate's report on this matter the following decision was made, "That we discontinue dealing with those bakers that have prevented their workers joining the union, and purchase bread from those who have not interfered with their men organizing; and that we notify the bakers why we take this action; further, that we inform the Trades and Labor Council of our action and urge the Council to prevail upon the delegates to ask their wives to take similar action."

This action of the Toronto League shows how the Leagues can use their influence. Actually the Leagues are UNIONS OF HOUSEWIVES, but because of the social character of the home, their work as producers is lost sight of. As the Leagues increase in membership, and signs are pointing this way, their influence will be strengthened, and they will become a force to be reckoned with.

WINDSOR

January 1927, p. 14.

A very successful euchre was held in the Machinists' Hall Saturday, Dec. 11th. The hall was packed. A personal canvass of the women present was made with the view of getting new members. The result was that eight new members were added to the League.

Comrade F. Custance, from Toronto, gave a short address on "The Importance of Women's Activity in the Labor Movement."

The following evening (Sunday) Com. Custance addressed the Labor Forum. Her subject was "Women's Part in the Labor Movement." The result of this week-end activity was encouraging. The W.L.L. was able to help meet the travelling expenses of Com. Custance and give a donation of $5 to the Woman Worker.

The secretary continues her report:

"We have enrolled 15 members now, but do not expect to stop at this small number, but hope to enroll many more after the new year. We have had two busy meetings since Com. Custance's visit, and another euchre party, which was well attended.

We are going to canvass the whole of the Border Cities to try to get subscriptions for our Woman Worker. Also we intend to take up educational work, so that when the need arises for one of us to speak we can do so."

Last Sunday at the Open Forum the speaker failed us. But there were a few members of the C.L.P. present, and these entered into discussion and did fairly well. The women who belonged to the Labor League were asked to speak. I went on to the platform, but as this was my first try I guess I was not a great success. But I will sure keep trying. There was a lot I wished to say, but could not say it as it should be said.

Well, dear comrades, we are sending another $5 to the Woman Worker. We know you are wishing us every success.

Alice Cray, Secretary.

SOINTULA

January 1927, p. 15.

Our group is gathering new members, and the pleasant side of such a fact is that the new members are young women. Previously, older women have taken all the interest in the organization of groups and reading circles, etc., but now it seems to change, which is as it should be, isn't it?

Young mothers in bringing up their youngsters should know how to train them, and the mothers, if they don't study working people's lives, will not know what to teach their children. These circles and groups really teach one an awful lot. Every working woman should attend.

Our group put up an entertainment on the 27th November, a big play being staged and, a splendid program given out.

A. MALM, Secretary.

REGINA LEAGUE REPORTS ANNUAL MEETING

February 1927, p. 12.

The annual meeting of the League was held on Sept. 1st, with a sign-up of twenty members. Our numbers are small, but we are all active members, and I think we can call ourselves pretty live ones. We have delegates to the Canadian Labor Party, Trades and Labor Council, Labor Temple Co., and Local Council of Women, and our delegates are always present at the various meetings.

During September our activities included running a refreshment booth at the Labor Day sports, which netted us a nice little sum to start our year's work. Whist drives and dances were held the last two weeks. We decided to have these, not with the idea so much of making money, but with the idea of getting people interested in the social side of the work.

Prof. Scott Nearing spoke to us one afternoon on the coal strike situation in Great Britain. We had decided to [...]have a special roll call on the first meeting of the month, so October saw this installed. Each member is expected to answer her name with an interesting "Item of Labor News." We think this is a splendid idea. It gives each one of us a chance to really take part in the meeting.

In November we staged a tea in aid of the miners' wives and children in England. We were able by this means to send $70.00 to the Fund.

In November we had a visit from Miss Jessie Stephens, who spoke at two meetings, and we were all very interested in what she had to say on her subjects—The Nine Days which shook Britain, and, Labor's Bid for Power.

We had decided to send up a candidate for election at our municipal elections to the School Board. We did all we could to get her elected, but were not successful. We shall have to try again this year.

Another speaker we had the pleasure of hearing at one of our meetings in November was Miss Becky Buhay. It was a surprise visit so were unable to give her much time.

Our work for 1926 terminated with our Christmas Tree entertainment for the children of our members and members of the Unions. We had a splendid time, the children enjoying themselves to the hilt.

Sandwiched in between all these special activities were discussions on reports of the delegates to affiliated societies, social afternoon the 3rd week of the month, and the study of Trade Unionism, by Karl Marx.

We are continuing the whists and dances through the winter.

E.E. CARVETH, Secretary.

LETHBRIDGE

April 1927, p. 13.

Our newly formed League received the three dozen of The Woman Worker and these were all sold. Our members enjoy the magazine very much. Would it be possible to outline a study course? Some of our women feel the need of this very much. We have so few who feel like speaking. A full report will be sent later when I have recovered from sickness.

Mary M. Cameron, Secretary.

BLAIRMORE

April 1927, p. 13.

We held our last monthly meeting on March 17th, and we then decided to have a social and sale of work some time in the spring when the times are expected to get better.

For this purpose we have started a sewing circle, getting work ready for the spring sale. The money we get from it we decided to send to The Woman Worker. What do you think about it?

We celebrated International Women's Day with the Coleman Finnish and Ukrainian women. Comrade W. Moriarty, who happened to be in this district, was asked to speak for us, and he did so in a clear and interesting way.

I might report that we have to thank Com. Moriarity for giving us advice about our work. He is acquainted with what is being done in the east of Canada by the Leagues. This was very helpful to us.

One suggestion, and which we think a very good one, was that in order to interest the wives of the miners in their conditions of life, that we bring before the notice of the Miners' Union the suggestion that they form a Women's Auxiliary of some sort.

At all times, we try to explain the object of the Women's Labor Leagues and to get the women to think for themselves.

Mary North, Secretary.

MONTREAL LEAGUE

December 1927, pp. 13-14.

It is nearly two years since our League came into existence, and we may say that during this time we tried to carry out the program of our movement. Our members have certainly learned what a working class organization is, what it means to be in the labor movement, and especially have they learned what it means for women to be organized.

The League has taken part in two conferences, one in connection with the Sacco-Vanzetti Release Campaign and the May Day Unity Conference. The League also helps the Co-operative Bakery.

Most of our work was connected with the Camp during the summer months. During the season we had 85 children at the Camp. Most of the children came from working class homes, and most of the mothers joined the League. We are planning to have our Camp for the coming summer in a most beautiful place and with more conveniences.

Our meetings are well attended. Out of 75 members 40 attended regularly.

For this winter we have worked out a plan of work which includes entertainments—a concert, a tea-party, banquet, and educational work—lectures on co-operative work, the women's movement, the bringing up of children and group study, using the book Women and Socialism by Bebel. We are also helping in the bazaar for the Kamf, a Jewish working class paper.

We are planning to open a Children's Home so as to give a possibility to working mothers to go out to work. At this moment we are carrying on a campaign for new members. It is in the interest of every working woman to join the League, for only by organizing can we carry on the struggle for a better and fuller life for the whole of the working class.

B. Shacter.

LABOR LEAGUES AT WORK , NAKINA, ONT.

May 1928, p. 15.

The Nakina W.L.L. (Finnish) held its regular monthly meeting on March 25th. At this meeting we elected new officers. Our meetings are held regularly the last Sunday of each month. Our sewing circle meets every Thursday evening at each of the members' homes in turn. At these meetings an educational book is read and discussed. It is interesting to listen how each of us voices our thoughts. We are no longer asking our men how we should think or how we should have to say aloud our thoughts.

Our Finnish organization made a trip to Long Lac with a one-act play on April 21st, where also the sewing circle disposed of its fancy work to the highest bidders. We realized a good sum for our work. For this we have to thank Hugo Siren, our auctioneer; Katri Matson, our cashier, and all the people of Long Lac who bought our goods.

Now we are all busy again with our needles for another sale at the end of the summer.

We have no hall here where we can hold concerts and so forth. But we have a spacious pavilion where, when summer comes, we are able to hold dances and concerts.

We send our best wishes to all the Women's Labor Leagues.

Sophia Mackie
Nakina W.L.L. Organizer.

OUR LEAGUES SUPPORT THE MINERS OF THE U.S.A.

June 1928, p. 13.

Meadow Portage League sent $15.00 and the Sudbury League $20.00 to the relief fund of the Pennsylvania miners.

This help we know is appreciated by the Miners' Relief Committee. The fight the organized miners are putting up is for a living wage and better conditions.

The miners have very good reasons for fighting. We have read only during the past few days what happened in those mines which were manned by non-union workers. Explosion. Over 200 men killed.

SUMMARY OF THE WORK OF THE THIRD ANNUAL CONVENTION OF THE B.C. DISTRICT OF THE CANADIAN FEDERATION OF WOMEN'S LABOR LEAGUES, FINNISH BRANCHES HELD ON MAY 20th, 1928, AT CLINTON HALL, VANCOUVER, B.C.

September 1928, p. 14.

The following branches were represented by delegates—from Vancouver, Webster's Corners, Ladysmith, Cob Tree, Chase River, Salmon Arm, Carlin, Sointula, each one delegate. The Vancouver Finnish Domestic Help had also one delegate.

The report of the secretary was read and accepted with a few remarks.

Many important resolutions were read from the different branches represented and fully discussed, among which were:

1. All branches to do their utmost in distributing and getting subscribers for The Woman Worker. 2. All branches to take an interest in youth education, and in youth and the War Danger. 3. Against intoxicating drink and drugs. 4. Militarism and women taking part in school meetings. 5. All branches in B.C. to do their best in helping the domestic servants to organize

and to help them get their own home, where they can meet and discuss conditions relating to their work. 6. Demand for Civil Marriage in Canada.

The Dominion Convention was discussed, but was tabled until word was received from the E.C. concerning same.

The next convention to be held at the time when the C.L.P. convention (B.C. section) is held in Vancouver. The meeting closed with the singing of The International.

A. Vakeva was elected to deal with English correspondence.

H.M. Sillanpaa, Reporter.

November 1928, pp. 14-15.   Box 1036
Sudbury, Ontario
Oct. 4th, '28

Mrs. Florence Custance,
211 Milverton Blvd.,
Toronto 6, Canada.

Dear Comrade:

We have received the 50 Woman Workers and the membership cards for the Domestic Servants' Union. We would wish another 50 membership cards, if possible, by return mail. Comrade Mrs. Lievonen has been out on a tour again and has succeeded in organizing a Women's Labor League at Garson Mine, with 11 members to begin with. We have also great hopes of being able to organize a Women's Labor League at Copper Cliff. Comrade Mrs. Lievonen is leaving shortly for Sault Ste. Marie and vicinity to help those Leagues out that way on with their work, and she would like to take some of those membership cards with her.

The Domestic Servants' Union seems to be growing nicely. They have well over 30 members. Perhaps I mentioned before that they held a very successful social dance some time ago. Last Tuesday evening they invited the Women's League to a pleasant social and comradely evening, the members of both organizations being privileged to bring a friend. They are collecting a membership fee of 15 cents a month, and intend to start two funds, one to aid members happening to be in need on account of sickness or unemployment and another towards getting a home or headquarters, where girls can meet and rest during off hours and when not in employment. They are not very clear yet about all this, neither are we, and we would be very glad of your opinions and suggestions in this matter.

We have a committee here, elected at the last district convention, whose business is to begin a traveling library, mainly for children and young folks. We are that far with the work that we have planned to start with five cases or boxes, built for the purpose, and plan to place them in five different places at a time in care of members of the Women's Labor League, each League to elect a reliable person to have charge of the loaning of the books and of, in due time, sending the case on. We have a fund of about $50.00, have ordered the cases, and now need books. We are asking all Leagues in this district to contribute to this fund by holding a social event of some kind for the benefit of it.

Now, we are asking your help, and the help of any one you can suggest, to aid us in getting and selecting suitable books. The idea is to obtain books that young people will read willingly, working class books, especially in story form and in fiction, both in Finnish and English, but mainly in English. We understand that it is not very easy to find such literature, for there is so very little of it, and we shall be very glad of all the help we can have from any source.

This is rather a long letter and is perhaps demanding more time than you could probably waste for anything like this, for we can imagine how busy you must be with the convention coming, etc. By the way, have you figured out or formed any plan that we should use to collect means towards the convention fund? Or are we to go about this in any way we find best in this district? Have you any estimates of about how much per member would be needed, etc.? We have very near 300 members in this district, counting Sault Ste. Marie and Bruce Mines.

Please let us hear from you and please send us the bills for the Woman Workers, pamphlets and the membership cards.

With comradely greetings.

Elizabeth S. Este.

TORONTO WOMEN'S LABOR LEAGUE
Annual Report of Work—1928-1929.
Affiliations

February 1929, pp. 13-14.

The League maintained its affiliations with the Central Council of the Canadian Labor Party and The Canadian Labor Defense League. It also affiliated during the year with the Miners' Relief Committee, organized by the Toronto Trades and Labor Council, for the purpose of raising assistance, money, clothes, etc. for the striking miners in the United States. The League donated, through collection, five dollars ($5.00) to this fund, and some of our members contributed clothing.

Organizing Work Among Women

There is not much to record in this direction. The task of approaching and organizing women workers in industry remains one of our problems and the lack of results in this direction is one of our shortcomings. During the strike or lock-out, in the York Knitting Mills in Toronto, in the early summer, the League attempted some work in this field, without any appreciable success. The League has also interested itself in the organization of domestics and waitresses in hotels and restaurants. This work is still in hand, with the prospects of better results.

Educational

In January, 1928, Com. Custance spoke to the League on "The Local and Trade Union Movement." In March, Dr. Marty gave a talk on our Educational System. In May the League endeavored to widen interest among working class women by calling a meeting in the Earlscourt district, one afternoon. The turnout, however, was poor and no further attempt was made in this direction. Lectures were also given during the year by Mr. Fester, of the Minimum Wage Board of Ontario, and by Mr. Kingston, of the Workmen's Compensation Board.

International Women's Day

Early in the year a "Women's Labor Council" was formed prior to the meetings for International Women's Day. Hopes were entertained that the Council might be of a permanent character. After the Women's Day meeting, however, which was held in the Don Hall, the Council has practically disbanded. This is regrettable, and an attempt ought to be made to revive this Council.

Support for Woman Worker

The League has good results to record here. From the Raffle held for this purpose, approximately sixty-six dollars were raised.

A very successful bazaar was held before the close of the year, which netted about $150.00 for the Woman Worker. A few of the comrades held affairs in their homes, which, while being highly enjoyable socially, also served the very useful purpose of assisting financially. Affairs were held at the homes of Comrades Trenchard, Machin and Macdonald. The league has taken the opportunity presented at mass gatherings of labor organizations to introduce the Woman Worker. Com. Kalmicoff has been particularly serviceable in this work. More must be done by the League members to secure subscribers for the Woman Worker.

League Meetings

The League has met regularly during the year with the exception of three months in the summer. The attendance has been fairly well sustained, although sickness at the latter part of the year affected the attendance somewhat.

Membership

In the year 1927-1928 the League membership increased considerably. This was due to the interest taken in the subject of "Birth Control" at that time. When this discussion ceased most of the new members dropped off. The work of the General Labor Movement failed to hold them. The total membership of the Toronto League in good standing is just a little over thirty members. A recruiting campaign ought to be put on soon to increase our membership.

General

During the year the League sent delegates to the Social Hygiene Council's annual meeting. Comrade Mrs. Machin attended this meeting. Arising from the report to the League a discussion on Mother's Clinics ensued and a resolution was adopted on "Maternal Mortality." Comrades Campbell and Morton attended, as delegates from the League, a conference of women's organizations in the interests of the League of Nations Society. A report signed by Com. Campbell was published in the November issue of the Woman Worker.

In general, the work of the League has been fairly well sustained. The evident world-wide preparations for war and the general attack on the militant labor movement, with the co-ordination of the forces of reaction, demands that we put forth greater efforts than ever to rouse the working women and draw them into the circle and organizations of the labor movement. In this the Womens' Labor League can perform great service to the working class movement.

Submitted by,
B. MacDONALD, Secretary.

VANCOUVER

February 1929, pp. 14-15. Vancouver, B.C.

Dear Comrade—

The Vancouver Branch of the Canadian Federation of Women's Labor Leagues held a whist drive and social on Saturday, December 15th, in the Jubilee Labor Hall, for the purpose of raising funds for The Woman Worker, and also with the object of trying to form another branch at Jubilee.

This was very well attended, and the proceeds amounted to $15.00, which you will find enclosed.

During the course of the evening, Comrade Mrs. Stevenson gave a very instructive and able talk on "The aims and purposes of the Womans' Labor League." She emphasized the fact that in the past most women's organizations have been dominated by the women of the leisure class, such as I.O.D.E. which uses its influence entirely for the ruling class. It holds itself en masse from the working women, yet it is none the less determined to bring that mass to its way of thinking. Then there is the different church societies. The daily papers, also, have a page wholly devoted to women and her doings, and our comrade asks, "Is it any wonder we find working women on the side of those who are fighting against the working class for the preservation of the present capitalist system?"

The question of war was also introduced, and the men and women present urged to understand that war had an economic basis, and it could not be abolished simply by talking peace and signing peace-pacts.

In conclusion, the speaker made a strong plea for all working women to join the Womans' Labor League, to study the economic and social conditions, and to work side by side with their men comrades in the labor movement and so bring about the New Social Order.

The organization in Vancouver is yet very young, but we are determined to make it a real live working women's organization. We are very enthusiastic about our paper, the Woman Worker, and will do all in our power to increase the circulation, and so directly benefit those whom it represents.

The League joins in sending to you their heartiest and sincerest wishes for renewed success, and trust that this new year upon which we have just entered will indeed be filled with an increased enthusiasm and zeal for making our organization a power for good which will be felt when any industrial crisis takes place.

With Comradely greetings,

Yours for success,
ISABEL WHITE,
Financial Secretary.